POLITICS OF
THE LESSER
EVIL

ANTON PELINKA

POLITICS OF THE LESSER EVIL

Leadership, Democracy & Jaruzelski's Poland

Transaction Publishers
New Brunswick (U.S.A.) and London (U.K.)

Library of Congress Catalog Number: 97-51254
ISBN: 1-56000-367-7
Printed in the United States of America

Library of Congress Cataloging-in-Publication Data

Pelinka, Anton, 1941–
    Politics of the lesser evil : leadership, democracy, and
Jaruzelski's Poland / Anton Pelinka.
        p.   cm.
    Includes bibliographical references (p.   ) and index.
    ISBN 1-56000-367-7 (acid-free paper)
    1. Jaruzelski, W. (Wojciech)   2. Democracy.   3. Leadership.
4. Poland—Politics and government—1980–1989.   I. Title.
DK4435.J37P454   1998
943.805'6'092—dc21   97-51254
                                                                    CIP

*T*able *of Contents*

*F*oreword

The German edition of this book appeared in 1996: "Jaruzelski oder die Politik des kleineren Übels: Zur Vereinbarkeit von Demokratie und 'leadership'" (Frankfurt am Main: Peter Lang Verlag). Since that time, the debate over the role of General Jaruzelski has continued. In Poland this debate has the character of a political fight. After its victory in the election of 1993, the "leftist" majority of the Sejm had ended the parliamentary investigation into Jaruzelski's behavior during the period of martial law. Legal investigations into the General's role in the crackdown on the strike movements in 1970, among other things, came to nothing. The question of whether or not a military invasion of the Red Army was imminent remains unanswered. What is certain is that there was no direct threat from Moscow. It is just as certain that the possibility of a Soviet intervention was a threat to be reckoned with.

Jaruzelski's position in 1981 will continue to be the subject of controversy both in Poland and outside that country. Yet the role Jaruzelski played within the framework of Gorbachev's policies beginning in 1985 has met with increasing interest in scholarly analysis. Jaruzelski's decision to allow the first free elections in a state of the Warsaw Pact accelerated the reforms that ultimately led to the end of the Soviet-type systems in Europe, to German unification and to the collapse of the Warsaw Pact and of the Soviet Union (*Zelikow, Rice* 1995, 70, 88; *Maier* 1997, 124, 182-185). The round table conferences between Jaruzelski and Solidarity became the lever for western, liberal democracy. With that, General Jaruzelski's Poland became the model for the transition of political systems.

The task of this book is not to deliver a final judgment on Wojciech Jaruzelski. Jaruzelski serves as a model, as an interesting case study that clarifies the essence of leadership, particularly the tendency toward the incompatibility of leadership and democracy. Jaruzelski's status as an individual who will remain controversial only serves to emphasize the paradigmatic character of his behavior.

I thank Irving Louis Horowitz for including this book in the publishing program of Transaction Press. I thank Renée Schell for translating the text from German into English and for her spirit of cooperation. I thank Ellen Palli for her fine technical preparation of the English text.

Anton Pelinka   Innsbruck   March 1998

1   *On Leadership*

This is a book about Wojciech Jaruzelski, about the role that he played in 1981 and about the role that was played to him in 1989. But these observations are not only and not even primarily intended as an historical representation. Rather, the person of the Polish General, Prime Minister, Party Secretary and President serves as an example of what it means to have to undertake political decision-making, with consequences for a society, for a people, indeed, for world peace. Jaruzelski had to make decisions under non-democratic circumstances. Jaruzelski will be treated here as a case study.

Wojciech Jaruzelski is a fascinating figure in part because, at first, he does not fascinate. He is the only General-Dictator produced by the communist world, a Leninist Bonaparte who nevertheless does not correspond to the expectations one might have for such a figure. He was not so much a social climber as a social dropout from an aristocratic family. His socialization was, as a matter of course, Catholic and nationalistic. He was more the type of a turncoat from the ranks of the ancien régime. The messages he promulgated as minister, head of government, party leader and head of state had nothing electrifying about them. He proclaimed no ideology; his words mobilized no emotion. His message was always "duty" and "fulfillment of duty." And, indeed, his career was largely one that was foisted upon him — most often he declined the offers made to him. To be sure, he turned down these offers only in order to yield to the demands of others that it was his duty to be minister or party leader. The rank of marshal was the only one he had successfully turned down time and again, for here, probably no one could have convinced him that this had anything to do with duty. Besides, the image of another marshal would have been overwhelming — that of Marshal Jozef Pilsudski, who cast an ambivalent shadow over all of modern Poland. (Rosenberg 1995; 125, 177).

The figure of the man in dark glasses with the stiff, military bearing and ascetic personal lifestyle does not invite "populist" identifications. Jaruzelski is most certainly not the leader onto whom the expectations and longings of the masses can be projected. His dictatorship has often been described as "socialism without a face," in critical distinction from the "socialism with a human face" promised by the Spring of Prague. Jaruzelski stands for no inspiring ideas, no mobilizing message.

This book will discuss and explore the decisive question for any systematic evaluation of Jaruzelski, that is, whether or not the imposition of martial law was really, as Jaruzelski himself claimed, the only means by which to avoid a Soviet invasion. This question is the point of departure for the actual topic: the compatibility of leadership and democracy. This question leads to the central theses of this book:

Thesis I: that political leadership always means having to choose the lesser of several identifiable evils;

Thesis II: that the inner logic of democracy leads to the narrowing and, ultimately, to the destruction of the playing field of political leadership.

This book is thus a book on the compatibility of democracy and political leadership. In this context, the term "leadership" will be preferred to the German term "Führung" for one reason, in accordance with the international discussion of political science: "Leadership" is accepted as a neutral term in the general scientific debate, even in the sense of a nonideological theoretical discourse. "Führung," on the other hand, carries the strong connotation of a variant of elitist theory bearing a positive valence in fascism, including the National Socialist principle of the "Führer."

Yet if "Führung" in the sense of "leadership" is inextricably connected with politics, then any tension that is claimed to exist between democracy and leadership must also include a tension between democracy and politics per se; then the entry into democracy is the beginning of the departure from politics.

Even a cursory consideration of this assumption reveals it to be at odds with political reality for several reasons:

—   In stable democracies, politics is increasingly perceived as a competition between individuals who lay claim to leadership for themselves. This indicates more an alternate meaning than a diminishing of leadership.

—   The findings of empirical social research and the claims of elite theory have led to a "realistic" understanding of democracy that stems from the unavoidability of democratic elites.

These objections make it necessary to differentiate between concepts of leadership — if political leadership is equated with the carrying out of political office, then the above objections must be accepted and the hypothesis must be seen as mistaken from the outset. If, however, one employs the typology suggested by James MacGregor Burns (Burns 1978) in order to differentiate between different concepts of leadership, then suddenly more arguments are found to support the hypothesis.

A concept of leadership that is unlimited by specificity, one which includes reference to all those who hold office and carry out political function makes sense, of course, for all sorts of empirical analyses of comparative political science — studies on aspects of socialization, recruitment, marketing and the acceptance of political leaders have, of course, their own redeeming value. For an approach based on the theory of democracy, as in the theses formulated above, we must differentiate between a broad, general concept of leadership based on functions and offices, and a narrower concept that marks the decisive criterion of leadership, that is to say, the effects of political action that we can recognize, describe, measure, and analyze.

Leadership is therefore not understood in terms of function or roles, but in terms of effect. The fact that someone is Chancellor of the Federal Republic of Germany or Prime Minister of Japan does not in and of itself make that person a leader. Not until that person (whether Chancellor or éminence grise) undeniably and unmistakably "makes history" is he or she a leader. Others, those who merely carry out the duties of their office, are, or at least tend to be, replaceable, when understood solely in terms of their office. But with that, the central theses of this book include the claim that the notion that history is created by people can only hold true for a predemocratic stage of development.

The question remains to be answered, why, then, leadership as a product is so much in demand, why, even in stable democracies worldwide the call is heard for more and more leadership. The need for leadership strangely contradicts the triumphant advance of liberal democracy: on the one hand, this success of existing democracy is applauded; on the other hand, a central result of this success of democracy is feared and criticized—the erosion of leadership. This study, then, will also address this contradiction.

It is undoubtedly true that people "make" history. In a democracy, however, these individuals lose their identity and instead, assume roles, holding functions that are defined on the political market and are, indeed, must, in this sense be neutral with regard to individuality.

This becomes clear when the extreme opposite of the actual existing democracy of the twentieth century is manifested: the forms of totalitarian dictatorship. Their style of leadership is completely different from that of democratic leadership with its roles and functionaries. One task of this book will be to demonstrate that this phenomenon has to do with content, and that this is one indication of the plausibility of the book's two central theses.

Wojciech Jaruzelski's role will continue to be controversial because he, as party leader in a communist dictatorship during the twilight of the Soviet-type systems neither had to nor was able to follow any certain role model. Jaruzelski intervened in the history of his country, and it was clear to him that he would, in his own words, "get his hands dirty" in the process. But denying this responsibility would have, in a certain sense, seemed to him even dirtier, like a flight from the responsibility of whose ethical dimension he was probably well aware.

His example is that of the exercise of personal influence on the fates of a large number of other people. He was only able to have this importance for Poland and for Europe because he made a choice between "evil" and "evil" and acted accordingly. The amount of power he had at his disposal would have been inadmissible in a democracy. Yet, when democracy triumphed in Poland eight years after the imposition of martial law, it triumphed in part also because Jaruzelski had helped to bring it about. With that, however, the power of General Jaruzelski came to an end. It had simply rationalized itself away, or rather, he had rationalized it away. The leadership with which he had violently suppressed the democratic movement in 1981 had dissolved into democracy.

2 Jaruzelski I: On the Gravity of one — of any — Political Decision

Martial Law — The End of Dual Rule — The Parameters — Purgatory instead of Hell — A Particular Type of Dictatorship — Jaruzelski as Leader

On the eve of December 13, 1981, Wojciech Jaruzelski made a decision that he had long considered and then prepared systematically: As Prime Minister, Minister of Defense and First Secretary of the Communist Party of the People's Republic of Poland (the Polish United Workers' Party), he imposed martial law on his country. The General had chosen this date with a sense of purpose: on December 11 and 12, a meeting of the "national commission" (of the ruling committee of Solidarity) took place in Gdansk, a final opportunity to reach a consensus between the two central powers that had been living a difficult, distrustful coexistence since September 1980; on the one hand, the Communist Party that, in the sense of the communist one-party systems, ruled the state as a dictatorship, and whose most important power base consisted of the Soviet Union and the Red Army; and on the other hand, the democracy movement of Solidarity, long since more than a union in the traditional sense, that was supported by the large majority of the Polish population.

The national commission of Solidarity did not compromise; a general strike was announced as well as a referendum on the power question (Jaruzelski 1993, 287-291. Jaruzelski 1996, 11-22). From the General's perspective, this marked the end, after more than 15 months, of the system that had set Poland's course since the massive strikes of the summer of 1980 and that, in many respects, resembled the system that had reigned in Russia between February and October, 1917. The coexistence of two centers of power — one that stood more or less for the status quo, and another that had radical implications far beyond this — lasted only a short time in the Russia of 1917 and also in the Poland of 1980/81. Yet, whereas in Russia the Soviets, pressured by the insurgent Bolsheviks, prevailed against the Duma and the provisional government that was based on it, that is to say, the radical power prevailed against the conservative, in Poland the conservatives triumphed over the radicals, at least in December, 1981.

This development had its reasons, and they were international in nature. The Europe in which the People's Republic of Poland was embedded was the Europe of the Cold War. Yalta and Potsdam and Helsinki stood for a system of order that prioritized security over freedom, at least over the political freedom of people in countries that had fallen to the Soviet sphere of influence in this postwar order. Whenever the political freedoms that had been denied were demanded, the troops of the Red Army — with the support of Polish, East German, Hungarian and Bulgarian troops in 1968 — had secured the priority of security over freedom very quickly. And the other side, the West, USA and NATO, had not, it is true, remained silent, but had signalled their basic agreement: this had been the case in the GDR in 1953, in Hungary in 1956 and in the CSSR in 1968.

For, in the West, there was a clear priority in this postwar order that had also been expressed in the "Helsinki Final Act" treaty in 1975. If the alternative to the postwar order was to be a war between East and West, then for the West, the Cold War was still the lesser evil vis-à-vis a nuclear war.

The possibility that the Soviet intervention would be repeated was articulated directly very early on. Erich Honecker had found direct words on the occasion of the departure of the Polish ambassador to the GDR, Stefan Olszowksi, on November 20, 1980: "The Revolution ... can develop peacefully or unpeacefully. We are not for the spilling of blood. That is the final means. But even this final means must be implemented if the workers' and peasants' power ever has to be defended. This was our experience in 1953, and it is borne out by the events in Hungary in 1956 and in Czechoslovakia in 1968" (Kubina 1995, 111).

Words could hardly be clearer. Nevertheless, Honecker had made this threat to Olszowski, a member of the Politburo and Secretary of the Central Committee of the Communist Party. The addressee of this memory of the history of Soviet interventions was, in November of 1980, Jaruzelski's predecessor as First Secretary (Party Leader), Stanislaw Kania. One year later, the threatening posture of the brotherland was more of an issue than ever.

It was Husak and Honecker who functioned in the summer of 1981 as representatives of the hard line vis-à-vis Polish developments at the meeting of the Communist party leaders of the Warsaw Pact states in the Crimea. Honecker declared to Brezhnev that the Polish situation, the dual rule of Communists and Solidarity, would "help the American course of confrontation"; also, that he "did not trust" Kania (Kubina 1995, 333, 335).

At a routine meeting of the Ministers of Defense of the Warsaw Pact countries held from December 1-4, 1981, the "extremely complicated situation in the People's Republic of Poland" was an important topic. The results of the talks were inconclusive: it was clear that Hungary, and particularly Romania, would hardly agree to a military intervention (Kubina 1995, 387-389). Yet in light of Romania's special position, which was the case even in 1968 and still had not been able to prevent the invasion of the Warsaw Pact (without Romanian troops), the opposition from Romania was hardly decisive.

All of this was clear to the Polish party leader and head of state in December, 1981. He must also have been aware of the fates of Imre Nagy and Alexander Dubcek. The Hungarian Communist and head of government in the fall of 1956 had positioned himself against the Soviet demands of hegemony, fallen from power through the direct military intervention of the Soviet Union, and been arrested and executed after a secret trial; the head of the Czechoslovakian Communist party had not taken Soviet threats seriously enough and, after his country had been occupied, was forced into a humiliating agreement in Moscow in August, 1968 and soon thereafter, at the behest of the USSR, deprived of political power.

Jaruzelski had one thing in common with both men: the belief in Communism, emerging from the national tragedy of their respective countries. Jaruzelski, exiled to Central Asia in 1940, had decided to participate in the liberation of his country from the rule of National Socialism — on the side of the Poles, who were both supported and exploited by Soviet politics.

In the Soviet Union, Jaruzelski underwent an extreme schooling in political realism. He, the Polish officer with the aristocratic background, whose formative ideology was that of Polish Catholic nationalism, and who must have experienced Soviet policy of the years 1939-1941 as anti-Polish, now perceived — after 1941— the Soviet challenges to Hitler's Germany as his only chance to contribute in a personal way to the liberation of his country. He was able to fight again, by the grace of Stalin. And he became a Communist (Rosenberg 1995, 140-144).

Once retired, the General, Minister of Defense and Prime Minister, First Party Secretary and President Jaruzelski wrote about the earlier motive that was to determine the course of his life: "Stalinism had committed horrible crimes. Nevertheless, Russia saved us from complete destruction" (Jaruzelski 1993, 342).

Even at that early date, the strategic motive that was to make of him an international political player was clear: to choose the least of all possible evils from the array of real, existing possibilities. For the young Jaruzelski, this was, after 1941, the alliance with the Soviet Union and, consequently, the integration into the Communist Party. For the Jaruzelski of the year 1981, the situation looked different. He saw unmistakeable signs from the USSR that presaged an invasion if the dual rule of the Communist Party and Solidarity was not ended. Brezhnev and, presumably to a greater degree, Honecker and Husak feared the spread of the Polish model to other states too greatly; the party leaders of the satellites, especially of the GDR and the CSSR, feared for their own rule. Jaruzelski saw himself, or at least believed himself to be in the same position as Alexander Dubcek immediately prior to August, 1968, who, even at a final meeting with Janos Kadar, the Hungarian party leader and most "moderate" among the interventionists, did not want to hear the overly clear warnings on August 17, 1968 (Mlynar 1978, 200). Dubcek's optimistic perspective was overrun by reality. These were the armored tanks that began moving in the night from August 20-21.

The research that began when the archives in the capitals of the former Communist countries were opened offers no clear answers as to the seriousness of the Soviet threat of intervention. It is certain that the Politburo of the Communist Party of the Soviet Union did not deliver an ultimatum to Jaruzelski; it is certain that top SED officials pushed the Soviets to exert massive pressure on the Polish leaders (Kubina 1995). It is certain that the model of Soviet policy did not exclude, indeed, did not want to exclude a military intervention in a "socialist" state. Whatever the threat of intervention may have looked like, it was a real, not an imaginary presence.

Jaruzelski saw himself caught between two alternatives: the first was to ignore the Soviet warnings and those of the other "brother countries" — and then to be able to choose later between the roles of Dubcek and Nagy, that is to say, between a resigned role and an aggressive, heroic one. For the Polish people, the result in both cases of the first alternative would be fundamentally the same: dictatorship ensured by foreign troops in connection with a presumably high cost in terms of human life. The second alternative was to remove the Soviets' reason for invading, in other words, to end the dual rule of his own accord, to eliminate the "Polish model" and return to the "normalcy" of Communist rule, to dictatorship. Such a dictatorship would be supported, of course, not by a foreign army, but by Polish troops, and would presumably demand fewer victims.

For Jaruzelski, the second option was the lesser evil. That was the one he chose. And he declared martial law, which had the immediate result of destroying the institutions of Solidarity and causing the arrest of its leading proponents.

In the process, Jaruzelski made certain assumptions that were at least in and of themselves quite plausible. They were not merely the result of his own analysis, they were, rather, an integral part of the European order as it had been established, at least indirectly in 1975 in Helsinki with the participation of the US.

— The US and NATO would not be prepared to counter an invasion of Poland on the part of the Red Army with military force. This reticence reflected the logic of the Cold War: why should the West react differently than it had in 1953, 1956 and 1968?

— The USSR was primarily interested in the stability of its own empire. With the democratization of any part of it, the party and state leadership in the Kremlin feared an infection that would destroy the "existing socialism." Why should the Polish model of the dual rule be less threatening that the model of the "Prague Spring"?

— The Soviet leadership could assume, just as the Poles could, a Western policy of non-intervention. Why should the Communist party leaders risk their position of power when an act of violence that was admittedly poorly justifiable in a political sense, but did not threaten peace or the system as a whole, could guarantee it?

— Soviet troops had recognizably begun with preparations for the invasion of Poland. Jaruzelski could not be sure, but: "I did not know that such preparations [for the military invasion, A.P.] had been made. But I felt it" (Jaruzelski 1993, 291). Later there were a number of confirmations that Jaruzelski's estimation had been realistic (Jaruzelski 1993, 281f., 290).

— Jaruzelski was the man of moderation inside the Polish (Communist) leadership. The other currents of the party would, when in doubt, force a hard line. Jaruzelski perceived his position in this way and even his opponents saw him as "approachable," in other words, as moderate (Walesa 1987, 283). When elected as First Secretary of the Central Committee of the Communist Party on October 16, 1981, Jaruzelski had to state "Except for me, there were only proponents of an even more confrontational orientation" (Jaruzelski 1993, 276).

— The declaration of martial law had no "irreparable consequences" (Jaruzelski 1993, 292). Poland was not involved in war or war-like acts of violence with unforeseeable sacrifices. The longterm option for a different development remained open in principle. "We Poles had to go through purgatory ... I only know that we have avoided hell" (Jaruzelski 1993, 292f.).

Jaruzelski made a decision. He acted. He sent Poland through purgatory. And future developments confirmed his belief that he had done his best for his country, in light of the alternative of hell. For the activists of the democracy movement, purgatory took the form of prison. Once again, Poland was made to conform with the model of a "Soviet type" system. The party's monopoly of power was reestablished, at least at first glance. Moscow had reason to be pleased. The threat of a military intervention was withdrawn. The time of Polish pluralism was over — until 1989 when the same General Jaruzelski, fortified by new political powers in the Kremlin, was able to bring about the dissolution of the monopoly of power.

Jaruzelski the dictator had held Jaruzelski the democratizer in reserve until conditions in Poland allowed a democracy. Yet, in order to keep Jaruzelski the democratizer in reserve and not have to make room for a Polish Husak, who was directly dependent on the grace of the Red Army, Jaruzelski the dictator first had to act.

In so doing, Jaruzelski would have lost any political innocence he had, assuming that, as General and Communist party leader, he had anything like innocence. Jaruzelski literally got his hands dirty. He carried the responsibility for the repression of Solidarity. He was thus the destroyer of a movement that had, by no means simply as a union, but rather in a heterogeneous form, brought a powerful piece of democracy to Poland (Ash 1984; Pumberger 1989). His authority forced the democrats into prison, hindered the publication of democratic newspapers, and led to the discrimination of all members of the opposition.

After 1989, Jaruzelski claimed to have done all of this with his eyes open. His decision was made despite the fact that he knew what it must mean for the democracy movement; despite the fact that he knew that he had to become, if not the executioner, then certainly the prison warden of Polish democracy. He saw himself "alone, desperately alone in power" (Jaruzelski 1993, 277). He felt the burden of responsibility for 36 million people.

On December 7, 1981, Brezhnev told Jaruzelski by telephone that the Soviet Union could no longer tolerate the Polish situation. On

December 8, Soviet generals intensified the pressure in a face-to-face conversation with Jaruzelski: "Do something, or it will end in disaster." On December 12, when he had already made his decision, Jaruzelski spoke by telephone with Suslov, the "head ideologist" of the Communist Party of the Soviet Union and with the Soviet Defense Minister Ustinov. Suslov confirmed to Jaruzelski that if he declared martial law, the USSR would refrain from any intervention, which, for Jaruzelski, sounded like a cancellation of the planned invasion. Ustinov remarked, according to Jaruzelski's paraphrasing, "Your problems concern the entire Warsaw Pact. If you don't solve them yourselves, we won't just watch and offer brotherly aid" (Jaruzelski 1992).

The declaration that Jaruzelski made and that was published in the Polish newspapers on December 14, did not reflect this international context. The pressure exerted by the Soviets went unmentioned. A catastrophic economic situation and the threat of the collapse of public order were the reasons cited for the imposition of martial law. Jaruzelski announced that the state council had transferred the highest decision-making powers to a "Military Council of National Recovery," referring to the Polish constitution and the determinations of an exceptional situation foreseen therein ("martial law"). Jaruzelski emphasized that the jurisdiction of this military council was only temporary and that the return to constitutional normalcy was, of course, fully intended (Labedz 1984, 7).

What should Jaruzelski have done after having become on October 18 the decisive figure of one of the two centers of power, as head of government and also party leader? Since he knew of the probability of a Soviet intervention ("brotherly aid" in Ustinov's words), should he have allowed further provocations of the Soviet Union, a country still governed by the same leaders whose decision in 1968 had sentenced to death the CSSR model of "socialism with a human face"? Should he have aligned himself with the democracy movement against the Warsaw Pact and the Red Army? Should he have offered himself —like Imre Nagy — as a martyr, or rather served the USSR first as an accessory, then as a dispensible retiree, like Alexander Dubcek?

If it is true that Jaruzelski had come to a clear insight of the Soviet will to intervene between Ocotber 18, when he was made party leader, and December 12 — what were his parameters? In any case, they would not have included one thing, namely, the Polish model with its two centers of power, its limited pluralism and its unique brand of partial democracy. If his political analysis was correct — and there is no doubt that it was at least highly plausible, then Solidarity was already finished. The question was only whether or not it would be finished off by an executioner or a prison warden; whether its substance would be destroyed, or whether it could be maintained. If the premises upon which Jaruzelski had based his decision, according to his own words, were correct, then he was the savior of Solidarity, of the democracy movement, and of Polish democracy.

There are those who doubt whether the analysis upon which Jaruzelski based his actions can survive critical scrutiny. Tina Rosenberg, whose analysis is based on various conversations, some with Jaruzelski, allows for a reasonable skepticism about whether the presumed Soviet threat was the decisive motive for the declaration of martial law. She brings forth indications that Jaruzelski was also filled with a genuine loathing for the chaotic tendencies of 1981 attributed to Solidarity; and that he, again (still?) in 1981, acted as a Communist believer. But even she concludes: "Jaruzelski made the decision he genuinely thought best for Poland — because he was a Communist, and because of the main reason he had become a Communist: his constant awareness of Moscow's power" (Rosenberg 1995, 222).

On December 12, Jaruzelski decided not to be interchangeable and to remain unmistakeable in the future. Had he not declared martial law — and only he was in a position to do so, the development of Poland would not have been determined by the two centers of power Solidarity and the government (including the Communist Party), according to his analysis, but by the intervening and aggressive USSR and by the resistance of Polish society, probably led by Solidarity. Jaruzelski himself would not have been able to play an independent role in this confrontation — no matter if he had put himself at the disposal of the Soviet powers as Kadar or Husak or not at all. If he had not acted on December 13, he would have been dispensable for the future history of Poland, like Nagy for Hungary after November, 1956 and like Dubcek for the CSSR after August, 1968. His decision saved the relative autonomy of the Polish Communist party and the Polish government. And it saved his own role as leader. Jaruzelski practiced leadership for the preservation of his own leadership.

The Jaruzelski of 1989 was quite different. At that time he practiced leadership in the dissolution of his leadership. He initiated a course of events that would, he must have known, eventually cost him his own position of power. Even if he, like Gorbachev, might have had illusions of the possibility of a new, stable division of power that would not be endangered by Soviet pressure, the results of the free Sejm elections of June, 1989 had to demonstrate that he had set a course of events in motion that he could no longer really control, that he could at most merely curb, and whose end would necessarily also mean his own end as leader.

In 1981 Jaruzelski opted for securing the center of power that consisted of the government and the Polish Communist Party by suppressing the other power center and by preventing the external threat of the massively influential power center in Moscow from directly invading Poland. By securing the ability of his own center of power to take legal action, he secured his own personal influence — and deferred the decision to the benefit of his own power. He secured his capacity for power as well as the ability to determine for himself when he would lose power.

The Jaruzelski of December, 1981 was surely not aware of this option, which then took effect in 1989. He could not foresee, years before Gorbachev's takeover, the collapse of the Soviet system (any more than anyone else), or how the transformation should really take place under his, Jaruzelski's, participation as leader. But the fact remains that he could be open for the possibility that then surfaced, namely to participate actively in the downfall of the Communist system and thus in his own decline.

Jaruzelski was not praised by the representatives of the democracy movement for his decision of December 12, 1981 — of course not. Who would praise the prison warden. And Poland did become a prison for all those who had participated in the struggle for democracy. Alexander Smolnar, who counts 3 million striking workers after the declaration of martial law, describes the consequences of Jaruzelski's decision as follows: "It was an incredibly deep shock. The resistance to the military police units and the military was limited. ... It was surprisingly easy to suffocate a movement that comprised millions and to force it from the public sphere. The traditional political system thus achieved once again a certain efficiency, even if the military, the police, and the administrative organs had to replace the disintegrating party in many functions" (Smolnar 1989, 8).

The Communist system was resuscitated, but not completely. The party "disintegrated" — a sign of a quiet transformation that could not be prevented by martial law and that helped prepare for an open transformation. This could be instituted as soon as additional signs were received from Moscow. "Since things had not reached a confrontation between state power and society in December, the repressions also remained relatively harmless. Leaders in the government did not want to deprive themselves of the chance to recreate certain connections to society. For the opposition, that meant the maintenance of a certain continuity and the possibility of achieving influence again quickly and rebuilding institutions. Only in the background, of course, and by no means in the framework of the previous 16 months of legal activity" (Smolnar 1989, 8f.).

In this context, Smolnar writes of a "self-imposed reduction of repression" and a "self-imposed restriction on resistance." Jaruzelski the dictator did not want to destroy his future options. Instead, he wanted to remain politically viable vis-à-vis Polish society, that is, vis-à-vis the democracy movement. And the opposition, conscious of widespread popular support, did not want to provoke a confrontation, also as a reaction against the self-limitation of state power. It thus remained politically viable, if only as a reserve, because it was capable of action, that is, of differentiation.

This "self-limitation" meant that Jaruzelski could free his policy from the excesses that were characteristic of dictatorships, particularly those of the twentieth century. No Communist system of that time — except for Jugoslavia's — was further from the Stalinist totalitarianism than Poland, even after Jaruzelski imposed martial law; or, to stay within the General's logic, by virtue of the very fact that martial law reigned, excesses of political leadership that were otherwise unavoidable could be prevented; because without martial law, the premises for the political leadership of Poland would come directly from Moscow.

Jaruzelski saw to it that there were no executions; he ensured that no one went to prison for years on end without public knowledge or even the semblance of a legal trial — a significant difference from the repression in Hungary in 1956 and thereafter. And he saw to it as well that the leaders of Solidarity were not humiliated for no reason and that no one was exiled against his (her) will — again, a difference from the repression in the CSSR from 1968 onward. General Jaruzelski's repression was a deep frost that did not kill, only paralyzed. The thaw that came several years later from the East allowed developments in Poland to continue from where they had left off abruptly in December of 1981 (Jaruzelski 1996, 332-337). And even the players were the same: Wojciech Jaruzelski, Lech Walesa, Jan Cardinal Glemp, Tadeusz Mazowiecki, Mieczyslav Rakowski and others.

Between 1981 and 1989, Jaruzelski was often compared to Janos Kadar; people spoke of a Polish "Kadarism" (Brus 1982). Kadar and the Jaruzelski of this period shared the fact that each allowed a maximum of political, economic and cultural pluralism within the framework defined by Moscow. However, unlike Kadar, Jaruzelski had been able to ensure that the Polish dictatorship between 1981 and 1989 was purely Polish, not Soviet; that no Soviet troops advanced with military force against Polish resistance; that the repression, even in December, 1981 and directly thereafter was contained and that it could remain so. Jaruzelski was able to avoid his opponents becoming martyrs. Nagy and Maleter were executed by Soviet authorities while Kadar was governor of Hungary by the grace of the Soviets. Jaruzelski arrested the leaders of Solidarity and saw to it that they went physically unharmed and could thus remain available for future tasks. And unlike Kadar, Jaruzelski was able to achieve the transformation of 1989 himself — he himself became a key figure of the process of democratization in Poland.

The death of Jerzy Popieluszko in 1984 gave the underground Solidarity something of a martyr. But Jaruzelski was quickly able to make clear that he held no responsibility for this murder. The fact that this was also acknowledged by Solidarity showed (Jaruzelski 1993, 352f.) that, despite the bitterness on the part of the democracy movement that had been forced underground, there was still the potential for dialog and cooperation between Jaruzelski-turned-dictator and the repressed Solidarity.

The dictatorship of Jaruzelski, unlike that of Kadar, was a national dictatorship even in its origins, free from the direct intervention of foreign troops. And Jaruzelski's dictatorship paved the way for its own downfall by gradually crossing over to democracy. In Hungary, this process was left to Kadar's successors.

Jaruzelski's dictatorship was unique: the dictatorship of a Communist party as rule by the military; or the military dictatorship in the guise of rule by the Communist party. Never before had a career officer achieved such absolute power in a Communist-ruled country. The Communist leaders who liked to appear in uniform — Stalin, Bulganin, even Castro — had advanced through the party to positions of command and appeared in military poses for specific reasons. Jaruzelski was, at first glance, the first (and last) Leninist Bonaparte.

He was a Napoleon without a mission, except for fulfilling his "duty," namely, to save Polish lives. And he was a Napoleon who saw the repressions of his dictatorship, and therefore his own role as dictator, merely as a painful transition, as a purgatory, a lesser evil. If ever a dictator had understood his personal power only as a means and not as an end, then it was this stiff, shy, not so bonapartist Bonaparte from the Polish aristocracy.

The Bonapartism of Wojciech Jaruzelski was a Bonapartism of an undemonstrative but therefore all the more believable personal modesty. Even his sharpest critics never tried to accuse him of a luxurious personal lifestyle. The accusation of corruption was never levelled at the General-Dictator. He was a Puritan, which everyone recognized. The Napoleonic gesture was just as foreign to him as Napoleonic rhetoric or a Napoleonic lifestyle (Rosenberg 1995, 126). But he was also a dedicated Puritan in his ability to make a logical, and in this sense, "necessary" decision from a political analysis he viewed as correct, and to accept the consequences of this decision.

One of the representatives of the democracy movement, Adam Michnik, directed this angry question to the then retired General and President Jaruzelski after the open transformation of Poland: "From 1980-1981 the hopes of Poland were directed toward the social and national minimum: toward a real pluralism. Did that really transcend the possibility of party leadership and the state?" (Jaruzelski 1993, 367f. See also Michnik 1985). Jaruzelski could only indicate once more that the signs from the Soviet Union had been unmistakeable. The "social and national minimum" did indeed transcend the possibilities of a Communist system that, on the periphery of a massive political bloc, was ultimately completely dependent on the center.

Events in the Soviet Union and in other countries of the Communist bloc proved Jaruzelski, not Michnik's skepticism correct. Not until the virus of pluralism, now called "perestroika" and "glasnost," spread through the Communist center could the "social and national minimum" that Michnik called for be established in Poland with the decisive aid of Jaruzelski. Before Gorbachev, it was simply not in Jaruzelski's power to guarantee this "social and national minimum" to Walesa, Michnik, and the others.

Jaruzelski's decision is paradigmatic. He made the decision as the leader of his country who held the ultimate responsibility. His position was not legitimated politically — he was in this position because the Communist center of power wanted it that way. But it was his decision that affected democracy — it extinguished the democratic freedom and political pluralism that had emerged in Poland in the space of 15 or 16 months. From the perspective of 1981, he was the gravedigger of Polish democracy. And yet he saved the memory and indeed, the structures of this democracy for a not-so-distant future, in the form of the outlawed, then partly legal democracy movement, Solidarity.

Jaruzelski's decision was leadership: his intervention in the course of Polish history was indispensable, unmistakeable, and unchangeable. He practiced leadership by accepting the choice Ulysses had between Scylla and Charybdis: between invasion by foreign troops and martial law supported by Polish troops. He did not want the former, but could have brought it about by not actively making a decision. But the latter he could bring about by his own decision. It was up to him what course developments in Poland were to take in the 1980's.

Either to exist as a relatively autonomous country within the Soviet bloc, like Kadar's Hungary, and to always run up against what was tolerated by Moscow, or to exist as a quasi-colony administered directly by Moscow, like the CSSR. It was also up to him to determine how many lives would be sacrificed to the political system of the Communist model.

Unlike Ulysses, Jaruzelski did not have the option of navigating between the two evils. He had to opt for one or the other. He was only able to decide what price he would pay for Poland's irrevocable dependency on the Soviet Union, not whether he should pay the toll of dependence at all. Which of these was and is the lesser of the two evils can be shown by examples.

The "case" of Jaruzelski demonstrates what is paradigmatic:

— leadership as a clearly personal, indispensable, unmistakeable, and unchangeable intervention in the political decision-making process;

— leadership as an option between alternatives that can be differentiated in relation to one another; leadership as a decision made betwen two evils of different dimensions.

Yet what is actually of interest is that the "case" of Jaruzelski is so paradigmatic because it unfolded under non-democratic circumstances. Jaruzelski was capable of leadership precisely because he had no democratic legitimation. If he had had to consider a majority opinion in the Polish public sphere in order to secure his reelection, among other things, or if he had had to consider coalition talks with implications for a government dependent on parliament, he could scarcely have made that particular decision. For at the end of 1981, the democracy movement was quite clearly in the majority; the majority was on the side of Solidarity. Should Jaruzelski have obtained an agreement with Solidarity as to its own dissolution, its own suppression, and to the arrest of its own representatives?

Jaruzelski's momentous act of leadership was only possible because he did not base himself on democracy but on dictatorship. Democracy would have made his leadership impossible, at least in its tendencies, and if it is true that his case was paradigmatic, not only his leadership.

The typologies attempted in the literature of political science confirm this, at least with regard to certain aspects. Jean Blondel, for example, distinguishes between "excessive," "ruthless" and "more humane 'populist'" leaders — and all of those whom he assigns to the first group (Mussolin, Hitler, Stalin) and the second (Mao), but also many whom he assigns to the third group (Nasser, Bourguiba, Tito, Nyerere) are examples of leadership beyond liberal democracy. Those whom he categorizes as belonging to the third group and whose leadership occurred within the framework and under the signs of liberal democracy are either leaders in the foundational period or in a decisive period of transition in liberal democracy (Nehru, Roosevelt, Churchill); and particularly with the last two, the efficiency in leadership is located in the realm of foreign policy which is governed by specific, more limited hallmarks of democracy (Blondel 1987, 195-203).

This is also the case for James McGregor Burns' notion of "transforming leadership" — this leadership is established either under nondemocratic conditions ("revolutionary" leadership) or under exceptional circumstances (Burns 1978, 141-254). Leadership in a typical, real, stabilized Western democracy is hard to imagine and seldom observed — leadership in a stable democracy tends to erode.

The subject in what follows will be the incompatibility of leadership as defined above and the existing liberal Western democracy. The choice between two alternatives of action; the determination of what constitutes the lesser evil; the logically resulting decision whose individual handwriting may not be avoided: this form of political leadership is foreign to Western democracy. Leadership as a contradiction to the internal logic of liberal democracy; leadership as inconsistent, romantic memory of pre-democratic circumstances — this hypothesis stands as a prerequisite to the one that follows.

Jaruzelski himself was not a leader who would have provoked romantic associations; he was no Robin Hood, no Sir Lancelot. With his stiff military bearing, untempted into "populist" behavior by pressure from the media of Western democracies, he represented the political decision-maker who does not owe his political power to election, and who is also not driven by the desire to win elections. To a great extent, he expressed the style of politics from within: the source of the interests that determined his actions was in him early on and remained permanently — "directed toward generalized but nonetheless inescapably destined goals" (Riesman 1950, 15).

In the latter period of Communist dictatorship, this type of leader was unusually viable politically and unusually effective. In a stable democracy, there would probably be little use for this type of stiff, military man who made no concessions in his style to modern media. This is the reason that the democracy that was brought about in 1989 also signalled the end of his career.

Jaruzelski was a Mr. Hyde who knew how to transform himself into a Dr. Jekyll. In 1981 he showed the ugly, brutal side that was prepared for dictatorship. But he did not lose sovereignty over the determination of his own role. He changed. He turned himself inside out. And as a democratizer, he brought forth his own friendly, conciliatory, integrative side. If he had not first been Mr. Hyde, he would never have become Dr. Jekyll.

Jaruzelski presented himself with categories which probably no politician in a stable democracy could dare face. He said of himself, quite the "inner-directed," consummate politician: "I cannot wash my hands in innocence. Incidentally, I do not believe that there is any politician of my generation who can make that claim" (Jaruzelski 1993, 343).

This sort of political understanding was fated to erode in the everyday world of democracy. The other-directed politican had to take the place of the inner-directed politician more and more — regardless of election results, and therefore dependent on opinion polls and the media. If they say "laugh," the other-directed politician laughs. If they say "cry," he cries. Can one even begin to imagine this for the Jaruzelski of December, 1981?

The end result of the stabilization of democracy is the transition from the inner-directed to the other-directed politician. And the latter is not a leader in the sense of a personal, indispensable influence on the course of history that is neither interchangeable nor mistakeable for that of someone else. Democracy makes the Jaruzelskis of the world impossible, along with leadership. Indeed, politics itself is ultimately made impossible. A stable democracy tends toward the erosion of leadership, and with that, it tends also toward the depoliticization of politics.

3 *On the Illusion of Democratic Leadership*

The Fantasy of Democracy — Heroes and (or) Managers — Politics and Policies — Leadership as an Exception to the Rule

Reflections on democracy are full of contradictions that culminate in observation, description, analysis, and evaluation of the relationship between the elite "on top" and the masses "down below," between leaders and those who are led, the governing and the governed, rulers and the ruled.

Language itself is necessarily partisan. To describe voters in a real democracy as "those who are ruled" or even as "the masses" expresses a certain partisanship. This is particularly the case from one language to another. To write about the "Führer" in German or the "Duce" in Italian is to provoke other, less neutral connotations than the English "leader."

Recognition of the indisputable fact that "rule" has existed in all historically observable political orders and that it was and is characterized by an overly regulated relationship between the elite "on top" and the masses "down below," between the more and the less powerful, extends to democracy as well. All forms of democracy that can be experienced are characterized by the existence of a minority that has the legitimate right to make decisions. The most radical forms of direct democracy have, admittedly, been able to reduce but not to eliminate this fact. Democracy, then, recognizes leadership, but only at first glance.

This is a nuisance insofar as democracy also includes implications summed up in the utopia of a society free from rule. Democracy is, after all, at least for many people and for many theories of democracy, not only a state of affairs, but also a promise. This promise extends beyond the circumstance of existing democracy.

In this way, democracy bears within it a tension between an experiential "real condition" and a desirable "imaginary condition." The phenomenon of leadership is fully realized by this tension: If the "imaginary condition" is characterized by the fantasy (or utopia or vision) of freedom from rule, this fantasy must include the erosion of leadership. Thus, the result is that democracy is, to be sure, not a sort of order without leadership, but it is the promise, or at least the memory of the promise of such a society without leaders.

The fantasy of democracy is different from reality, the democratic as well as the non-democratic reality, above all by dint of the erosion of leadership. The fact that leadership is diagnosed in a dictatorship, of course, is perceived as logical and consistent within the terms of the system. Leadership within democracy, on the other hand, would be a contradiction, if not to existing democracy, then certainly to the imaginary democracy. And even in existing democracy, leadership is consistent with the (democratic) rules of the game only in a limited way. Leadership must be legitimated, controlled, and subject to recall from "below."

Leadership within democracy is like the Kulaks and small business owners in Lenin's NEP (New Economic Policy): as a temporary evil which one hopes to be rid of as the situation develops.

But the debate on leadership in democracy exhibits characteristics that are much different. It is not characterized by a distrust of leadership but by a desire for leadership. In its vulgar form this debate is characterized by the call for the "strong man." And even in the variant of the debate known in the political and social sciences, the desire to work out the optimal preconditions of leadership is evident.

Peter Bachrach's skepticism vis-à-vis all forms of elitism is one of the exceptions. His "alternative" theory of democracy illustrates that not only "social" elites, empowered above all by an economic advantage, are existing in permanent tension with democracy, but also "political" (or functional) elites, whose advantage is produced directly or indirectly by elections (Bachrach 1967). For Bachrach and the critical theories of democracy, democracy is also about the constant containment and dismantling of the existing elitism. Democracy is a reduction of leadership.

Jean Blondel's understanding of leadership offers insight into this tension between leadership and democracy. He criticizes the division that tends to be made between the heroes and the "mere" office-holders and therefore the dichotomy that Burns makes between "transforming" and "transactional leadership" (Blondel 1987, 19-26). With that, we have reached a point at which the subliminal tendency toward the heroization of leadership not only contradicts the utopian democracy, but also is not so easily aligned with existing democracy.

In this existing democracy, leadership, according to Blondel, is aligned especially with the improvement of social and economic conditions (Blondel 1987, 195). The question is only to what degree the functional elites who stand for leadership in existing democracy — the presidents, prime ministers, secretaries and chancellors — are capable of taking on the responsibility for social and economic conditions. How can the President of the Republic of Chile take on responsibility for the world market prices that are decisive for the welfare of his country? How can the British Prime Minister be responsible for the course of industrial labor conflicts in his country that may, in turn, have to do with the transfer of production sites to Malaysia or India?

The more globally interconnected the criterion of socio-economic success that is used to evaluate leadership, the more senseless it is to want to ascribe this success to individual nations; the less the evaluation of national leaders is aimed at the actual addressees; and the less realistic the personal attribution of success or failure.

The contradiction between global political interconnectedness and national expectations of leadership is also the result of national limitation of democracy. This limitation refers to a national political system whose results depend increasingly on transnational events. Such events cannot be attributed to individuals. The terms of trade recognize no responsible individuals that would offer themselves as "bad guys" or "heroes."

The political interconnectedness leads to alienation between leaders and their constituents. Karl Mannheim said decades ago that this would lead to an ever increasing distance between the masses and the upper classes and to the "call for the leader" (Mannheim 1958, 69). The more leadership in the sense of personal accountability and responsibility for politics disappears, the stronger the "Volk" will react with the demand for recognizable personal leadership. The gulf between the reality of politics and the expectations of politics grows larger.

Politics itself widens this gap by responding to and thereby encouraging the demand for recognizable personal leadership through a technical mystification of the actual conditions. The stylization of politicians as decisive personalities on whom the quality of society is significantly dependent, although their actual possibilities for structuring or restructuring society in a stable democracy are negligible, strengthens a false perception and therefore, ultimately, a false consciousness. This politics of marketing personalities as leaders who are not leaders because they can't be, contradicts both the fantasy and the reality of democracy; and this contradiction feeds and strengthens itself constantly.

This is not to say that the personality factor is of no consequence in a stable democracy. The above mentioned distinction made by Burns can assist here again (Burns 1978): Transactional leadership as the qualities of management that can and must be expected of one who holds political office just as they would be expected of the head of a corporation — this is also needed by a stable democracy. It is particularly the ability to communicate that must be demanded of politicians in the framework of transactional leadership — the task of mediating between the different agencies of government, bureaucracy, justice, parliament; but most importantly, the mediation between the sum of these agencies, that is, between the political system and its addressees, that is, society.

Leadership must ensure legitimation. In a democracy, this form of leadership is subject to a clear form of checks and balances, namely, election results. Successful leadership is the kind that is in demand and that guarantees the election. And leadership must ensure integration, must synchronize the different agencies of government, must especially integrate the rulers and the ruled. This kind of leadership is different from Jaruzelski's, one which corresponds to the concept of "transforming leadership": This is not measureable in terms of election results but in terms of social data and political output. When this output, in the form of unemployment statistics, per capita income, violent deaths, literacy rates, etc., is dependent on the work of one person; when this work is unmistakeable; when the real history of society is written significantly and unmistakeably by one person, then we can speak of substantial, "transforming leadership." And in terms of its logic, this cannot be unified with democracy in the long run.

Democracy tends to dissolve this "transforming" leadership in a manner that corresponds fundamentally with the literal definition of "rule by the people." And yet history is written and democracy is taught as if this were not the case. Henry Kissinger, for example, tends to portray the history of states and diplomacy of the 19th and 20th centuries as the work of great men (Kissinger [no date]; Kissinger 1994). And the almost mythical perception of the role of the individual in history (especially American history), greatly influenced by John F. Kennedy, reveals a similar perception that emphasizes individual personality (Kennedy 1956).

Yet whereas Kissinger can illustrate that he is primarily interested in the representation of politics in the international sphere, that is, a realm that is no democracy in itself, Kennedy confronts the contradiction between the romanticized and heroicized expectation of leadership and the reality of democracy, without accounting for this contradiction. How should a President of the United States, following the spirit of the Constitution and promise of any democracy, obey the impulses emanating from the people and yet, following his own conscience, lead the nation? The image of the people's servant and the image of the leader of this same people cannot be understood together intellectually. Fairy tales, of course, are not required to submit to such a demand for intellectual consistency.

And they are fairy tale-like expectations with which especially the President of the United States is confronted. Since he is, in his historical, constitutional embodiment, an "elected monarch," all citizens can project their predemocratic desires onto this President in the best democratic consciousness. The degree to which predemocratic patterns determine these projections is evident in the particularly extreme blurring between public and private: Presidents and their families are, in fact, royals.

This expectation is an undercurrent of the thesis of two presidencies, one for domestic, the other for foreign policy. This explanation, developed by Aaron Wildavsky even before Nixon's "imperial" presidency, accounts for the contradiction between predemocratic expectation and democratic reality (Shull 1991). An American President can actually practice leadership in foreign policy and be more than a first-level manager of a massive governmental machinery caught in the spotlight. Even in the late 20th century, a President can write history in foreign policy. In domestic policy, on the other hand, his hands are tied by public opinion whose short-term developments affect the presidency through the Congressional elections every two years.

In this way, foreign policy, which carries a special weight for the leadership of a super power, can continually nourish the expectation of a particular role of non-routine political leadership, without conflicting with the erosion of leadership in a stable democracy. Here, the imperial nature of the US presidency finds the support that is inconsistent with the way in which precisely the American president is tied so tightly to Congress, public opinion, and the media.

Yet leadership in domestic policy, assuming stable conditions in a democracy, is conceivable only in the sense of management and communication. The political content and the actual political form must be determined by the political market. "Transactional leadership" means exactly this: that interests present in a society are represented and tranformed into decisions. The politician is the broker: he deals in interests. The skill that the individual broker develops can and must vary. But it may not be mistaken for the actual driving force of the political process: the interests.

It goes without saying that leaders, that is, the elite, have their own interests, just as these interests must be taken into account in the analysis of the political process. But the elite's interest in maintaining or expanding its own position is a secondary one. Particularly in a stable democracy, this interest on the part of the leadership will concentrate on promptly recognizing social interests, foretelling their dynamics correspondingly, and reacting to them in the best possible way and then, in the sense of the axiom of self-interest, coming to a decision. Leadership as a brokerage means that the self-interest of the political leadership is the result of a social parallelogram of interests and not an autonomous part of it; a dependent, not an independent variable; a reactive, not an active factor.

Even where Burns, in the framework of his concept of "transactional leadership," finds formulations at first that appear to expose a greater autonomy of routine leadership in stable democracies, nothing changes vis-à-vis the dependence of elite self-interests on social interests. With specific reference to the "opinion leadership," Burns writes this of the "market place" on which the relationship between leadership and followers insists in the exchange of gratification, a variant, therefore, of the sociological exchange theory (Burns 1978, 258). And even the notion of the arousal of public opinion (Burns 1978, 259-265) remains within this framework: in order to stimulate something, it must be present. In order to recall interests and encourage their articulation, the corresponding social factors must be given. Particularly in a stable democracy, these cannot simply be politically decreed.

The central distinction that Burns makes between "transactional" or routine and "transforming," or non-routine leadership corresponds to the difference between politics and policy (Easton 1953). In a stable democracy, all the hallmarks exhibited by Burns' typology of "transactional leadership" — public opinion, bureaucracy, party, legislative and executive branches — are nothing more than a naming of the usual players of a democratic political system, that is, a naming of politics. The criteria that he lists for the typology of "transforming leadership," on the other hand, have nothing to do directly with politics — ideas, morals, reform, revolution, ideologies. He thus describes what precedes or follows the political process to be be carried out by the players of politics — policy, that is to say, results, content, and the consequences of politics measureable in society itself.

With its own logic and consistency, democracy destroys the possibility of tracing policies back to the work of individuals. This work becomes routine — interchangeable, mistakeable for that of another. Individuals and their political activity become a dependent variable, activity in the system that reduces the personal sphere of influence to almost nothing. In a democracy, the tangible force of the political system which subordinates all decisions to the concern over the results of the next election transforms these decisions into processes that can be calculated according to their tendencies and therefore subjectively interchanged.

This is the form of leadership present in a stable democracy — the optimal observation and analysis of the political market; the availablity of the optimal supply for the satisfaction of present demand; and the optimal marketing in order to reach an optimal market share. There is no other form of leadership (in the sense of "transforming leadership") in a democracy, with several exceptions:

— in phases of a decisive new beginning of democracy (for example Charles De Gaulle, 1958)

— in niches of politics not encompassed, but tolerated by democracy (most importantly, foreign policy)

— leadership from the outside in the sense of moral and intellectual leadership (for example, Martin Luther King Jr.)

In all of these exceptions, however, leadership in a demcoracy is tied to an ex-post facto acceptance. The logic of the political market and with it the logic of existing democracy reaches for this sort of leadership not, admittedly, from the start, but after the fact. At some point, "transforming leadership" must be converted to "transactional leadership."

De Gaulle's transformations from the Fourth to the Fifth Republic had to be implemented after the fact in the political market in the form of a referendum. The General's "authority" alone would not have sufficed, as it also had not sufficed in 1946 when his notion of the Fourth Republic failed for lack of acceptance. British foreign policy of 1940, for which Winston Churchill carried the ultimate responsibility, and Roosevelt's American foreign policy before Pearl Harbor are the expression of a non-routine leadership, but without the objective measure of success, i.e., the victory in World War II, the acceptance and the political perception of both cases of leadership would have been a different matter. And Martin Luther King Jr. was able to influence American politics in the 1950's and 1960's as a moral authority only because the time was ripe in American society for the recognition of the untenability of racial discrimination.

The evaluation of the compatibility of leadership and democracy is also a semantic problem. If one insists on a broad definition of leadership and also includes forms of routine leadership in the concept, the question becomes moot. If, however, one limits the concept to the non-routine forms, to "transforming leadership" and to the unmistakeable and non-interchangeable effects of the individual on history, then the question remains.

But limiting the question to the compatibility of non-routine leadership and democracy has not only an operational but also an explanatory component. If one follows the broad, general notion of leadership, then an extremely ideologically colored view of democracy is advanced, at least indirectly. And this is valid both generally and specifically:

— In general, a broad, undifferentiated concept of leadership promotes a romanticized view of political events, whereby heroic individual fighters "structure" history. Politics is made naive and brought down to the intellectual level of comics.

— Specifically, a broad definition of leadership promotes the marketing strategies that emphasize the personality factor within a stable democracy and that use the (quite correct) reference to the ruling consciousness to confound the gaze at the complex realities that lie behind it.

The reduction of the concept of leadership to "transforming leadership" also corresonds, then, to an analytical need to shed an ideologically critical light on the wordiness of the meaning of the individual personality and the historical power of political leadership.

Behind the central hypothesis of the virtual incompatibility of leadership and democracy is also the claim that this corresponds to the essence of democracy; and that if the hypothesis survives the tests, then democracy will have earned a certain balance of success. Because both theories of democracy bear themselves out: the identity-based theory, which assumes an equality between those who govern and those who are governed and therefore also the dissolution of any form of rule of one human being over another; and on the other hand, the empirical theory, which views the essence of democracy in the marketplace and resolves political decision-making in the satisfaction of political demand.

This is not to say that it makes no sense to conduct research on routine leadership in stable democracies. In the process of analyzing political systems, it makes sense, of course, to investigate how and why certain people rise to positions of political power; which prerequisites are advantageous to whom; which expectations the public has of governments and leaders; how decisive the arguments of the top candidates are in the outcome of an election; which image is "effective" and which is not. This type of approach is, of course, a self-restrictive one that presupposes a limited concept of leadership, in essence excluding everything that does not suit the notion of "transactional leadership."

Investigating routine leadership can bring about numerous insights into the role and meaning of political parties, into the ways in which political recruiting functions, and into the effectiveness of certain campaign practices. As far as the recognition of the development of democracy is concerned, however, this limited approach does not bring us much further — with regard to democracy theory it falls flat.

Democracy has come a long way — it can feel vindicated. Yet, at the same time, democracy is still in its infancy. For any assertion about the success rate of democracy refers to the social realms to which democracy applies and in which it has borne itself out. The assertion has little validity for the far more numerous realms in which it has no place:

— Democracy has little weight in the sphere of international politics. The pleasure with which the collapse of communism in Europe has been met with increasingly new, self-reproducing officialdom contradicts the alleged victory of democracy. When Azerbaijan and Armenia, Bosnia-Herzegovina, Croatia and the "rest" of Yugoslavia confront each other with military force as soveriegn states, these tangled relationships are surely not determined by democracy, indeed, they cannot be determined by democracy. The triumphant cries of hurrah vis-à-vis the new sovereign states are cries of hurrah for the reduction of democracy that cancels out the spread of democracy internally; they are also cries of hurrah for the unavoidably escalating danger of war brought about by the increase in the number of sovereign states. "Every state is free to use force in its relations with other states ..." (Elias 1987, 9). The more states enjoy this freedom that accompanies their sovereignty, the higher the probability of war. Democracy ends at every border based on the sovereignty of a nation-state. Any action beyond these borders follows a logic different from that of democracy, even if the states in question are democracies. For real democracies, foreign policy is the great deficit of democracy, and for that very reason, foreign policy is the refuge of heroes.

— Democracy does not encompass society in its entirety, only in parts. The containment of power and its embeddedness in a logic that makes routine and ultimately cancels out any form of leadership is therefore valid only for the sectors of society controlled by democracy. Beyond real democracy lies any amount of power and rule that is not overly regulated, or at least not in a democratic sense. There is also any amount of leadership. The form of social power that is external to democracy is of great relevance to democracy as a factor of the field of politics that determines the interests. For this reason, the question of the limits of democracy and possible shifting boundaries is so important. It concerns the debate between two concepts of leadership: the confrontation between the leadership that tends to erode due to democracy and the brand of leadership that goes unchecked by democracy.

Democracy has won — leadership is dead. Leadership is alive and well — democracy lies out of reach.

4   *An Impossible Encounter — The First*

"But the art of policy is to create a calculation of the risks and rewards
that affect the adversary's calculations."

(Kissinger 1994, 481)

"With this quote he proves once again that he is your dutiful pupil, Messer Niccolo. Policy as a sort of aesthetic design, reduced to strategy and removed from any goal. And anyway, art as policy! Small wonder that such a cynical notion could appeal to the messieurs Cesare Borgia and Richard Nixon."

"What a grotesque misunderstanding. You only demonstrate how it is you succeeded in rising to the honors of the altars of the Holy Roman Church, but that it was not given to you to influence England's politics, Sir Thomas. You confuse the role of the field chaplain with that of campaign analyst and by doing that, you only help to ensure that no one explores the significance of the strategist. You are quite like the Prussian King — he wrote an 'Anti-Machiavelli' with the sole purpose of punishing the bearer of bad tidings. The tidings themselves are meant to disappear as much as possible. That I call true cynicism."

"I really have nothing in common with the allegedly Great Frederick. And I believe I have sufficiently proven that I do not cave in to the thrones of princes. It is not like me at all to sing the praises of the powerful, not even by disguising it as their 'education.' I gladly leave that sort of labelling hoax to you. What I care about is simply the unavoidability of morality in politics, which can be proved empirically. Politics is never free of values, that is, never free of morality; and this can also be an immorality, but who am I telling this to?"

"You act as though you had established clear parameters for 'good' and 'evil,' as though someone had a corner on 'morality' and someone else were left with 'immorality'. Intellectually, that can't be taken seriously. Besides, the fact that Henry made you a head shorter does not impress me in this regard. You are of good use now to the other side as an instrument of propaganda — for the Pope and for the Catholic monarchs, especially for those in Spain. You obviously never uttered a critical word about their Inquisition, including the dress rehearsal for the Holocaust. In 1522 you welcomed the Spaniard Charles of Habsburg in London with highest honors. And the following year, Wolsey wanted to send you as ambassador — you, the moralist — to the land of the Inquisition. So much for your morality."

"Your attacks become personal, Messer Niccolo. Evidently you notice that your position is intellectually untenable. Of course I am not concerned with a concrete morality, and certainly not my own, at least not in this stage of the debate. I do not have to offer a confessional catalogue that tells the powerful of this world what is 'good' and what is 'evil.' I gladly leave this sort of political advising to you. I am concerned with the statement that politics is more than the struggle for achieving and maintaining power. First, we need to differentiate: there is power and then there is power. Ask the serfs who are subject to princely powers if they would not rather be citizens subjected to the power, for example, of your city, even if it is expressly not a 'republic.' And as soon as we differentiate, we come to an historical dynamics: existing circumstances are not always the same. They can be 'better' or 'worse,' depending on the time coordinates. But if we admit this, then we have arrived at the unavoidability of morality, any morality at all to begin with."

"Historical dynamics — there's a notion I can deal with, Sir Thomas. But you do not strike me as the most suitable person to be discussing historicity. You invented that literary opium that competes with the preachers of all time by making everyone so drunk with the invention of paradiesical conditions that they forget the repulsiveness of their own existence. You developed this monster, this utopia that tells of the end of history by promising a heaven on earth. And now you of all people come to me with your historicity? And what is 'morality,' what is differentiation in the time coordinates for instance, for your country? Would it have been better or worse if the House of York rather than Lancaster had won the War of the Roses? Certainly, your Henry would not have ascended the throne in that case; and the propaganda machine of the Windsors, led by this Shakespeare, could not have made a hunchbacked monster of Richard, according to your example, of course; an embarrassing example of discrimination that makes me long for political correctness. But otherwise? Richard's successor would surely have had successors who would have sent some other Lord Chancellor to the scaffold. That would have cost you your sainthood, but would it have been otherwise significantly 'better' or 'worse' than the other outcome?"

"You confuse me again with a Baptist. I am no fundamentalist, and I am no Thomas Münzer. But I also have nothing in common with this Martin Luther who aligned himself with the German princes, a pattern that you should recognize. I am also no Leninist who offers the blue print of the near future. But to return to your attack on utopia, Messer Niccolo, either you did not read the book, or you have completely misunderstood it. First of all, it is what it is meant to be: a novel. Second, it is not meant to construct a concrete, real utopia. That is why it is called 'ou topia', because it cannot be located in any time or place. But you seem to have no sense for literature,

with your preference for the real politics of daggers and poisonous drinks, just as you have no sense for the power of imagination ..."

"...now you even refer to the anarchists of the Paris May and demand that imagination be in power ..."

"... I have nothing in common with the anarchists and you know that. Why this cheap polemics? It is a simple attempt to try to hide your lack of knowledge of historicity."

"Well, if you are quite serious, Sir Thomas, than recall your 'utopia,' or at least contradict its dominant interpretation. Write an 'Anti-More' yourself that explains that you did not mean to call for the end of history, that you did not mean to propagate the opium dream of a society free of conflict and distract from the morass of politics. These secondary utopians have always seen to it that politics remains secret knowledge whose entrance is disguised by a doctrine of virtue that alleges to proclaim the good, the true and the beautiful, not the real. These utopians have called out to all those who want to push forward from this doctrine of virtue to a real doctrine of politics 'Shame, you're all Machiavellians! You care about dirty things like the relations of power!' Distance yourself, will you, from these utopians who were and are the most self-satisfied justifiers since they cast veils over the notion of concrete rule. Make it clear that your morality is not the conventional 'utopian' sort and then perhaps we can engage, finally, in an intellectual debate. Distance yourself, sir!"

"That's how far it's come, that you, Messer Niccolo, set conditions, and moralistic ones at that, for deigning to agree to a dialogue. Evidently you realize that you are not only not catalyzing any sort of dynamics with your snapshots of what you call reality; beyond that, you cannot even convey any serious intellectual returns. Or do you believe that it is particularly original to tell the powerful that they owe their power to power and that they must exploit it as ruthlessly as possible in order to stay in power? If that is your political theory and you block off any further development, then I praise those whom you call 'utopians.' Political theory cannot be reduced to knowing more and more about less and less relevant details. When, for example, has the Prince (General Secretary, Führer, Prime Minister, etc.) thought to destroy those to whom he owes his own rise to power? Must not political theory also be developed further toward answering the question of which goals power can serve or be useful to — those of the Prince, the President, the party functionary? Your political theory is a theory of 'politics' — of the machinery of interests, transformed into access to power. But we need also a theory 'policies' — of the effects and results of concrete power relations."

"But I have nothing at all against asking these questions. It's simply that I find it all rather boring. Somehow you always know who is going to say what. The Pope decrees that everything lies in the divine nature of man.

But what this means, now that varies. Up until the 19th century, the Popes always held the opinion that the oh-so-practical institution of slavery could be reconciled with the notion of human dignity and that it thus corresponded to natural law. Which does nothing to prevent today's Pope from pretending that his Church has always been the champion of the disfranchised. Mr. Brezhnev and Co. have never had difficulties presenting their personal family vacations in palaces on the Black Sea taken over from the czars as the expression of revolutionary progress. The New World Order of the U.S. is valid when the oh-so-democratic rule of the Kuwaiti royals is threatened, not when self-determination in East Timor is at stake. You, Sir Thomas, pose the question of morality — how dreary. I see only interests everywhere, especially when the lips fairly drip with the salve of values and ideals. And when I hear of 'alternative goals', I only ask who wants to sleep with the ruler now."

"Save the polemics for your function as court jester with the Borgias or with the Duvaliers or, for all I care, with Mao's grandchildren. The bloody robbers always like to hear that there were no alternatives to their deeds and that they are therefore 'right': that walking all over the weak merely corresponds to outside pressures: that 'rule' and 'rule' can always only mean the same thing; and that, therefore, it makes no sense to tend the only driving force behind every change, namely, the conscience. You, Messer Niccolo, fulfill perfectly the task of a tranquilizer that the powerful keep so that it can grant them cynicism and a restful sleep."

"You repeat yourself. The powerful have always denounced me because I return their shameful ideologies, their extremely dubious justifications to what defines their rule, namely, self-interest."

"Your oh-so-humble dedication to the most holy father Clemens VII, with which you open your history of Florence, is probably also an expression of your critical distance from the powerful!"

"Sir Thomas, now you confuse the necessity of earning one's daily bread with the content of my writings. No one has made me a saint. And the willingness with which you offered the House of Tudor your unbearable polemics against Richard III, a House which was able to use this 'morality' to justify its rule, was just as foreign to me as the 'morality' of your 'Dialogue on Heresies' with which you backed up the Inquisition in the case of poor Richard Hunne. For you advised the rulers to kill for reasons of morality. If I advise the powerful to kill, then it is for reasons of rule and its logic. And I find them, I do not make them. Reading my books is forbidden under many systems as subversive. And I am subversive, because I do everything possible to remain intellectually pure. And the architects of all political façades fear this, the destructive power of analytical thinking that results in the dissolution of the morality that blocks people's intellectual

capabilities. The true revolution exists in the destruction of myths, including, of course, the myth of revolution."

"You remind me of a monk holding a string of beads, mumbling the same thing over and over, not caring whether it's the redundancy of the rosary or the 'Om Mane Padme Hum.' Your thought, whose supposed subversiveness you are so proud of, is the only real banality, the only real calculable quantity, the thing that has been known for a long time. 'People have interests but no ideals.' So what? Don't you ever yearn for new intellectual ground, even if it means the risk of being unprotected and therefore, making a mistake? Your fear of producing ideology paralyzes you and makes you impotent and therefore uninteresting. Your theory is one long déjà-vu experience."

"If attention should be bought with entertainment value, then one can simply produce comics and sell them as theory. If I make the desire for what is new the guideline for theory, then your 'theoretical' writings would have to be the first to be tossed as the oldest 'old hat,' Sir Thomas. Incidentally, desire: I felt desire, of course, while writing my 'Mandragola' .... No, I must insist: the only guideline in the evaluation of what passes as theory is reality. Otherwise we end up with salad bar theories from which everyone takes what suits his interests and which would ultimately only reflect the existing power relations. Whatever you care to say about my 'Prince,' the fact that the real princes of the world do not like my book, speaks for me. For those in power want nothing so little as to be exposed for what they are: driven by ruthless self-interest."

"To bring it to a point, Messer Niccolo: Do you really believe that Caligula and Roosevelt both signified one and the same thing? Does the simple fact that both 'ruled' really suffice to equate them? And is not precisely the very quality you supposedly so treasure, namely, the ability to analyze, completely lost with such gross simplifications? If everything in politics throughout the millenia is already there in your 'Prince' or in your 'Discourses', then aren't you the author of a boring catechism that deprives us of the essence of analysis, the capacity to differentiate?"

"Well, now, you know of course that I cannot agree with these simple equations. I may emphasize the historical dimension somewhat less than Marxists of all stripes, but I use it myself when I strip the Church of its supposedly timeless doctrine and expose it for what it is: an institution dependent on history and social change. I do not deny the fact that Gregory XIII and John Paul II contradict one another when it comes to democracy and human rights, rather, I emphasize this. What they have in common is the method of producing ideology, not the content."

"Perhaps we can leave polemics behind in this point, despite our differences. If there is change in content, not in methods, of course, then it

must be of interest to you to observe and describe the extent and orientation of this change, and not to cover everything with the claim that it's always about the self-interests of the powerful. And if everything is not the same, what makes the difference? For you, everything may be evil, but all evils are not necessarily alike or equally evil!"

"If I were not interested in evaluating, that is, in differentiating, or, you might say, in moralizing, I would not have so much fun catching the holier-than-thou preachers at their own game. Of course, my preference for criticizing ideology is something very moralistic and my uncontrollable desire to prove the cognitive dissonance between the claims and realities of all the clerical hogwash is, strictly speaking, something very moralistic. Moralistic, that is, if one does not understand it as a system of thought that blinds its representatives to their own dependencies and interests and if one avoids declaring one's own highly personal wishes to be science. In other words, if morality does not become ideology, then I am for morality. And if you want to compare and measure the evils of this world — Caligula and the Medicis, Robespierre and the Bourbons, Columbus and the Aztecs, and of course Stalin and the Social Democrats — in order to avoid silly comparisons, I'm with you on that. I must ask you just one thing: Leave your eschatological dreamings of the true, the good and the beautiful; leave your utopia at the door."

"Now this I don't quite understand, Messer Niccolo. Agreed, if you mean that in the current sense of our discourse we need no sketch of a best of all possible societies. But we must have our points of reference, a standard by which we determine why, for example, Hitler and Franco cannot be equated. And if we do not openly dedicate ourselves to the search for an evaluative standard then precisely what you have wished to exclude will come in through the back door: interests that are not declared openly, namely, ideologies. We may not need a utopia for our discussion, but we need the discussion of what we will discuss. Again, just as an example, do you evaluate the right of non-European cultures to develop in their own way as more important, even independent of the typical, Western claim to universal human rights? Or the right of a presumably small minority of women to emancipate themselves from and against their own culture according to Mr. Jefferson's claim, say, in Bangladesh in the late 20th century?

"This Thomas Jefferson — talking big in Philadelphia about the inalienable rights all are born with and then having his slaves serve him in Virginia ..."

"Granted, we are familiar with this objection, and it simply proves that we must differentiate ..."

"But, Sir Thomas, you must allow me a little jab: to praise the welfare of all in 'Utopia' and then, as Chancellor of England ..."

"A role I failed in ..."

"But not because of your oh so progressive social policies, but because you did not leave Henry to his women!"

"This return to personal polemics only shows your instinct to flee, Messer Niccolo. Whenever things turn serious and you must take a stand on an aspect that makes you uncomfortable, you fear having to leave the cynical shallows of simple empiricism — and that you don't like."

"And you speak of polemics! But polemics aside — I have never liked the bearded living room revolutionary who let his millionaire friend finance his bourgeois lifestyle in London — this mixture of smallmindedness and prophecy! But I find him compelling in one regard: when he comes with his dialectic, borrowed from Hegel, of course, but nonetheless, further developed and made useful for political analysis. Nothing is what it appears to be on the surface and everything has a bit of contradiction, and thus resistance and movement. That I find fascinating when it does not lead to the end goal, in the form of a perfect society, unlike what Marx says. Dialectic minus the classless society, that could bring us further along, Sir Thomas!"

"I believe you when you say you like Marx' emphasis of contradictions, but not his quasi-religious aspect. I can also well imagine that the Communist paradise on earth is just as repulsive to you as my 'utopia.' But let's stick to your notion of the end. Even if we know, with a certainty bordering on the absoute, that neither my utopia nor the Marxist one can ever become reality in any developmental period of society, don't we still need a similar image as a starting point toward making a discriminating evaluation? If we say, for example, that the misery of the English proletariat during the time of Marx was greater than under Mrs. Thatcher, don't we have a concept in the back of our mind that one could call utopia, or, so you don't object to the word, 'a system of norms' or 'concept of justice'?"

"Agreed. Of course, I assume that it is negative to practice a 'morality' different from what one preaches. But I do not claim that this personal norm of mine is the product of a scientific, epistemological process. It is, rather, the expression of my own, unavoidable partisanship. In the sense of certain knowledge it can be 'right' if I said the Prince must, for example, 'preach water' to ensure his rule. He himself may drink water under no circumstances, he must stick to wine, by himself as much as possible. He must insist with all his power that all others keep contracts and promises made before him; he himself must not follow this law. Whether you or I personally like this circumstance in the sense of what you have called a 'concept of justice' is another matter."

"But I do not believe, Messer Niccolo, that that can be so easily separated: Justice as a private opinion, in the sense of a hobby, and the demonstration and tracing of real power relations as a scientific statement.

Simply the fact that you are occupied with the techniques of attaining and maintaining power and not, say, with the life history of St. Hieronymus, is an expression of partisanship that, at least indirectly, has to do with morality (or even a 'concept of justice')."

"If you choose an early father, let it at least be St. Anthony. He at least resisted some interesting temptations in his desert. But, of course, you are quite right, in the sense of a truism. Of course I am bound to my personal interests, including those I am not conscious of. And of course these flow into my choice of objects of analysis and thus into my analysis, in the sense of the given partisanship you mentioned earlier. But do we really need to discuss this obvious fact any longer, Sir Thomas?"

"Not as far as I'm concerned, Messer Niccolo. But it seems important to me to have clarified this. All too easily, and somewhat, well, rather more than somewhat, arrogantly, you claim to be purely a critic, above the morass. And in your duties for the various lords of Florence? You, the average political advisor, you of all people should not stylize yourself as a pure critic. But if you take my remarks to be self-evident, then I withdraw the accusation of arrogance ..."

" ... after you have expressed it just to be on the safe side, so that any imaginary jury will think me arrogant in spite of your withdrawal ..."

" ... now, just a moment: This is not an freestyle exercise in a competition that is supposed to determine the best political theoretician of all time! The time of scholastic disputes is long gone! But I still have the impression that you, Messer Niccolo, assume that you would have to win such a competition, if things went as they should!"

"Whereas you, in the humility of the martyr who has officially beeen called to heaven, are of course beyond such vanities!"

"I understand that the circumstances around my martyrdom disturb you; but not even I can change that now. But let's return to the relationship between scientific analysis and practical politics: you emphasize the separation, I emphasise the interconnectedness of these two fields. But I do not level the two plains; and if you do not see the separation as absolute, then we have a methodological basis for our discussions!"

"You are a harmonizer, Sir Thomas! But I can declare myself in agreement as long as this harmony is understood dialectically. But I am concerned with the connection to praxis. Do you agree that whoever enters politics must get his hands dirty? To remain with your image: Whoever differentiates between the evils of this world and works for substituting the lesser for the greater evil must deal with the lesser evil. He must become an evil himself, even if it is the lesser."

"I must confess that that is too abstract for me. Of course a reflection on the means and the end is necessary; and a means that is not really a good one can be used if it brings about a significantly better result ..."

"Too scholastic, Sir Thomas! The question is quite simple. Agree with me: He who does not want to get dirty at all, he who want to maintain his personal integrity (whatever that may be) may not be active in politics. Such a man would have to become a hermit or live on a desert island like the one on which your countryman Daniel Defoe had his Robinson settle. But work that is socially perceptible, that is, politics, can not be effected with this ethical fundamentalism of the individual."

"You put too fine a point on the matter and thus you simplify things. Under certain circumstances — yes! If the 'City of the World' is so far removed from the 'City of God' that every attempt to bridge the gap seems doomed to failure, then we must agree with your 'either-or.' But if ..."

"You are such a victim of theology — now you come with your St. Augustine! What you really mean is that a Christian hegemony, and by that I mean a hegemony of the rulers who call themselves Christians, like the Borgias or the Tudors, silences the Augustine in you. As soon as the princes call themselves 'Christian' or even 'defenders of the faith', than you, Sir Thomas, turn soft with flattery. And by that I mean of course, in your case, not for the usual opportunistic reasons, but as a result of deeply internalized reflexes that only let you differentiate between tyrants because they sacrifice to different gods. The fact that the work for the representative of Christ on earth has the same, unavoidably dirty consequences as the work of, say, a Montezuma ..."

"I thought we were finished with the ridiculous comparisons, Messer Niccolo ..."

"Yes and no! By that I do not mean that politics in the sevice of Julius II must mean the exact same amount of dirt as politics in the service of Attila. Quantitatively there can be significant differences, although I would never assume that the politics of the king of the Huns must necessarily make one dirtier than that of our most militant Pope. I mean it qualitatively: whoever enters politics and though it be with the most subjectively honest intention of doing so in the highest sense of justice, will not be able to do it without getting dirty. Or, expressed differently: If social ethics is at stake, the would-be politican must learn to do without his own individual ethics. Whoever cannot give up the luxury of a purely personal conscience, must leave his hands out of politics. And he should do what the afore-mentioned St. Anthony did. The desert beckons. To be alone as a human being between the snakes and other beasts, that and only that is freedom from politics. That and only that is the guarantee for clean hands. You, Sir Thomas, must have sensed just that as you climbed the career ladder of practical politics higher

and higher, as your friend Erasmus of Rotterdam continued to refuse to serve a prince. And this humorless, bloodless Raphael with no profile whom you had tell the story of your utopia, this alter ego of yours, he refuses to hire himself out to princes. You are split between standing on the sidelines and going along. You practiced your politics with a guilty conscience, otherwise you wouldn't have distanced yourself from politics in a utopia, this strangely boring land that is missing the very ingredient that was the content of your life: the personal power of princes."

"I have the impression that you are speaking out a fictitious window. Do you think you're at an intellectual beauty contest again? Why these sidesteps, what are you yielding to, why don't you want to think together progressively? And what you have confessed in your fiery rhetoric is enough for that anyway, Messer Niccolo: even the dirt that you diagnose as unavoidable must be differentiated — whether you call it quantitative or qualitative matters little to me. Let's simply call the dirt evil and then we'll have reached the point we have already agreeed upon. Not every evil is alike. For that reason, it is necessary to differentiate and evaluate. And only after that does politics become truly interesting, because it can be understood as more than a mere technique to push through one's own interests. Only then can we decide and choose because we have the means to judge what is better and what is worse. By the way, the guilty conscience you accuse me of is perhaps the best driving force for that, the best motive. If we do not feel a fundamental discomfort — a guilty conscience, in other words — in doing what we do, why should we attempt changes? Why fight for something better when we don't regret what is wrong, for which we share the responsibility?"

"Sir Thomas, but now you must add: 'Better' or 'worse' must always been seen in connection with concrete interests, otherwise one conveys the false impression that there is such a thing as an objective commonwealth. And we have already agreed that there is no such thing ..."

"Objection, Messer Niccolo: we have agreed to leave that question out of the equation for the time being!"

"Fine, for all I care. We agree to disagree and we'll continue to discuss what we agree on."

5 On the Tendency to Ban Machiavelli to Hell

The Conversation in Hell — Machiavelli, the Subversive Man of Reason — No Special Morality for Politics — Politicians as Scapegoats

In his book of 1864 entitled "Dialogues in Hell between Machiavelli and Montesquieu," the Frenchman Maurice Joly placed Niccolo Machiavelli in hell in order to have him discuss power and law with Montesquieu (Joly 1990). The book was published anonymously in Brussels and smuggled into France. Joly was discovered by the French police, arrested and ultimately sentenced to 18 months in prison by the imperial court (Joly 1990, 367-369). The reason: Machiavelli stood for Napoleon III.

"Machiavelli stood as the embodiment of a policy of violence next to Montesquieu, who represented the politics of law; and Machiavelli was supposed to be Napoleon III who would represent his despicable politics in person" (Joly 1990, 367).

The notion of what Machiavelli means and what he stands for was and is so evil that a roman à clef in the form of a dialogue in hell that stylized the French emperor as Machiavelli was enough to put its author in prison in the final period of the Second Empire.

James Burnham, alternating between Marxism and the theory of modern management, illustrates why Machiavelli continues to be banned again and again: he publicizes knowledge about the nature of domination (Burnham 1943). Frederick II represents the tendency of the powerful to brand as a cynic anyone who describes power and to punish the messenger for the message and thus to deflect moral outrage about the realities of power from its practitioners to its critics.

"If men generally understood as much of the mechanism of rule and privilege as Machiavelli understood, they would no longer be deceived into accepting that rule and privilege, and they would know what steps to take to overcome them. [...] Small wonder that the powerful — in public — denounce Machiavelli ... They can recognize an enemy who will never compromise, even when that enemy is so abstract as a body of ideas" (Burnham 1943, 77).

Machiavelli stands for the attempt to understand and explain politics, not to use it as a screen for the projection of desires. Thus,

Machiavelli stands at the forefront of attempts to deal with politics in a scientific, scholarly manner. And that is why he must be banished to hell.

There is a reference in "The Prince" to Ferdinand the Catholic: "A certain prince of the present time, whom it is well not to name, never does anything but preach peace and good faith, but he is really a great enemy to both, and either of them, had he observed them, would have lost him state or reputation on many occasions" (Machiavelli, The Prince, XVIII).

This statement exemplifies Machiavelli's subversive quality. With reference to a reality that can be tested, he claims that there is a dissonance between expectation and reality. And he ascribes to this contradiction a stabilizing function for rule. It can, under certain circumstances, be advantageous for maintaining dominance to preach a certain morality, yet practice quite the opposite.

This thesis must first be proved. However, if such proof is undertaken, the existing rule may sustain damage whether the thesis is proved or not. The contradictions between morality and reality would be exposed. The morality that was preached would sacrifice its capacity to act as a disguise for a reality that ran contrary to it.

This cannot be in the interest of those who rule under the protection of the disguise. For this reason, Machiavelli's empirical claim must be moralized. What is formulated as a description of reality must be denounced as a normative challenge. Machiavelli is transformed from a critic of the sermon to the preacher; his diagnosis is taken as therapy and damned moralistically, and with it, Machiavelli himself.

The damning of Machiavelli corresponds to a Manichean principle of the dichotomous order of things. Something is either "good" or "evil." Since reality cannot be presented as purely "good" by those who claim to be able to see, the truly good becomes transcendental: "True justice exists only in the commonwealth whose founder and ruler is Christ" (St. Augustine, City of God, Book II).

Machiavelli is not concerned with "true justice" as understood by Augustine. But those whose task it is to console themselves with this "true justice," "all the 'official' thinkers, the lawyers and philosophers and preachers and demagogues and moralists and editors — must defame Machiaevelli" (Burnham 1943, 77). That is why he must go to hell. He, man of reason that he is, does not simply dare to condemn the conditions of this world in an abstract manner; instead, he represents them concretely, illuminates and sheds light on them. And, in turn, those who want to leave the concrete in the dark cannot forgive him for this because it does not serve their interests. This is another reason Machievelli must go to hell.

Machiavelli allows the relativization of good as well as evil. His standard does not allow the "either — or," the "everything or nothing" that avoids all measurement. For him, politics and human life can be represented in contexts and deconstructed into causalities.

In the first book of the "Discourses," Machiavelli writes about the unavoidability of thanklessness in politics. It is precisely those who owe their power to the powerful who must approach them with particular mistrust (Machiavelli, Discourses I, XXIX). Machiavelli describes here the inherent social and political principles of power. He thereby deconstructs the catalog of virtues into functions. Ultimately, every virtue must be tested in terms of its functionality. Nothing stands alone, everything has its place in a context. There are no "primary" and "secondary virtues"; no division of virtues into those that stand alone and those that are derived. In this sense, all virtues are "secondary."

This separation of morality from politics can be interpreted in different ways. Burnham refers to the connection Mussolini liked to construct between Machiavelli and Italian faschism (Burnham 1943, 75). But this view is anything but necessary, especially in light of the ethical reflections of the Florentine, that always reappear at the end of his undeniably brilliant analysis and that is likely the driving force behind his criticism of, for instance, the realities of the Church (De Grazia 1989, 88-121).

Machiavelli delegates morality. He transports it to the prepolitical realm. Politics itself, as a process of the use of power and the control of power, produces and possesses no specific morality of its own. Virtù, that is, competence, energy, effectiveness is what characterizes politics after Machiavelli, not morality (Münkler 1984, 313-328). But politics finds that morality is present, especially after Machiavelli, and it must cope with this circumstance, it cannot ignore it.

Morality comes from society, that is, from the field of politics and its soil. Machiavelli banishes it to that realm, and with good reason. Neither Cesare Borgia nor Louis Napoleon Bonaparte nor Richard Nixon have the competence to form the morality of their time. They simply lack the necessary instruments; or, alternatively, they lack the power. This competency is distributed more diffusely among family, religion, economy and culture.

This separation of morality from politics undermines the longings that are projected onto politics. Even in today's politics it is not only leadership that is called for, but morality as well. And not the generally accepted, everyday morality, but a specific, significantly higher morality. Leaders must be "better" people. And this moral difference is, in turn, ambivalent. It is, on the one hand, a political straitjacket for those who make the political decisions; on the other hand, it is an instrument of domination. The Führer doesn't smoke, the Pope doesn't marry and the President doesn't lie. In a society in which drug addiction is normal, sexuality is natural, and stretching the truth is a matter of survival, idealistic images are projected onto a few elite people who reflect them or, rather, act as though they do.

This longing for a higher morality in politics is the expression not only of a premodern understanding of politics, but of one that predates history. Political decision-makers are expected to embody moral standards that combine many roles into one. These standards have no correspondence with modern (or postmodern) society with its complex division of labor. Politicians are shamans, high priests, faith healers. They are responsible for the health, welfare and morality of society at large, and for this reason they must separate themselves from society through privilege, but also through extreme moral requirements.

In their develomental history, "Comparative Politics," Gabriel A. Almond and G. Bingham Powell, Jr. describe the ways in which this notion of multiple roles in one functions in "primitive political systems" — with the Eskimos (Innuit), the African Beduin peoples and the Bergdama in Southwest Africa (Namibia). An "omni-functional" social system goes hand in hand with the factual lack of differentiated social roles, with the exception of a headman, or chief, who is considered omnipotent. He does not rule dictatorially in the sense of modern dictatorships, but is nonetheless ultimately burdened with the expectation that he will fulfill all the tasks of the social system (Almond, Powell 1966, 218-223).

Modern democracy, especially at the end of the 20th century, is characterized by an advanced division of labor and of functions. Religious functions have long since been weeded out and more or less abandoned in the wake of secularization. As far as the market assumptions of liberal democracy are concerned, economic functions are largely beyond the competence of politics in the strict sense. Social functions enjoy a wide distribution and are by no means located solely in the central realm of politics. Nonetheless, politicians experience the pressure of expectations that demands their personality as payment, as if they were still the headmen of the Bergdama people. And if they succeed in keeping up appearances and maintaining the façade of a special morality, they are richly rewarded, both materially and otherwise. But when the fiction of a specifically political morality collapses, then woe unto the politicians. They are driven out, like Nixon in 1974.

All the expectations of virtue held by an unvirtuous, or not so virtuous society, rest on the heads of the politicians in a sort of recasting of the scapegoat of the Old Testament. They cannot fulfill these expectations, yet they must act as if they fulfill them. But in democracy as it exists today, serious deviations from these expectations cannot be hidden for long. Once they are discovered, sanctions will follow.

Machiavelli destroys this extreme discontinuity by his functionalized, realistic image of politics. He removes the basis for the expectations that the people have of politics. In so doing, he removes politics' claim to being a system of the good, the true and the beautiful.

Machiavelli is like a somewhat naive modernizer who demonstrates to the shaman cults that have survived into late modernity their own functional anachronicity. Such a man of reason must not be accepted. The politicians and people alike must declare him immoral, label his teachings as unethical and condemn him to any and all imaginable punishments.

Machiavelli must go to hell so that the contradictions between atavistic images and late modern realities do not become part of the collective consciousness. And yet he, the "immoral," is a moralist of almost childlike proportions. René König even calls him a "romantic dreamer," an interpretation that is diametrically opposed to the conventional image of Machiavelli (König 1979, 328). König refers here to the final call of the "Prince," the call to free Italy from the barbarians. This passage does indeed read like a nationalistic call to arms. And the quote from Petrarch with which Machiavelli ends his "Prince," is more than surprising: "Valour against fell wrath / Will take up arms; and be the combat quickly sped! / For, sure, the ancient worth, / That in Italians stirs the heart, is not yet dead" (Machiavelli, The Prince, XXVI).

This pathos at the end of "The Prince" must also be seen in the context of Machiavelli's self-promotion. He wanted to bring himself into the business of politics again, to break out of his political isolation, to serve a political master. This is why he formulated an ideological call, in the spirit of the times, and placed it at the end of "The Prince."

If Machiavelli were a moralist, would he count on his analyses being enlightening? We find one possible answer in his view of treachery. Machiavelli says that a "smart ruler" cannot keep his word and must not keep his word if this would cause him harm and if the reasons for his promise are no longer present. The ruler must and should do this above all because people, and therefore also those who are governed, are always corruptible.

"If men were all good, this precept would not be a good one; but as they are bad, and would not observe their faith with you, so you are not bound to keep faith with them" (Machiavelli, The Prince, XVIII).

In other words, the morality of the ruler is no higher than that of the people. There is no special morality of power. Those being governed can demand the same morality of their rulers that they themselves have. Machiavelli's notion of morality corresponds to that of an identity-based democracy. But do those being governed want the sort of democracy that allows those in power to be as corruptible as society in general? Or isn't it more likely that they want those who govern them to have a special, higher morality, one that they demand with such intolerance because they feel "guilty" themselves and therefore want to, and must, project their own unresolved, moral claims onto ruling figures? Does democracy the way it exists today even allow an egalitarian morality, or is it not the case that the elite in a democracy must be thought of in terms of a special, stricter morality?

Richard Nixon was the victim of a conception of morality that was professed by society in general, but hardly present everywhere. He lied to his own advantage. He veiled truths that had become disadvantageous to him. He manipulated his colleagues, he pitted them against each other. He acted contrary to the norms, but conformed to reality. He broke so many written and unwritten rules. And the society in which behavior like Nixon's is an everyday occurence brought about his fall under considerable expenditure of moral outrage.

That was a shining moment for American democracy: no one stands above the law. The President who had been elected by a landslide in November, 1972 was exposed as a liar. He had to resign. That, however, was not a shining moment for identity-based politics. For a society in which lying and cheating are "normal" in the sense that they are everyday occurences, would otherwise have deserved a lying and cheating President. The public that generally accepted at least an ordinary lie was outraged at Nixon the liar. Democracy in its present form demonstrated that those in power and those who are governed are not bound by the same moral standards; rather, that those in power must fulfill significantly higher expectations.

The moralist Joly attributes the following words to his Machiavelli (Napoleon III), evidently to be read as cynicism: "I could even return real freedoms to the people, because one would have to have lost all sense of politics if one could not recognize that my laws have come to fruition in my own time. I have achieved the goal I indicated to you. The character of the people has changed" (Joly 1990, 343).

Naturally, Joly is wrong. The "character of the people" demands the scapegoat, especially under democracy as it currently exists. The "character of the people" cannot be manipulated as the theatrically amoral Machiavelli would have us believe in the above-mentioned dialogue in hell. What should be criticized in a contemporary dialogue in hell is not subjection to real politicians, but subjection to a specific ritual. Those who are powerful outside the realm of politics are removed from this ritual. Those who wield power within politics are fully vulnerable to it.

Politicians who are caught with the average morality, exposed as liars, found to be maximizing their incomes or to be driven by self-interest do not fare well. In a democracy, they are punished for these things because they are not "better" than their judges. But someone who exposes this democratically obtained, anti-egalitarian morality fares no better. He will be banished to hell just as surely now, presumably, as during the Second Empire.

It is particularly the stable Anglo-American democracies that demonstrate this split in moral expectations and demand higher moral standards of leading politicians than of their constituents. The stability and continuity of democracy evidently serve to nourish this contrariness. The very matter-of-course and everyday qualities of democracy lead to politicians being held to higher standards, above and beyond those of society in general.

The distance between the expectations of leadership and the everyday notions of morality create what is known as "charisma." It is a dangerous phenomenon because it is illusionary and cannot actually be defined. In the last years of his life, Albert Speer described charisma as "the most dangerous quality there is" (Sereny 1995, 14).

Speer had in mind the charisma of the one person who had determined his life charismatically for many years. Speer knew that whoever longs for charisma will find Hitler.

6   *On the Limits of Idealism*

Democracy and Fundamentalism — Stalin as a Realist — Hitler as an Idealist — American Idealism — Idealism à la Lyndon B. Johnson — Kennedy: Idealism as Public Relations

Whoever believes with a certainty bordering on the absolute that he or she knows what is "right" for the community (the people, the nation, the class, the party), will tend to reject as an affront the idea of putting to a vote what is "right." Democracy is difficult to mediate when the confrontation of clearly defined values and interests is — presumably — at stake and when these can be clearly categorized as "good" (or "right") and "bad" (or "wrong"). Democracy needs a certain measure of skepticism, self-doubt, and the readiness to imagine one's own (political) defeat and accept it. Democracy needs the basic virtue of relativism (Kelsen 1963). Absolute certainties fare poorly with the democratic process that can bring about one result, but just as easily another.

    Those who measure all political articulations by a single position and who make all interests dependent on a single priority do not muster up this basic virtue of relativism. The antithesis of relativism is fundamentalism: that concept that says that everything must be subordinated to a single goal or system of values or catalog of virtues. A religiously defined order can be fundamentalist. There is much that points to the fact that monotheistic religions or religious communities in particular tend toward fundamentalism. But a secular system of thought can also be fundamentalist, or a politics based on such a system, especially radically revolutionary movements or parties are susceptible to this. The path toward inquisition, to the stake, or to the guillotine is the logical consequence of a way of looking at politics as a struggle between the powers of light and darkness.

    Fundamentalists at least have morality on their side. There is a clear, ideological line from the moralist Robespierre to the "moral majority" in the U.S. of the late 20th century. What the radical Jacobins and the Protestant fundamentalist have in common is that they see politics as a part of an approach to thinking that is based on the concepts "true and "not true." And the Ayatollahs and agnostics of all denominations agree that we cannot vote on truths.

This fundamentalist approach to thinking views politics not only as a religious or secondarily religious doctrine of virtue; it also tends to lend a scientific conceptuality to politics: "right" and "wrong" form a dichotomy that stems from the world of the natural sciences. Utopian literature, beginning with Plato, is full of expectant connections between the triumph of scientific thinking, social construction and eschatological prognosis of the end of the world and the end of politics.

The fundamentalist approach to thinking is carried by an anti-political longing; it is anti-political. The various lines of conflict, or cleavages, that pervade all social realities are cancelled when they dissolve into a single, all-conquering cleavage — of class (the Marxist trap), race or nation (the social Darwinist or national trap), religion (the confessional trap), the environment (the ecological trap), or gender (the sexist trap). Common to all of these fundamentalist longings is the fact that, rising from the depths of relativism, they ultimately lead to a loss of politics.

Fundamentalism is concerned with clear boundaries between categories conceived of as high and low. Everything that does not correspond to a set, singular contradiction is defined as a secondary contradiction and thus more or less pushed aside. The burden of constantly differentiating, discriminating and comparing two evils is cast off intellectually. It is no longer a matter of weighing the various advantages and disadvantages, it is a matter of "either-or"; a Manichean black and white line drawing that allows only victory or defeat.

The Lenininists fell into this trap of absolute certainty. In the firm belief that, as the avantgarde, they had to rush forward, ahead of the working class consciousness, they emphasized the determinism that was potentially inherent in Marxism on the one hand; on the other hand, they exaggerated it such that it turned inside out (Popper 1970). By referring to the unavoidability of the socialist revolution, they, impatient intellectuals that they were, wanted to force the revolution onto an historical situation that was not yet ready for it. By trying to rush history, they lost the real Marxist standard of measurement. The result was a theoretical arbitrariness that gradually gave way to a traditional pattern: the Leninists, to the extent that they weren't murdered first, became Stalinists whose politics in the sense of "socialism in one state" was oriented on a national interest that was defined in the sense of "Realpolitik." This included such pre- and un-

Marxist concepts as "spheres of influence" and the "balance of powers" (Kissinger 1994, 332-349).

The de facto idealism of the secularizing missionaries of Marxist-Leninism, which understood itself as "scientific," quickly became a foreign policy à la Bismarck and a domestic policy à la Genghis Khan under the pressure of "Realpolitik." But this rapid switch occurred not under the conditions of a liberal democratic political system. Stalin did not have to win any elections. The concessions, to which he saw himself forced, were not the ones to which, say, the opinion polls would have forced him, in order to satisfy these constituents and neutralize this segment of society. Stalin made concessions to the "objective" givens — to the strength of the German Luftwaffe or to the geopolitical position of Leningrad, or even to the level of development of Soviet agriculture. This sort of realism always meant for *Stalin* the weighing of alternatives and, ultimately, politics by means of opting for the supposedly, factually lesser evil.

In a democracy, which is particularly characterized by the constant competition for votes, "idealism" has a special meaning, namely, that of limiting fields of action and therefore making politics itself more difficult. If by idealism, the orientation of political action toward given value systems is meant, then we must assume a certain banality: in no modern system is there such a thing as politics without idealism as a contributing factor. And in no modern system is idealism (or even just the sum of idealisms) the single decisive factor. And in no political system can "idealistic" factors be separated from the factors that cannot be subsumed under idealism. All too often, interests tend to bind themselves to ideas in order to make them selling agents of their own cause.

Nevertheless, the factor of idealism exists, and it cannot simply be dissolved in the concept of interests. That was also Stalin's misunderstanding. He grossly underestimated both the independence of Hitler's idealism and the idealistic American tradition. In 1940 and 1941 he had counted on Hitler's sense of "Realpolitik" and had considered Hitler his equal. In so doing, he overlooked the extent to which the "drive to the East" that strategically expressed the racist mass murders belonged to the — idealistic — essence of National Socialism. Unlike Stalin, Hitler was no Machiavellian who deduced his actions logically from a parallelogram of strength that was drawn as objectively as possible.

But the idealism with which Hitler was able to bewilder the Machiavellian Stalin in a way that was almost decisive, geopolitically speaking, was, in turn, an idealism void of a democratic framework. This idealism was, in its nature, a reaction to secularization and enlightenment, to the decline in values and to relativism and therefore, to democracy. Hitler's idealism pushed, consequently, toward self-annihilation. Through the loss of politics, through the conscious-unconscious, goal-oriented destruction of political options, through the "politics of burning ships" (Haffner 1978) that, in the end, made any politics impossible, this idealism reached the point which it had aimed at all along: absolute nothingness. Hitler's refusal to engage in foreign policy after the attack on the Soviet Union beyond intimidating satraps, and to see more than a simple chain of commands and punishments in domestic policy proves this. The pleasure with which Hitler declared war on the U.S. in December, 1941, although the pact with Japan had not in any way forced him to do so, and the consistency with which he forestalled every effort of Ribbentrop, Himmler and Göring to regain political capacities in foreign policy (efforts which were extremely deficient in any case, since they were limited by the constraints of National Socialism) confirm the murderous and, ultimately, suicidal tendencies that stemmed from the idealism of refusing to conduct politics.

In an open system of liberal democracy, an immanent system of checks and balances prevents a dominant idealism from taking on such far-reaching consequences. And yet the directions of development and efficacy even of an idealism under democratic principles are the same: idealism hinders the political capability of the system; it limits the political playing field for policy-makers; it complicates the weighing of options and, thus, leadership; and it conflicts, in the end, with the logic of the "lesser evil."

An example of this immanence is the formulation of the unconditional surrender announced by Roosevelt and Churchill in Casablanca in 1943. This formulation was criticized again and again because it not only limited the playing field of the Allies vis-à-vis the Axis powers; but also because it prevented arguments for internal resistance, for instance, in Germany. If a government comprised of German resistance leaders could not count on more attractive conditions of surrender for Germany, what strategic or foreign policy-related attraction should such a resistance have?

The criticism of the formulation in Casablanca overlooks its domestic and idealistic function. It was Roosevelt who suggested this formulation and pushed it through. It was part of his policy to continue to mobilize public opinion in the U.S. by drawing clear lines between "good" and "evil" after he finally had "his" war for the liberation of the world, and especially of Europe, from the terror of Nazism. Casablanca served this purpose well, and Roosevelt had little problem with the character of this idealistic formulation that tended to limit politics, because once the idealism of the most powerful democracy in the world had been set into motion, it was not to be distracted by political finesse.

Stalin had simply overlooked the fundamentally idealistic character of the American political system. He, who, according to Henry Kissinger's dictum, always had a strategy for (foreign) policy, but never any principles (Kissinger 1994, 348) could not understand that with the full-blown outbreak of the Cold War, the foreign policy of the United States was determined by fundamental principles that had to construct a strategy of containment. The politically reductionist consequences of U.S. strategy stemming from the idealism of the Cold War were pefectly clear: "Realists" like Walter Lippmann criticized the fact that containment amounted to a paralyzing of the U.S. in terms of foreign policy (Kissinger 1994, 463-466).

Politicians oriented toward action, like Nixon or Kissinger, always had to struggle with this idealistic principle of U.S. policy. Nixon stumbled over the cognitive dissonance between his lip service to American idealism and his own behavior, which deviated from it; and Kissinger was never to lose the "Dr. Strangelove" image that made him appear to be a cynical Machiavellian devoid of any values (Isaacson 1993, 653-672). What they had in common was the desire to broaden the political playing fields for domestic and foreign policy in the United States, and the fact that they brought these politically expansive tendencies into conflict with the unavoidably reductionist idealism of the American public.

Kissinger's perspective on the connections between morality and politics demonstrates on the one hand the unavoidability, indeed, the desirability of the factor of idealism; on the other hand, its limitations. Kissinger's praise of Roosevelt's foreign policy contrasts with his much more critical view of Wilson's foreign policy. Wilson was a moralizing preacher who did, in fact, awaken a short-term and militarily strategic idealism that had slumbered in American society since its inception, and instrumentalized it, in the sense of an alliance, by means of entente. But he neither succeeded in transforming the U.S. power into a lasting order of peace, nor was he able to transfer the idealism of foreign policy to one of domestic policy. The result was the reaction of isolationism that removed the United States from the international political arena for two decades. The fascination with Roosevelt lay with his pairing of idealistic conceptualization and political praxis in terms of domestic as well as foreign policy, as well as his combination of principles and strategies.

Without idealism, the U.S. would not have been able to carry out its real-political function beginning in 1938. Without idealism , there would have been no "Realpolitik", and, of course, without "Realpolitik," there would have been no results for those idealistic goals. The strict opposition between "Realpolitik" and "idealism" leads one astray because it either fails to recognize idealism as the motor behind real, political energies, or it overlooks the unavoidability of social and other consequences inherent in any politics.

Without ideals there are no social movements that become political parties from which the personnel for political leadership is recruited for the decision-making processes. The simple reduction of this transformation of social energies to socio-economic interests (a potential Marxist misconception) or to elite interests (a potential conservative misconception) does not account for the complexity of this process. Idealism is, on the one hand, an accompanying and strengthening factor of politically motivated interests. On the other hand, it is itself very much capable of releasing motivating energies. Idealism in the sense of not primarily material interests is just as indispensable as an independent factor in the understanding of religious wars as for the analysis of modern revolutionary processes. Events in Iran in 1978 and 1979 are just one example for this.

In a democracy, an idealism that determines politics in any significant way can ultimately stem only from what is called "civil society," that is, from the socially anchored values that establish themselves in interest that are not primarily material and that, in this way, influence political decisions. The idealism of the policy-makers then constitutes the reaction to the idealism of the social interests — nothing more and nothing less.

One example for this context is the emergence of the American civil rights legislation in the 1950's and 1960's and the key role that came to Lyndon B. Johnson as Senate Majority Leader and then as President. Until 1948, Johanson was a member of Congress who represented a relatively poor constituency in west Texas and who was in this role, building on his first political activity as administrator of the New Deal programs, "liberal" in the American sense, that is, egalitarian in his social policy and open toward the needs of the socially disadvantaged, among them not only whites, but blacks as well. In 1948, Johnson was elected to the Senate by a slight majority. Now he represented the entire state of Texas and thus a constituency that was, on average, much more conservative and also much more racist than his earlier constituency had been. In 1948, black voters in the southern state of Texas were excluded de facto from the right to vote due to legislative manipulation. For that reason, they could not form a counterbalance to the racially motivated sector of the white electorate, the majority of which was interested in maintaining legal discrimination against blacks (Kearns 1976, 240f.).

In these years as Senator from the state of Texas, Johnson created his reputation as a conservative Democrat and as such, he became Senate Majority Leader. When President Eisenhower, in the wake of the groundbreaking decision by the Supreme Court in 1954 (Brown vs. The Board of Education) wanted to enact corresponding civil rights legislation and thus put an end to racial discrimination in the South, Johnson had a decisive function. He represented the majority in Congress that opposed Eisenhower and he was a Southerner whose constituency expected him to protect their — the white Texans' — privileges. Regarding legislation, there was no getting around Johnson.

Working indirectly with the Eisenhower administration, Johnson arranged for certain of the laws desired by the government to be passed, whereas others remained mired in difficulty. The law that was finally passed in 1957 gave the Justice Department new jurisdiction to protect civil rights even vis-à-vis the individual states; at the same time, however, the original regulation that had allowed the Justice Department (that is, the Federal government) the right to intervene directly in conflicts between individuals and states by dispatching officials, was eliminated.

Johnson "sold" this result, which carried his mark as much as that of the government, to each audience differently: To Senators and other opinion-makers in the South, he emphasized that the real "monstrosity" of Eisenhower's suggestions had been avoided through his, Johnson's, doing — the "worst part of the nigger bill," as he expressed it to his colleague from the South, Sam Ervin (Kearns 1976, 157). On the other side, he was already working energetically on correcting his image as a politician with obligations to the conservative South. For this reason, he emphasized to his liberal colleague from the North, Paul Douglas, that this law was "long overdue" and had been passed "for the benefit of Negro Americans" (Kearns 1976, 157). To one part of the public, Johnson spoke of "niggers," to the other, of "Negro Americans."

Johnson had, of course, understood that if he ever wanted to be more than a Senator from Texas, he would have to correct his image as a conservative Southerner. And so, in the following years, he foregrounded the aspect that, for the first time in many decades, there was a civil rights bill, and the other aspect, the fact that he had ensured the harmlessness of this same law, faded into the background.

In this regard, Johnson could argue with the logic of the "lesser evil." Without the concessions that the law ultimately made to the Southern states, the passing of any legislation would have been uncertain. Better a bill that was watered down than no bill at all, for the Johnson of 1957. The Johnson of later years was, admittedly, a different one. Public opinion in the U.S. had shifted markedly due to the influence of the idealism that was addressed by the civil rights movement. And Johnson was no longer a Senator who wanted to be re-elected in his homestate; Johnson wanted to become, or rather, remain President of the United States.

As President, Johnson ensured that the civil rights legislation of 1965 went beyond that of 1957, for which he, as majority leader, had also been responsible. As President, he knew he was no longer dependent solely on the state of Texas, but on the electorate of the entire United States. And the majority of this electorate had had enough of the race discrimination that wore the cloak of legality in the South. The President now had to take into account the values of the U.S., just as the Senator from Texas and the member of Congress had had to be in line with the values of the state of Texas or of his west Texan constituency. The question regarding the values and morals of the individual Lyndon B. Johnson is beside the point. They cannot have been too clearly defined because otherwise one could not have expected Johnson's elastic conformity to the respective situations.

Too much idealism and too much morality on the part of policy-makers only impedes democracy. Idealism and morality must come from below, if they are to be politically effective, as called for by the spirit and process of democracy. The idealism and morality of political leaders in democracy must remain within the constraints defined by the dominant public. Whoever demands an idealism of the policy-makers that significantly transcends these constraints, encourages the dictatorship of a particular morality — one's own, of course. Whoever does not approve of the dominant idealism can, within the framework of democracy, work for the transformation of this dominant, public idealism. The democratic moralist turns not to leadership, but to the basis, to society. "Moral leadership" takes place beyond the offices and institutions of democracy.

Clearly, political elites in democracy do not want to calmly accept this tendency toward the limitation of their political playing field, a tendency that is immanent to any democratic system. For that reason, politicians always play a game of roles: one player, called leadership, must rely on the idealism that is present in society and that expresses itself in concrete articulations, say, in the form of opinion poll results.

The player then diagnoses a need for idealism, also for idealistic leadership. He does not react by openly pointing to the tendency toward the incompatibility of policy-makers' individual idealism and the mechanisms of democracy: such openness is harshly punished in this game. He must, rather, pretend to be idealistic, without really being so. Our player, if he wants to win, must be a pseudo-idealist. And he does the most justice to this role by believing in the appearance he has fabricated himself. Then his credibility is optimal.

Johnson's predecessor in the Oval office, John F. Kennedy, presents a particularly impressive example of this sort of idealistic façade. There is hardly any other political career in an established democratic system that has been planned out as precisely, hardly any other campaign was programmed as exactly and was as scientifically engineered in the sense of a long-term marketing plan as Kennedy's (Kearns, Goodwin, 1988, 866-943). Kennedy's public appearance was styled for the market; even his policies as President, for example, his civil rights policies, were chosen with an eye to his chances for re-election.

And yet, or more precisely, for that very reason, Kennedy succeeded in distinguishing himself as the frontrunner of a new idealism. In truth he was not the frontrunner, he was the product of this idealism. But in order to demonstrate leadership to a political market thirsting for idealism, he formulated his praise of the courage to be unpopular. He wrote his book "Profiles in Courage," in which he (or his ghostwriter) portrayed individuals from U.S. history who had put their own convictions, in other words, individual idealism, before their chances for election and who had, for that reason, failed in their personal careers (Kennedy 1956).

Kennedy wrote in his book about the "purpose of courage" and demanded that politics have the courage of idealism against popularity. He praised Senator Robert A. Taft for not sacrificing his principles to his interest in becoming the Republican candidate for President in 1948 and 1952. He spoke for something that was foreign to no one more than to Kennedy himself. He constructed a façade of idealism behind which idealism was clearly forbidden.

Kennedy suggestively let himself emerge as the representative of an idealism that would include the unconditional courage to be unpopular, and hid behind this façade his own unconditional will to direct his politics toward avoiding all obstacles and to winning the election. Kennedy was the prototype of the politician who recognized the incompatibility of the (individual) idealism of a leader and of democracy, just as he recognized the necessity of keeping this insight to himself. It is only with great difficulty that the policy-limiting consequences that amount to a prohibition of idealism vis-à-vis successful democratic leadership can be compatible with the idealistic image needed by the successful democratic leader.

7 Charisma

Many years ago there lived a politician who thought so much of his own charisma that he spent all his money in order to be recognized by all as a charismatic leader. He did not care about his army or culture or politics, unless it was to show his charisma. For every occassion he had a special form of charisma, and, as they say of another politican: "He is in Parliament," so they say here: "He is demonstrating his charisma."

One day, two swindlers showed up who passed themselves off as political advisors and as weavers on top of that. They claimed to be able to weave the most beautiful charisma imaginable, in the form of robes. Not only were the colors and the pattern unusually beautiful, but the charisma one could produce from them also had the magical quality of making everyone who was unfit for his profession or was unallowably stupid, invisible.

That would be an incredible charisma! the politician thought. If I had robes like those, I would see which men in my kingdom are unworthy of their office; I could tell the smart ones from the stupid ones! Yes, this charisma must be woven for me immediately! And he gave the weavers a handsome price, so that they would begin their work ...

This was no sooner said than done and implemented.

And so it happened that the politician went to the festive tribunal on the solemn day of the party convention, and all the people in the convention hall cried out "Oh heavens, how beautiful the politician's new charisma is! What beautiful qualities of leadership he wears on his robe! How becoming everything is!" No one wanted to let the others know that he saw nothing, because otherwise he would have been unworthy of his office or would have been incredibly stupid. None of the other robes had created such luck before. "But he has nothing on!" one delegate suddenly cried out. And he cried it louder and louder. The other delegates turned, outraged, and especially the top party members, their political advisors and all the media experts cried: "Out with him or her! Questioning charisma cannot be allowed! What is left of our meaning as politicians and for the politicians if everyone simply says the truth?" And they drove the delegate out of the convention hall.

Our politician assumed an even prouder pose, and the political advisors went and carried the train that was not there. And all of them were convinced that this charisma was simply wonderful and simply indispensable, because charisma exists when everyone believes in it.

The two swindlers, then, were not really swindlers. They had really produced charisma.

8 *On the Attempts to Tame a Myth*

Is Personality really Everything? — Charisma as Product
— The Erosion of all Ethics — Leadership as a (necessary?)
Illusion — Vietnam

"Does leadership make a difference?" is one of the eternal questions of political science. What meaning does it have for a concrete, political decision that not X but Y is Prime Minister? What is the unique, incomparable contribution that can not be exchanged or substituted that Z (and only Z) makes as a leader for the society and politics of a country?

Personality is everything, says a market-oriented form of the understanding of democracy and its development. In the course of the stabilization of democracy, the tendency is that a "pragmatic" approach to politics rather than an "ideological" one prevails. Closed "Weltanschauungen" and class-based parties are transformed into loose parties of the people that can hardly be distinguished in terms of a consistent traditional party platform, but differ only in the personalities of their leaders. The "mature" democracies, according to the hypothesis, are characterized by their presentation of personalities rather than ideologies.

At first glance, the evidence seems to support this hypothesis. Anthony Downs, for instance, attributes a decidedly non-democratic theoretical function to a policy decision thought to be "ideological." Politicians, according to Downs, formulate political goals in order to win elections — and they win elections by no means in order to realize these goals (Downs 1957, 21-31). Thus it becomes clear that a de-ideologizing process goes hand in hand with the stabilization of a democracy.

Seymour Martin Lipset can be invoked for this hypothesis as well. Democracy does not need the "ideological" person who views everything as a dichotomy and therefore contributes to an ultimately centrifugal development and thus to the destruction of democracy. Democracy needs the "political" person who is, of course, not indifferent to an "ideological" view of politics, but who also balances this view with a certain amount of distance and disinterest and thus experiences politics not as the single most important life experience, but as one of many such realms (Lipset 1960).

These rejections of the compatibility of democracy and a dichotomous, extremely ideological understanding of politics that sees only black and white, can be seen as the rejection of a naive conception of democracy: democracy as a system toward the definition of truth that is strictly and irreconcilably opposed to untruth. This is the sense in which Downs and Lipset should be understood. They destroy the claim to absolutes that have no place in the day to day workings of a stable democracy. Parties that conceive of politics first as part of an antagonistic conflict, for instance, in the Marxist sense, in which only one side can "win" and, as a consequence of the enormity of history, must win, undergo a gradual process of de-ideologization (for example: the history of the European adaptation of social democracy); or, they do not allow democracy at all (for example, Lenin's Bolsheviks).

Downs and Lipset cannot be used as support for a theory of the importance of personalities if this is meant to express the objective, not the subjective meaning of leadership. Of course, in the process of development and stabilization of democracy, often called "Americanization" in Europe, the voters' orientation toward party, ideology, and tradition can increasingly yield to an orientation toward personality. Of course, we can show empirically that the weight of the "ideology factor" is declining and the weight of the "personality factor" is increasing with regard to the influence of political action in stable democracies. But this says nothing about whether or not this perception, which is expressed in concrete behavior, also reflects the actual significance of the elected official. "Personality" as a decisive factor of the election is one thing, and this factor always affects the "image," the subjectively perceived public image of a party's top candidate. The actual effect of this person as a leader is always a different thing altogether. Whether or not a (re)elected official has an unmistakable influence on actual political developments as a leader, i.e., as President, Prime Minister, or Chancellor is completely independent of the voters' perceptions of personality and of the trend toward making personality the decisive factor. These are two independent levels of politics.

Of course, these two levels are connected indirectly. A stable democracy is based on a market mechanism that continually increases in strength and that forces parties as well as candidates, themselves in a constant state of competition, to conform constantly to the political demand, i.e., to the preferences of the voters as determined by the ever-present opinion polls. This market mechanism leads first to the erosion of "ideological" differences between the old parties that were aligned with a particular "Weltanschauung" or class. It also leads to a convergence not only of the parties but of the personalities. Personalities confront one another and, as a consequence of the availability of opinion polls results, can only promise the same, or at least an analog of the same leadership in the sense of content. These personalities (must) try to balance out this interchangeability by means of a difference in style and form that is often grossly exaggerated. Leadership is writ large, is promised and demanded, but leadership is produced and portrayed only as an empty shell, not as content. As soon as a particular content is successful on the political market, the competition will offer the same content. And then the uniqueness of political content is gone. Leadership will, of necessity, become interchangeable.

Max Weber's notion of "charismatic" leadership is irreconcilably opposed to this mechanism of adaptation and convergence. Weber was interested most of all in the "rule due to obedient submission to the purely personal 'charisma' of the 'leader'" (Weber 1968, 10). Weber's typological references point in a particular direction: He associatively combines "charisma" with prophets, warlords, magicians, gang leaders and condotierri; that is, with examples of political activity that have one thing in common: their non-democratic parameters. The voluntary element ("obedient submission") that belongs to charismatic leadership and differentiates it from an authority based on force should surely not be understood as the only constitutive element of democracy. Not charismatic leadership, but rather the functionality of a career politician embedded in the routine of a stable system with calculable processes who lives not only for politics but also from it, makes leadership and democracy compatible.

Weber, of course, also assigns an ethical postulate to this politician characterized by routine: the ethics of responsibility. This, and not the ethics of principles that exists in the ethical gesture should determine the (democratic) politician. This is the assumption that "one must take responsibility for the (foreseeable) consequences of one's actions" (Weber 1968, 58).

From here, it is only a short step to the theory of the lesser evil that, for Weber, becomes the essence of the ethics of responsibility and thus the essence of democratic leadership: "No ethics in the world can avoid the fact that achieving 'good' goals in many cases means the acceptance of morally questionable, or at least dangerous, means as

well as the possibility or probability of negative consequences ..."
(Weber 1969, 58).

Presumably, General Jaruzelski was not thinking of Weber in
December, 1981. He also does not refer to Weber's theoretical construct
in his memoirs. But Weber delivers precisely the logic that makes
Jaruzelski's argumentation understandable.

It is no coincidence that Weber connects this logic of the lesser evil
to politics in general. Politics is always one step ahead of the ethics of
principles; dealing with the associated risks constitutes leadership. But
if leadership means the uniqueness of one person's mark on history
and if the routine of a stable democracy tends to destroy this
uniqueness, what remains of leadership?

Charismatic leadership would remain; or, to speak with James
MacGregor Burns, "transforming leadership." This is defined by a
qualitative relationship between "leader" and "followers": the
leadership changes the followers decisively (and thus, the society). But
the variations in transforming leadership show that stable democracies
leave hardly any room for this. Burns names "revolutionary"
leadership that can establish democracies but that has no place in a
stable democracy; he also names the "heroes and ideologues" that
belong in the routine of a democracy just as little as the "intellectuals"
who practice their leadership as moral authority; in other words,
persons, as outsiders, influence awareness and thus the political
marketplace but are not themselves subject to the rules of this
marketplace, at least not in their capacity as heroes, ideologues and
intellectuals. What remains, according to Burns, is "reform leadership."
It is no coincidence that the examples Burns gives for this type stem
from early phases of stabilization within democracies — Great Britain
and the U.S. in the 18th and 19th centuries (Burns 1978, 141-254).

The stabilization and routinization of politics, which is the goal of
any democratic system, hollows out the assumption of transforming
leadership. The leaders remain those who use democracy without
being subject to its iron rules: the moralists, who, with their ethics of
principles, influence the political demand and thus the political supply
via the consciousness of the voters, without having to practice politics
themselves. It is left to the Savonarolas and Gandhis, the Marxs and
Sartres to proclaim morality without being indebted to politics,
without having the work of weighing the difference between two evils,
without having to subject themselves to democratic competition. When
they try undertake this, it usually ends badly. The tragedy of the
Kingdoms of God from Calvin to Lenin is, in any case, the stronger

evidence compared to the generally successful transformation of Gandhi's vision into practice.

But even Gandhi's vision was and is the result of the stabilization of democracy in India, exposed to the process of erosion that accompanies the transition of an ethics of principles to one of responsibility that is inevitable in the course of political realization. Indian troops and the wars they led against Pakistan (1947, 1965, and 1971) are the expression of this transition from charismatic (transforming) leadership of an intellectual and moral nature into a leadership characterized by democratic routine.

Leadership by intellectual and moral strength must appear as an unbelievable luxury to those embedded in the rather ironclad rules of a stable democratic system. The ability to express and propagate opinions that do not need to be continually corrected vis-à-vis the patterns of the current market strategies based on the latest opinion polls is, in any case, beyond what is allowed politicians in a democracy. It is a type of leadership that more or less assumes democracy as a condition but does not need to adhere its rules.

What remains within the framework of these rules is, according to Burns, "transactional leadership" (Burns 1978, 257-397). People take part in political processes as individuals. They can carry out their contributions to political decisions in parliaments, governments, parties and the media. But when democracy is stable, one has only to read the weathervane of opinion polls correctly or, to influence the demand as "opinion leader" in the sense of intellectual and moral strength, without direct dependence on the political market, that is, without holding an office and without having an institutionalized function.

Of course, it makes sense to make use of various disciplines to explore scientifically which sort of person tends toward a leadership function under certain circumstances. Naturally, we can use insights from psychology to gain knowledge about who under what circumstances would turn out to be more of a "Führer." It always makes sense to work out a typology of experienced leadership in the framework of the historical social sciences: the Napoleon type, the "man on horseback," who inhabits the gray zone between the military and politics (Finer 1976) and finally, the prophetic perfectionist who holds society in a state of constant restlessness through continual (cultural) revolutions in order to avoid stabilization, routinization, and thus the erosion of leadership.

But it is noteworthy that the typologies of leadership are, in general, following the approach of "transforming leadership," based on examples of dictatorships or democracies in crisis or in transition, e.g.,

Lenin, Mussolini, Hitler, Stalin, Mao in the first category, and Roosevelt, Churchill, De Gaulle, Adenauer, Nehru in the second (Blondel 1987). When there is a reference to stable democratic conditions, the question of the indispensability of a specific person remains open, as with Burns and his "transactional leadership," and other factors (the strength of the bureaucracy, the relationship to the opposition, etc.) are invoked. The lack of a typology of political leadership in the sense of personal uniqueness is surely no accident in stable democracies.

The skepticism voiced by the hypotheses of David Wilsford is merely the result of the tendency of democracy and leadership to be incompatible. Even charismatic leaders, according to Wilsford, could only hasten or delay reforms, not bring them about or hinder the direction of structural change (Wilsford 1995, XIVf.). If this is assumed for charismatic leadership, one can only imagine what the case must be for routine leadership!

The only thing that remains is to advance the illusion of leadership. He (she) is the successful leader in a stable democracy, who knows how to sell his (her) way of conforming to the market as leadership in order to satisfy a pre-democratic longing for clarity and an atavistic need for an ordered relationship between leader and followers. The one who can give the illusion of an ethics of principles, especially to himself, and who, in so doing, can, perhaps, avoid considering and perceiving the ethics of responsibility and thus avoid reflecting on the difficult work of constructing the thick, hard planks that constitute politics is the successful one. The one who creates the greatest possible gap between the Sunday rhetoric and the weekday praxis and who hides this from himself, is the successful one.

The ones who are most effective at encouraging the illusion of leadership are the one who, as leaders, believe in it themselves. As Secretary of Defense under Presidents Kennedy and Johnson, Robert McNamara was an important decision-maker who attempted to trace the path to catastrophe in Vietnam decades after his years in office. McNamara's readiness to criticize himself is impressive. But he insisted on one element of the old justifications: domestic policy had never been a motive for the policy in Vietnam; it was geopolitical considerations, especially as a result of the domino theory (which McNamara criticized after the fact), that had been the priority (McNamara 1995, 102, 115).

Yet, almost in the same breath, he describes an interesting experience: shortly after the fall (and murder) of Ngo Dinh Diem (the critical evaluation of American participation in Diem's fall is one element of McNamara's self-criticism) and after the murder of President Kennedy, the new U.S. President, Johnson, sent him to the new president of South Vietnam, Nguyen Khanh. Johnson gave McNamara the following key task: "Bob, I want to see a thousand pictures of you with General Khanh smiling and waving ..." (McNamara 1995, 112).

Johnson received his photos; they made their way through the international press. And McNamara, who had never been elected and who was therefore unacquainted with the legitimation techniques of an election campaign, felt like a "politician." For the man most responsible for the U.S. policy in Vietnam, aside from the two presidents, "politician" is a negative word. Above all, it stands in opposition to "leadership." Leadership has nothing to do with the calculations of domestic policy, and just as little to do with politics.

McNamara had, of course, realized that the constant media duet between Khanh and himself was supposed to serve the on-going campaign of the new U.S. President. This was detrimental to the image of the South Vietnamese President. He came increasingly under the suspicion of being dependent on foreign powers. But Johnson had his photos. And in spite of this, McNamara still wants to claim that considerations of domestic policy played no role for American policy in Vietnam. And this insistence has the character of faith: "Every president quite properly considers domestic politics, but I do not believe that the Kennedy and Johnson administrations' errors in Vietnam can be explained on that basis." (McNamara 1995, 115).

McNamara clings to a myth. For this reason he escapes from the world of reality into the world of faith. The world of reality was to teach him, the successful manager of the Ford Corporation, the Defense Department, and the World Bank, a lesson.

David Halberstam speaks for this world of reality. He writes, in agreement with McNamara, about the doubts that plagued President Kennedy in the last weeks of his life: Were the escalation and increase in U.S. military personnel, for which he was largely responsible, together with the increasingly direct responsibility of the U.S. in and for Vietnam really the most suitable means of reaching the goal — the prevention of a Communist government in Saigon? And Halberstam summarizes:

"In the last few weeks of his life, he (John F. Kennedy — A.P.) had talked with some aides ... about trying to paper it over through 1964, keeping the commitment away from Goldwater as a target, and then trying to negotiate his way out." (Halberstam 1972, 367). Thus, Kennedy did, in fact, use the Presidential election of November, 1964 and the expected criticism of his probable Republican opponent, Barry Goldwater, as a guideline for his policy in Vietnam. But this does not correspond to the image that McNamara would like to see: leadership without such obviously "dirty" calculations as taking into account the chances for reelection.

McNamara thus succumbs to a surprisingly naive miscalculation. At the beginning of Kennedy's presidency he discussed with him the chances of a second presidency. As a result of this exchange of ideas, he drew a diagram that showed a negative correlation between the "power" of the President and the length of his administration. In other words: a newly elected President is strong in the beginning, only to become weaker (McNamara 1995, 93). But although McNamara assumed a presidency of 8 years, he did not take into account the gap that the reelection would mean. Elections did not exist for him, or he wanted to negate their negative effect on the illusion of leadership.

Richard Nixon had different ideas. He gambled everything on reelection and saw the high point of his power not after his first, but after his second election. The Nixon drawn by the observers of the time between November and December of 1972, directly after his landslide victory over George McGovern, is Nixon at the peak of hubris: ruthless toward the opposition, arrogant toward his own followers (Ambrose 1991, 11-37). Nixon's assumption of the connection between length of time in office and power was certainly more realistic than the one McNamara had drawn with reference to Kennedy. But Nixon also miscalculated with regard to the theory of presidential leadership that underlay his behavior: The checks and balances of the American system saw to it that even a President elected by such a wide margin could not remove himself too far from the demands of the political marketplace, that is, from the rules of the democratic system, without being punished. (See figure).

Upholding a theory of democratic leadership that constitutes more than perceiving the function of officeholders whose work has become routine is like trying to fit a round peg into a square hole. It should be democracy, and it should be as stable as possible; it should correspond to the will of the people, it should realize the common good and should reflect the good, the true and the beautiful for the largest number of people. And it should be leadership, as the responsible role of highly qualified and highly moral and non-interchangeable individuals who are not afraid of making unpopular decisions.

Relationship between presidential power and the length of time in office

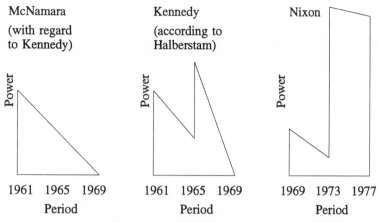

(McNamara for Kennedy in McNamara 1995, 93).

It should be A and it should be B. And A and B should be in harmony with one another, although A and B are like fire and water.

Does leadership make a difference? In a democracy, so goes the answer, not really. It is precisely the task of democracy to remove the personal significance of individual leadership. In a democracy, so continues the answer, as much as possible — as an illusion.

9   On the Skepticism Toward Too Much Democracy

Constitution against Tyranny — The Fear of the Majority — Lincoln's Contradictions — Babeuf's Impatience — Democracy from Above?

When the success of the American Revolution against the British troops seemed certain, the revolutionaries began constructing a political order. Should the 13 colonies form a federation, that is, a union, or simply join together as a loose confederation? That was one question that had to be decided. And secondly, should there be a government that was as strong as possible, or a minimum of government, of institutions, in other words, that could make binding decisions for all?

The Federalists more or less prevailed in deciding both of these central questions. These were advocates of a union with as strong a government as possible, proponents who represented largely the urban bourgeoisie. A union with a strong government was also supposed to be able to serve the interests of industry, trade, and commerce, which the small towns and plantation owners, to whom Thomas Jefferson was committed, could not serve.

The most important concept of the Federalists was the notion of checks and balances. The powers that were divided into three and conceived of as separate entities, following Locke and Montesquieu, were supposed to be, at the same time, so closely interconnected that one could not act without the others. The reason for this was the fear of tyranny: the tyranny of an individual, the tyranny of a minority, and most of all, the tyranny of the majority.

James Madison expressed it in this way: It was of the greatest importance in a republic to not only protect society from oppression by the government, but also to protect the segments of society from one another. And then, "If a majority be united by a common interest, the right of the minority will be insecure" (Hamilton, Madison and Jay, On the Constitution, No. 51).

The Constitution of the Republic should, then, also offer protection from the majority. In other words, the Constitution should contain guarantees against an undifferentiated rule of the people. The political order should be able to confront any form of the concentration of power, that of the rulers as well as that of a minority in society, but also the tyranny of the majority. The form of order, the Constitution, should not simply express "government by the people" but a complex system for balancing the various political interests.

The polemical guard against a possible tyranny of the majority was a semantic trick designed to hide the fact that it constituted a reduction in democracy. Democracy should be there, but not too much. The people should have a voice in determining their government, but only a limited one. The democracy of the Federalists and therefore of the U.S. was characterized by a skepticism regarding the "people" from the beginning. Democracy as it existed, expressed by and regulated by a constitutional system based on the theories and interests of the Federalists, wanted to see democracy limited for democracy's sake.

James Madison had therefore distinguished between "republic" and "democracy." The first was representative, governed by delegates and the election of a small group of representatives. In addition, the republic was intended for the state large in area with its many citizens; whereas democracy was intended for the smaller units, the cities and rural communities that allowed direct democracy and whose functioning could be observed in the townships of New England (Hamilton, Madison and Jay, On the Constitution, No. 10).

Above all, the Federalists wanted to secure the ability of the union to make decisions and take action. Alexander Hamilton expressed this in the section "The Need for a Government with the Power to Govern" (Hamilton, Madison and Jay, On the Constitution, No. 23, No. 26). The Federalists wanted to guarantee the capacity of the union to carry out politics. And for that reason, the rights of the people had to remain limited. The Constitution of the United States not only does not allow for direct democracy; direct election was originally limited to only one of the two houses of Congress.

In light of the federal structure of the U.S., this concern regarding the capacity of the U.S. to make decisions and take political action had largely to do with foreign affairs. The other responsibilities remained emphatically with the states. With foreign policy, however, there was supposed to be clear leadership on the part of the President, but checked by the Senate. Leadership should exist, but be carried out by both organs of the Constitution that were indirectly, not directly democratically elected, in accordance with the will of the Federalists. The "people" were supposed to participate in U.S. politics only in a highly indirect and fragmented manner.

The "people" were accepted as the source of the legitimation of power, but for the formation of policy, and the realization of leadership, it was considered potentially inconvenient. Leadership and democracy in a constant state of tension: this is the basic chord of representative democracy as it was constructed for the first time consistently and with exemplary results around the U.S. Constitution of 1787.

This notion of a democracy limited for its own good clashes with the claim and the mythos of democracy. "We, the People of the United States" — it is difficult to bring this legitimation into harmony with the Federalists' skepticism toward the majority and therefore toward democracy in general. And if this "We, the People" does not actually exist, but is to be neatly divided into majority and minority, those who govern and those who are governed? Or, perhaps, into wealthy and poor, masters and slaves, men and women? Does the "people" then not become an artificial construct, an ideology? And what is the nature, then, of democracy in the face of such a critical and analytical observation?

This tension between radical democratic semantics and the structures that limit democracy was brought to a head by Abraham Lincoln. As President he referred to the indivisibility of the Union and insisted on it with military force. As President during the Civil War, he limited citizens' rights as well as states' rights. From the point of view of the Federalists, it would not have been far off the mark that Lincoln's murderer had cried out theatrically "sic semper tyrannos!" after the fateful assassination. And yet it was this Lincoln who had hollowed out the complex system of checks and balances for the sake of his own personal power and who had, in 1863, coined the classic formulation of identificatory democracy: "Government of the people, by the people and for the people." Lincoln neglected the Constitution's reductionist rhetoric that was so skeptical of democracy. He shifted and broke the system of checks and balances. But while he was a radical democrat in his rhetoric, in his practice he was more of a dictator who saw himself called from a temporary republic to a rule by exception (McPherson 1991).

Lincoln proved his leadership in a manner unlike any President before him and in a manner to be repeated only by Franklin D. Roosevelt after him. There is little doubt that Lincoln had a decisive influence on the course of U.S. history. Without his leadership, the military and political outcome of the Civil War would have been doubtful at best. Without his leadership there might never have been a Civil War. In his leadership he consciously used a dual strategy. In his language he was radically democratic, in his practice, authoritarian. The fact that he did this with reference to the exceptional situation of war, and that he always referred to the noble goals of the Union in order to justify his actions, does nothing to change the quasi-dictatorial character of his style of government.

Lincoln also won the Civil War by means of the dialectic of his dual strategy. With his rhetoric and metaphors he helped decisively to win the war (McPherson 1991, 93-112). This was how he created legitimation for his actions. He gave the war between the racist but non-slaveholding North against the racist, but slaveholding South an agenda. He gave the war a purpose.

Lincoln referred to the abstract people without allowing the concrete people to truly participate in his decisions. He owed his reelection in 1864 to the military victories that occurred just at the right time, not to his allowing the citizens to participate in his politics. Lincoln is thus the typical representative of democratic rule by the elite (Bachrach 1967). He covered over the democracy deficit of his politics with a radically democratic flood of words. He made decisions in an elitist way but was able to disguise his decisions democratically. He was a master at packaging elitist rule as democracy.

The Federalists' skepticism toward democracy is causally linked with their skeptical anthropology. Robert A. Dahl sees the first fundamental of what he terms "Madisonian democracy," which corresponds to Madison's concept of "Republic," in an almost Hobbesian skepticism toward human nature. The skepticism toward democracy is based on the assumption that, all things being equal, every person (or group of people) would tyrannize others (Dahl 1956, 6). Humans act as tyrants to humans, if they are not prevented from doing so.

This image of humanity is an excellent foundation for the elite character of democracy as it presently exists. In order to prevent the outbreak of the wolf in the human, the rule of the elite, like Leviathan, is needed. Their rule is not legitimated by divine right or by aristocratic heritage. They take on the work of governing in order to protect the governed from their own self-destructive tendencies. But, unlike Thomas Hobbes, the contract between the rulers and their constituents, between the elite and the masses is not merely fictional, it is real and therefore subject to annulment. What is democratic about this form of rule is that the elites must win an election in order to rule.

For reasons made necessary by the marketing techniques of the election, the elites may claim that they are prepared to carry the burden of leadership only for the common good, that is, for the good of the people. The "classic" theoreticians of the elite, Gaetano Mosca and Vilfredo Pareto, were always aware that the actual motivation of the elite had to be self-interest, not humanistic altruism (Bachrach 1967).

This fundamental cause of elite rule can not be admitted in so many words. The marketing techniques of radical, democratic rhetoric are needed. The identificatory formulations à la Lincoln are needed. And this rhetoric can develop a life of its own and in this way present a danger to the complex, dialectical balance between façade and content, between claim and reality, a balance that is necessary for the stability of democracy as it exists.

The tendencies to take democracy literally and to evaluate the elitist factor not as an unavoidable concession to the limits of human nature (as the Federalist Papers do indirectly) or to the necessity of the division of labor in society (as Madison's arguments for the Republic do directly) but rather as the wrong path constitute, on the one hand, a corrective to the self-interest of the elite; on the other hand, the radical democratic critics are also seen as potentially totalitarian. For, if one follows the Federalists' skeptical point of departure, then the release of the "people" from their chains, that is, the liberation of the will (and the interests) of the majority from the limitations of checks and balances would open the door to tyranny — the tyranny of the majority.

For these reasons, the origins of a "radical" or "totalitarian" concept of democracy (depending on one's viewpoint) can be seen in the theoretical and historical opponents of the Federalists. J. L. Talmon views Jean Jacques Rousseau as the first representative of a "totalitarian democracy," the Jacobins as pragmatic improvisers in the tradition of Rousseau and François Babeuf as the theoretical perfector (Talmon 1986). The potentially totalitarian aspect is the undifferentiated concept of the people, which is expressed in Rousseau's volonté générale, while avoiding the differentiation into majority and minority, but also men and women, wealthy and poor.

In many ways, Babeuf stand for the bridge between radical democracy and socialism. He and his comrades thought the Revolution's formulation of equality through to its consistent, economic end — to the dissolution of private property. In this sense, early socialism begins with Babeuf. But the Leninist temptation also begins with Babeuf: As a counter balance to the self-interests of the People's Assembly, he argued for its maximal connection to the plebiscitarian will of the people. This corresponded exactly to the approach of the (pre-Leninist) democracy of councils, of soviets. As a counter balance to the "merely" quantified, plebiscitary will of the people the (Leninist) idea of the revolutionary avant-garde presented itself to him and, consequently, the revolutionary dictatorship (Talmon 1986, 201-221).

The empirically correct insight into the elite character of representative democracy, the Republic in Madison's sense, but also the Assembly government of the French Revolution: this recognition can be the reason for the demand for more and more democracy, for more decision-making responsibility, for more participation. This is a logical criticism of the attempt on the part of the representative democracy to make leadership by various office-holders possible by emphasizing the division of labor and thus by reducing democracy. The dynamics of this "Babouvian" criticism is directed toward the capability of existing democracy to allow leadership by limiting democracy. The radical democratic élan is directed, then, first and foremost toward the Madisonian limitation of democracy.

But nothing demands leadership and intervention into history like the radical will to change. If the limitation on the elite character of the political system alone does not bring about the desired revolutionary changes, then the radically democratic and radically egalitarian "Babouvian" affect threatens to shift to its opposite. The radical anti-elitism becomes the desire for a new elite. Babeuf's "Conspiracy of Equals" intellectually anticipates a great deal of the fate of the October Revolution.

The dictator who refers to his mission to complete democracy, who also, unlike Lincoln, sees himself as a dictator not temporarily, but permanently, who does not, of course, allow his rule to be described as a dictatorship: This dictator grounds leadership in perfection and in perfected (self-)delusion. He brings leadership to the "Babouvian" (Leninist, Maoist) point.

Joseph II's characterization of his rule is often quoted: "Everything for the people, but nothing by the people." This agenda is the antithesis of Lincoln's identificatory definition of democracy. There is a good deal of Josephism in the Federalists, curbed by the success of the American Revolution which they had to administer. "The people" could no longer be degraded into the recipients of charity and other enlightenment benefits in the manner of Joseph II.

Franklin D. Roosevelt also had a bit of Josephism in him. His politics can be viewed as a sort of middle ground between the Babouvian, Leninist impatience and the "Nothing by the people!" Roosevelt knew that he would have to justify his political leadership at least ex post facto. At the latest, by the next election — and Roosevelt was the record holder among U.S. Presidents concerning reelection — the results of his leadership had to meet the approval of the majority of the "people," that is, of the active electorate. Regarding foreign policy, Roosevelt was ahead of his time, but he succeeded in reconciling his people with the results of his foreign policy and creating legitimation for himself due to a number of factors, particularly the fact that the Japanese and German leadership played into his hand indirectly. It was a policy "for the people," not "by the people," but with a built-in veto of the people.

The trend toward more and more egalitarian claims (also to a greater claim to democracy) has always been accompanied by the confirmation of the elite theories. It was French aristocrats, the Lafayettes and Mirabeaus who contributed significantly to the fall of the monarchy. It was capitalists, the Engels and Owens who, in theory and to a lesser degree, in practice, wanted to contribute significantly to the fall of capitalism. It was the bourgeoisie à la Lenin and Trotsky who destroyed a bourgeois republic; and it was the sons of landowners like Mao and Deng who prepared the end of the rule by landowners. Marx was correct in this sense when he wrote that the old order bears within it the seeds of the new and thus carries within it its own destruction. But it was not only the powers of revolution that were cultivated by the old order, it was also the deserters from the anciens régimes who participated in the revolutionary upheaval of this very regime.

It was also Communists like Gorbachev and Jaruzelski, grown skeptical through experience, who made their decisive, elitist contribution to the end of Communist dictatorship. The dictatorship of the Communist Party did not collapse under the attack of the revolutionary masses; rather, it imploded; and the sparks that caused the implosion were set off by the Communist Party Secretaries themselves.

The elite theory, or rather, its proponents can feel vindicated, because the result of the fall of a government by the elite was always only the foundation of another one; but also because the deserters of the declining elite contributed decisively to the takeover of the ascending elite. What could this pattern mean for the expansion of democracy? Who are the deserters and where does a new elite form?

It is difficult to imagine an expansion of democracy through revolutionary pressure in the stable democracies as they exist today. The socially, politically, and culturally weak in these democracies are too much the victims of mechanisms of exclusion (Dahl 1989). The "proletariat" in wealthy countries has come to the petit-bourgeois reflex of maintaining their own level of wealth. Nationalistic thinking dominates too much, and the supranational mechanisms of a direct articulation of interests are too clearly missing for a revolutionary pressure on the part of the globally excluded to be effective. The "proletariat" of billions in the economically weak regions of the world is not truly capable of conflict, and is therefore not capable of revolution.

The motor behind the process of democratization, and in this sense, its leadership, could very well be accepted, elite standards of democracy that prevail at first intellectually and then also materially. These standards correspond to the concept of human rights, to the idea, virulent since the bourgeois revolutions, that all people are endowed with inalienable rights, which cannot be denied by political means. The discrepancy between this claim and the reality that lags behind can cause disturbances mediated by the elite: a sense of moral outrage capable of changing society and expanding democracy.

The transition in South Africa from apartheid to a system corresponding to western standards of democracy followed this pattern: Without the growing international moral indignation that had economic consequences for the country, the South African anti-apartheid forces alone would have not been strong enough to force deep-seated changes. Only the economic pressure caused by international moral motivation brought the division of one part of the old elite, in the person of Willem de Klerk, and the alliance with the new elite represented by Nelson Mandela. The process of democratization in South Africa was the product of this alliance of elites.

Leadership can indeed by observed in these experiences of a qualitative leap to democracy. Mandela, as well as de Klerk followed a non-routine understanding of their roles because for this leap to democracy, roles were not written. There were no scripts. Mandela especially, but also de Klerk could not simply be replaced. Their contributions were unique and indispensable.

In this sense, the limits of existing democracy can only be transgressed, or more precisely, expanded from "above." The skepticism toward too much democracy is quelled through leadership by the elite. In this way, leadership, in its concrete sense, has consumed its historical function. If it is successful, it is no longer needed. A democracy in South Africa can stabilize because of the historical interventions that Mandela and de Klerk stand for. But the hallmark of this stabilization would be that the South African democracy no longer needs heroes, just as the Polish democracy no longer needs a Jaruzelski.

10 On the Unavoidability of Lying

The Galilei Strategy — Joan of Arc or a Politician? — The Art of Deception — Dr. Jekyll and Mr. Hyde — Dr. Strangelove

In Bert Brecht's and Margarete Steffin's Galileo Galilei, the protagonist's grand lies are made understandable: Galilei makes an arrangement with the Church and the Pope that allows him to continue his research. This arrangement consists of Galilei's rescission. The Earth, he agrees, not the Sun, is the center of the universe. Against his better knowledge, Galilei accepts the interest of the Inquisition not to shake the foundations of the old image of the world. Galilei lies and with this lie, saves himself (Fuegi 1995, 369-371).

But it is not his desire to live longer that makes Galilei's action a model for others. Instead, it is his intention to save research by denying it, to serve truth by putting it aside. In order to continue being able to trace the foundations of the modern, scientific view of the world, he publicly claims the opposite of what he knows to be correct, real, and true.

In the literary adaptation of the conflict between the Pope and Galilei, the struggle is not about truth. Each of them agree that Galilei does better justice to the truth than can be managed by the doctrine of the Church that professes to know the truth. In the case of the Pope and Galilei, it is about politics. The Church, represented by a knowledgeable Pope, does not want to see the results of science spread without the correct dosage and filtering process. The Pope wants to control the truth politically — that is why he must insist on checking, relativizing and, if necessary, negating this truth. Galilei wants truth as such, but in order to seek and find it, he needs a minimum of freedom; in particular, he needs his own life. But it is the Pope, and only the Pope, who can guarantee him this, because the Pope can use the Inquisition to take from him his freedom and his life.

Galilei is the non-politician who, through the confrontation with the politician, in this case, the Pope, becomes the *homo politicus* by recognizing and respecting the rules of politics. And these rules are not those of science.

Science is, at least in its tendencies, oriented toward dichotomies. A statement is either "true" because it is not falsified, or it is "false" because it can be refuted using scientific methods. Politics, on the other hand, is not dichotomous. It is always about weighing different goals whose evaluation is dependent on very different systems of reference, especially on the interests of the agents. Galilei, by accepting this logic, accepts the necessity of choosing between two evils— either burning at the stake as a heretic, or living and conducting research in partial freedom; being burned with the knowledge of having been "right" or ensuring the possibility of continuing his research by conceding publicly.

He chooses what appears to him as the lesser evil. And he tells the untruth — for the sake of the truth. He lies because, in the confrontation with the politician-Pope, he has become a politician himself. He does without the heroic gesture, becomes a coward and for that very reason, a hero.

The situation of General Jaruzelski in 1981 was not so different. He would have had the chance to place himself at the forefront of the Polish democracy movement, to enter into a direct confrontation with the USSR and the Red Army, like Imre Nagy in 1956. Jaruzelski could have opted for the role of hero, but he chose, like Galilei, the role of the coward. And like Galilei, he saved the possibility of helping Polish democracy to a breakthrough under different circumstances in the future. He told the untruth when he justified declaring martial law by citing the domestic situation in Poland — he lied. He played the role given to him by the Kremlin in order to prevent the invasion by Kremlin troops. And so he helped to maintain a situation that led to democracy as a result of the different circumstances in the USSR, and thus, to his country's being detached from the Soviet Union. The "round table" discussions and the free Sejm elections of 1989 would not have been possible if Jaruzelski had wanted to play the national hero in 1981.

It is only possible to evaluate the actions of Galilei-Jaruzelski after the fact, of course. The diffuse nature of that December in Poland as well as the impossibility of foreseeing the collapse of the Communist system during the final years of the Brezhnev era doubtless hindered a clear political course that would have included the developments of 1989. But the fact remains that Jaruzelski, by means of his Galilei-like refusal to become a hero in direct confrontation with the hegemony of power, could ensure his political viability for the future. Jaruzelski did not want to be a hero; he wanted to be a politician. And for that very reason he was effective; he had an indispensable, unique influence on

Polish history, he practiced leadership. Galilei did not want to be a hero, he wanted to be a scientist, but in order to do so, he had to become a politician.

Becoming a politician means doing without the claim to innocence, and literally getting one's hands dirty. The judge Azdak in "The Caucasian Chalk Circle" is also a politician who not only does not make the claim to innocence, he makes corruption the object of his actions. He lets himself be paid, not for his office but for each individual sentence. He conforms to each person in power. But this corrupt Azdak, a caricature of justice, is, at the same time, a subversive fighter for justice, not in the sense of the positivistic law in the interest of those in power, but in the sense of the (political) law of the struggle of the oppressed (Fuegi 1995, 445f.).

Azdak is corrupt in order to be a judge at all, in order to be able to disguise himself successfully in a society of corrupt people and secure a foundation for political effectiveness. If Azdak rejected corruption, he would reject politics and thus remain ineffectual.

This dialectic is radicalized by Brecht and Steffin in the didactic play "The Good Person of Sezuan." To be "good," Shen Te must be "bad" at the same time; to be politically effective in the sense of changing the relations, she must agree to the relations. She must become a part of the conditions in order to disrupt them. Consequently, Shen Te divides into two roles, two people. First she is the "good" Shen Te, then she is the "bad" Shui Ta (Fuegi 389f.). In order to do "good," she must first become part of the "bad." Whoever preaches only justice, but does nothing toward bringing it about, is denying politics. But someone who struggles for the transition and thus thinks strategically, that is, politically, arrives ineluctably at the question of weighing two evils. Shen Te alone is ineffective — only with the strategic schizophrenia of simultaneously being Shui Ta can she effect change.

The dialectic of the Shen Te-Shui Ta character is criticized by Hannah Arendt on moral grounds: "Lying seems to be the tool not only of the demagogue, but also of the politician and even the statesman" (Arendt 1987, 44). This structure of "not only ... but also ... and even" is telling: The demagogue is likely the routinized leader who, caught up in the overwhelming day-to-day logic of the political marketplace, observes it constantly and seeks to influence it and is, in turn, determined by it. The lies of this democratic leader are easily forgiven; the lies of the statesman, however, who hovers above the morass of the demagogue (and thus above the morass of the political marketplace) are greeted with surprise and disbelief. Clearly, it is the dependence on the political marketplace that, for Arendt, binds politics and lies so closely together. Nevertheless, Galilei and Azdak are political activists beyond the marketplace and their politics assumes lies, indeed, their politics is lies.

In 1981, Jaruzelski was free of democratic limitations. In the framework of what he intended, he also had to lie. For reasons of foreign policy, that is, as a statesman, he could not openly acknowledge his motivation for anticipating a threatened Soviet invasion; therefore, he had to lie. And he had to violate personal and social ethics in other ways as well. He would have remained ineffective against the threatened invasion of Poland if he had not become involved in the dirtiness of politics, in martial law. The Jaruzelski of 1981 is Shui Ta. Only with his dictatorship does the Jaruzelski of 1989 become possible. He is Shen Te, who would, however, not have existed without Shui Ta. Arendt's moral resignation leaves no room for such a dialectic.

Like Azdak or Galilei, Shen Te is a leader in disguise. They are all characters who have their unique, indispensable influence on the course of history. But in order to remain effective, they must disguise themselves as cowardly and corrupt; they must lie and deceive. But they are effective, whereas "Johanna at the Slaughterhouse" is drawn by Bert Brecht and Elisabeth Hauptmann as the tragedy of the "pure," as the failure of the heroine who is ineffectual and unsuccessful for that very reason (Fuegi 263f.). Johanna appears as a leader, not disguised, but as a Joan of Arc of the class struggle. She does not sink to the level of lies and corruption; the end does not justify the means for her. And so the result of her heroism is nothing but disaster.

Jaruzelski had the same option as Joan of Arc: he could have placed himself at the forefront of the democracy movement as the "national Pole." Even if Solidarity would probably not have accepted him as one of its own, the democracy movement would have been just as unable to deny a Polish head of government who mobilized his nation against an invasion as the anti-Communist democrats of the CSSR had been unable to withdraw from the call of the Prague Spring. He would have hindered Poland's pioneering role in the transformation of the Communist system, but his place in the books of Polish heroes would have been secure for the next few centuries. He ruined his chances for this place because he got involved in politics, because he did not want to demonstrate, but to practice leadership.

If Jaruzelski had rejected any political function from the beginning, he would have avoided the necessity of stylizing himself either as hero or as politician. The third option is standing aside, ignoring the situation. It is the position of Yogi, the Holy one, who is not at all indifferent to the social conditions but who confronts them with interiority because social action is foreign to him. "... nothing can be improved by exterior organization and everything by the individual effort from within" (Koestler 1964, 10). Lying cannot be justified because the Yogi does not even recognize the strategy of Galilei.

The Yogi has no social ethics, at least not in the sense of social concepts. He deals with an extremely individual approach. This can be understood "critically," like Augustine's dichotomy that is, at least latently, Manichean. With his reference to the perfection of the future "City of God," Augustine also criticized the corruption of the real "City of the World," which was not worth struggling against.

This form of criticizing the political evils is the epitome of the unpolitical. And the unpolitical creates unavoidably political consequences, whether they are desired or not. The unpolitical that is based on the alleged purity of one's own position is embodied by Martin Heidegger in his post-Nazi period. In 1949 he wrote, "Agriculture is now a motorized food industry; in essence, it is the same as the production of corpses in the gas chambers, the same as the blockade and the starvation of the countryside, the same as production of the hydrogen bombs" (Ettinger 1995, 57).

This generalized criticism of civilization that equates Auschwitz with the new agrarian technology is, of course, massively political in its pseudo-hypercriticism and its rejection of politics. It serves the process of making things relative — in Heidegger's case, making National Socialism relative. And it creates legitimation: if everything is the same, nothing needs to be changed. This negation of politics sees everything as dirty; it rejects the necessity of dirty hands and only succeeds in making things even dirtier. Hypercriticism is exposed as lack of criticism.

But even the consistent antithesis to the escapism of hypercriticism has its faults. The readiness to dig in, everywhere and anywhere, to view and practice everything as "political," that is, as instrumental, leads to results that are not so opposed to hypercriticism, namely, the moral indifference to reality. The hypercritic wants to remain "clean"; the hyperactivist is always prepared to get his hands dirty. For the one, any means is too dirty, for the other, no means is too dirty. The result in both cases is the tendency toward indifference in the face of real dirt.

The politics of dirty hands is leadership and thus, in the final analysis, politics in general. This is true for democracies and non-democracies. But politics does not have to be indifferent to the amount of instrumental dirt. It can differentiate not only with regard to its goals, but with regard to its means.

In both war and peace, Mao Zedong followed the 2,000-year-old "classic" Sun Tzu (Salisbury 1993, 210). Lenin was influenced by Clausewitz. The founders of the Soviet Union and the People's Republic of China were instrumental from the outset: they used strategy and tactics to reach a given goal. The transition between war and peace was fluid. Politics as an instrument was not evaluated in terms of itself, but in terms of its functionality in relation to the goal.

From this perspective the switch to a murderous class struggle is consistent. But not only the annihilation of the landowning class and the murderous reduction of the class of farmers, even the art of deception could be grounded in this way: "He will conquer who has learnt the artifice of deviation" (Sun Tzu, n.d., 63).

Politics as the art of deception reigns also in existing democracies. In the space of a few pages, Robert McNamara gives succinct insight into the strategies and tactics of deception used in the U.S. presidential election of 1960 on the democratic side alone. Franklin D. Roosevelt, Jr. helped Kennedy by spreading the rumor that Hubert Humphrey had evaded the draft during World War II (Humphrey was one of Kennedy's opponents inside the party). Roosevelt, Jr. was rewarded by Kennedy with the post of undersecretary of commerce. In the service of Lyndon Johnson, John Connally had, in turn, spread the untruth at the Democratic Party Convention that Kennedy had Addison's disease. After his victory, Kennedy saw to it that Connally was bound to the government through his position as undersecretary of the navy — evidently he would have been too dangerous as an outsider (McNamara 1995, 19).

The topic of the "missile gap" offers a more complex view of the art of deception that played an important role in the election campaign itself. Kennedy, supported by an air force intelligence report, claimed that the Soviet Union had achieved superiority over the U.S. in terms of missile production. This topic helped Kennedy to improve his image vis-à-vis Nixon who was, at least at first glance, a more believable anti-Communist. Kennedy demonstrated that he was not soft on Communism and he showed his proficiency in foreign policy. But after the election, which had been won only by a small margin, it became known that the air force intelligence report was based on false information. There was indeed a "missile gap," but in favor of the U.S. (McNamara 1995, 20f.). Kennedy had not lied directly but he had negligently used a source made available to him in order to improve his image at Nixon's expense. The question of the "correctness" of the claim could not really be checked during the campaign due to the complexity of the issue.

Presumably, Kennedy had not read Sun Tzu. But within the framework of the Chinese military theorist's logic, he acted correctly. And Kennedy's actions could be traced and were thus interchangeable because they were logical and correct. Kennedy played according to the rules of the system and this gives politics a certain instrumental value, even in a democracy. In a democracy the rules are clear and strict, acting according to the rules can thus be counted on and this is true even for the art of deception. Whoever gave Kennedy the air force intelligence report knew that Kennedy would use the information the way he did.

Kennedy used the secret report against Nixon, whose attitude toward the art of deception was of a less well-defined caliber than Kennedy's. Years later, Nixon was to find out that the art of deception can only be applied successfully when it leads to the desired result: deception. In other words, Nixon was caught lying. And that does not go unpunished in a democracy.

Kennedy, who flourished with his careless use of lies and Nixon, to whom such carelessness brought a fateful end, are the two sides of leadership, the Dr. Jekyll and Mr. Hyde of political leadership in democracy. Both sides belong to reality just as much as the need of the politician to disguise his identity as Mr. Hyde as much as possible.

The Jekyll and Hyde dilemma of democratic leadership brings a non-transactional leader who is committed to reforms into a stalemate situation. Whoever plays by the rules is not a leader but a routinized office-holder, an interchangeable cog. A leader, on the other hand, can not always stick to the rules. A leader must command and apply the art of deception.

The routinized politician who always plays by the rules remains other-directed. He obeys the impulses that, in the end, can be traced back to the political marketplace. His actions can be scientifically deduced. His personality is therefore dispensable. The politician who transcends these boundaries and is inner-directed must act with no regard for the political marketplace in order to avoid its sanctions, even if this means transgressing the rules.

Within the general politics of existing democracies, Dr. Jekyll must never be caught being Mr. Hyde. Admitting the necessity of breaking the rules in order to reach certain goals would be counter-productive for these goals. The sanctions of an enraged electorate would crash down all too quickly. Only in the domain of foreign policy is the "necessity" of means that are other than "moral" openly admitted, even in stable democracies. The school of the "realists" has been debating for decades the issue of the unavoidability of "evil" means for the implementation of "good" ends (Morgenthau 1958; Isaacson 1993, 653-657).

This openly debated knowledge on the part of the analysts of International Relations is in no other field as complex as in the field of the weapons of mass destruction. In 1945, the U.S. stumbled naively, without public reflection, into the role of the world's first atomic power. But as the proliferation of atomic capabilities commenced on an international scale during the course of the Cold War, intellectual and moral distinctions had to be made. Nuclear physicists like Oppenheimer and Szilard were opposed to the spiraling development of atomic weapons, whereas others, such as Teller, approved of this policy. But for a long time the politics of nuclear proliferation was actually unpolitical. The clear idea was lacking as to how atomic bombs were to be dealt with in the Cold War, beyond the hope for their function as deterrents.

The first one who forced a public debate on the politics of the atom bomb was Henry Kissinger. His book "Nuclear Weapons and Foreign Policy," published by the 34-year-old Kissinger in 1957, provoked a debate on the political instrumentalization of the absolute evil, the undifferentiated mass destruction of human beings. The book established Kissinger's career as a sought-after political advisor. But it was also the beginning of the Kissinger-controversy: Kissinger as an amoral "Dr. Strangelove" who, like this film character, analyzes world politics in a Machiavellian manner even in the nuclear age and calculates both advantages and risks such as fleets of atomic bombs as if they were mercenary armies in the conflicts of the Italian city states around 1500 (Isaacson 1993, 86-90).

In 1957, Kissinger pleaded for a politics of the atom bomb — not for its invention, since the bomb already existed, not for its military readiness, since this already existed, and also not for its disarmament, since this would not have been politically feasible. His plea was to learn to live with the fact that the bomb existed, that is, to learn to deal with it politically. What would later be called the strategy of the "flexible response" during the Kennedy administration, namely the development of levels of strategy between atomic destruction by the atomic bomb and rejection of the atomic bomb, was what Kissinger thematized.

Kissinger was a proponent of *Realpolitik* and for that he became both famous and infamous when, as National Security Advisor and then as Secretary of State under Nixon and Ford, he not only analyzed but "made" world politics. This *Realpolitik* was suspicious to widely differing powers. The right wing of the Republican party criticized Kissinger in 1975 and 1976 as the evil spirit in the White House of Gerald Ford. Kissinger's politics of arrangement with the USSR was a source of constant annoyance to the right, for whom "détente" was a dirty word (Isaacson 1993, 693-699). And even earlier, Kissinger had become a symbol of all that liberal Americans rejected of U.S. policies as a world power, especially because of his policies in Cambodia.

The domestic conflict caused by the U.S. military intervention in Cambodia showed the limitations of the "art of deception" that a stable democracy generally allows in foreign policy. Kissinger's role in the U.S. offensive into Cambodia of April 1970, a country not yet fully involved in the Vietnam War, was and is still today an example for many of where *Realpolitik* can lead when it is not balanced by a sense of morality. The means of lies and deception that was employed not only in foreign policy but in domestic policy as well, and the means of the expansion of military force did not lead to the declared end: peace in Indochina and thus peace in Cambodia.

Kissinger's politics was, for his critics, a decisive contribution to the undermining of Norodom Sihanouk's presidency (already effected by the American policy of non-military intervention) and thus to the clearance for the genocide of the killing fields, for which, of course, the Khmer Rouge and not the U.S. is directly responsible. But especially when one practices *Realpolitik*, the actions of the "Realpoliticians" must be measured by the unintentional results of their politics. And the unintentional results of Nixon's and Kissinger's policy in Cambodia were the killing fields (Isaacson 1993, 256-284).

It was not easy for Kissinger to learn to accept the moral rejection that came to him from his own academic milieu, his own former colleagues and friends, after the invasion of Cambodia. For that was the real expansion of the war that Nixon and Kissinger had promised to end. In his memoirs he attempted in detail to depict the American intervention in Cambodia as a reaction to destabilizations in North Vietnam (Kissinger 1979, 515-557). Numerous reports reveal the degree to which the animosity of the criticism directed toward him affected Kissinger in the wake of the "Cambodia adventure." For his colleagues at Harvard University, Kissinger became a symbol for the political misuse of science. On May 8, 1970, after a meeting with his academic critics, which Kissinger had wanted to use as a rapprochement, he had to admit in resignation, "The meeting completed my transition from the academic world." It was not the opposition of his friends and colleagues that hurt him so much as their self-righteousness (Isaacson 1993, 281).

Kissinger's hands had gotten too dirty for his friends. But in their criticism he could see only the hypercriticism of self-righteous objectors. "Dr. Strangelove" saw himself as misunderstood. He had to see himself as misunderstood.

11 On the Misery of Collaboration

The Tragedy of the Jewish Councils — Collaboration as a
Lesser Evil — Philippe Pétain — The Collaboration of
Azdak and of Schwejk — Collaboration is not always
Collaboration — Collaboration as an Attempt at Political
Action

The literature on National Socialism knows a particularly complex
subject: the Jewish councils, those organs instituted by the National
Socialists that carried out the business of the mass murderers employing an autonomy that often appeared only cynical. (Trunk 1972)
But only too often, there slips into the story of the most tragic and
perhaps also the worst type of collaboration an argument that must be
taken seriously: It is true, the Jewish councils were not able to prevent
the Holocaust, they were not able to prevent the mass death. But often,
very often, they believed they were able, for some few individuals, to
postpone and perhaps even to avoid the fate of the Holocaust.

The possible justification of the collaboration of the Jewish
councils is the theory of the lesser evil. Without the willingness for
cooperation that appeared voluntary from the outside —and what sort
of cooperation would the mass murderers have accepted besides one
that was unconditionally willing — assistance even in individual cases
would have been impossible. Through their collaboration, the Jewish
councils were able to remove individual human beings from the lists
of those slated for the death transports, or to see to it that individuals
were not put on the lists to begin with. The tragic dilemma, of course,
was that, as a rule, the rescue of certain individuals was simultaneously a death sentence for others. For there were, after all, quotas to
be filled for the transports to Auschwitz and elsewhere; and if one
man or woman was not to be transported to death, then, unavoidably,
another had to be sent. All of this happened on the basis of decisions
made by the Jewish councils themselves (or by a single Jewish
collaborator).

The debate on Jewish councils after the end of the National
Socialist regime demonstrates that this collaboration apparently
unavoidably led also to corruption. Members of Jewish councils used
their privileges (relatively speaking) not only to save themselves and

their families for as long as possible; it came down to the commodification of survival. (Yivo 1972) Hannah Arendt, who started the debate with her reports on the Eichmann trial, reproaches the Jewish councils with the responsibility for Jewish life: in many cases the collaboration of the Jewish councils would have been a greater and not a lesser evil. This, because the Jewish councils all too often had lulled the Jews into a false sense of security; at times, in fact, during which flight from the ghetto would still have been possible. (Arendt 1995, 161f.)

The state of Israel has always had to struggle with the painful historical fact that it owes its existence in large part to the survivors of the Holocaust, whereas others were not able to survive. The criteria that determined who survived in the ghettos and camps, and even earlier, when there was "only" the quasi-legal discrimination of the Nürnberg laws, are factually unclear. Many survivors had to ask themselves over and over, or be asked, why they of all people had survived, why not the others, of whom there were so many. Where does collaboration begin? Perhaps when Zionist representatives bargain with Adolf Eichmann about the possibility of emigration to Palestine, as, for example, Teddy Kollek did in the spring of 1939? (Segev 1993, 31) How great is the distance between the actions of Kollek and his contact with Eichmann and the actions of the Jewish councils?

What options were open to Jewish representative bodies when they were put before the choice by the dictates of the National Socialists either to maintain a minimum of self-administration, as in Poland in the fall of 1939 or in the Soviet Union in the summer of 1941, or to relinquish the opportunity for this arrangement? The National Socialists, after all, usually saw to it that the Jewish councils retained the illusion that there were concrete opportunities for securing Jewish survival. And for the sake of this illusion that could be, and even had to be based on the hope of German defeat as the war went continued, the Jewish councils were able to develop motives that had nothing at all to do with corruption or with the individual will to survive.

One extreme case, that also demonstrated the extremity of the boundaries between lifesaving politics and the potential corruption of collaboration, was the story of the "King of the Jews," as Mordechai Chaim Rumkowski, the Jewish Elder in the ghetto of Lodz ("Litzmann-stadt") was sometimes called. Rumkowski worked closely with the National Socialists and saw to it that their machinery of destruction was attended to, until, with the last of those in the ghetto, he himself was taken to Auschwitz, which he was not to survive. One of those from Lodz who did survive wrote the following about this collaborator: "It is still difficult for me to evaluate Rumkowski's role today. He was a tool and still tried to save what could be saved." (Zelman 1995, 51) What else was he supposed to do when he took on the role of Elder?

Another extreme case was Paul Eppstein, the Jewish Elder of Terezin (Theresienstadt). He was deeply implicated in the corruption surrounding unequal distribution of food in the camp. He used internal conflicts with other members of the "autonomous" Jewish camp leadership to strengthen his own position with the SS. The SS, in turn, played a particular game with him: In June 1944 he posed as "mayor" of the Potemkin village ("The *Führer* gives the Jews a city ...") that the SS was presenting to representatives of the International Red Cross. But by the fall of 1944 even Eppstein had fulfilled his duty. When most members of the Jewish council of Terezin were deported to Auschwitz, he was arrested by the SS on a pretext and shot to death on the same day. His successor was Benjamin Murmelstein, who survived, instrumentalized to the end by the SS, despised to the end by the Jewish survivors. Murmelstein apparently saw himself as a latter day Josephus Flavius, as a Jew who was used by the Jews' enemies, but also an accepted Jew, since he was a necessary, and for that reason, a particularly tragic Jew. (Adler, in: Yivo 1971, 70-82).

What should Eppstein and Murmelstein have done, once they had accepted their roles? Would Eppstein's refusal to play the part of a happy Hitler-Jew have saved the life of a victim? And would Eppstein's or Murmelstein's refusal to take on their roles in the first place have changed anything? The Jewish councils were not the murderers. They were replaceable cogs in a machine run by others. They were not really able to conduct politics. Their submission to the illusion of being able to prevent the "worst" through their collaboration simplified the work of the murderers, but the murdering worked smoothly even without them.

It is not the blurring of the roles of perpetrators and victims that is the problem for the Jewish councils — there was no such blurring of roles. The Jewish councils' problem is their influence on Jewish consciousness after the Holocaust. The actions of the Jewish councils, or of some of their members, contradicted the need to see the victims as heroes. The problem for the Jewish councils is the perception of their political function in the debate after the Holocaust.

The Jewish councils are one extreme form of collaboration, the quislings of Europe are the other. This can be shown using the examples of Pierre Laval and Philippe Pétain. (Webster 1990)

What were the options facing the last Prime Minister of the third French Republic in June 1940? Forced by the majority of the democratically elected parliament of this republic, he saw at first no alternative to the surrender which was, in fact, dictated by Germany. And in accordance with the clear majority of the French public he followed a politics of appeasement toward the German occupying forces.

And this made it clear to Vichy France that an ultimately victorious Germany would be prepared to accommodate a compliant France with the status of favored satellite, a secondary power in the "new Europe" to be dominated by the National Socialists. If the first calculation was "right," i.e., the insight that the French capitulation was unavoidable, then the second step had an understandable, even a forceful logic: to secure a maximum of autonomy and of future influence for the national interests of France.

To achieve this, sacrifices had to be made. It was by no means clear with the crassness as of 1942, even for non-antisemites in the summer of 1940, that the victims were, for the most part, Jews: French Jews, or Jews that had fled to France from other European countries. And in the summer of 1940 very many, surely the majority of the French population could not perceive that the alternative De Gaulle was more than a satellite at the side of a Great Britain not really capable of victory.

And so the Marshal saw in Pierre Laval a politician of the Third Republic — by no means from the extreme right — who promised to ensure continuity for a legitimation, but who, at the same time, was supposed to be and, indeed, wanted to be an unconditional facilitator of German interests. With the rationalization that all other options were an (even) greater evil, Vichy France set out on its path to the overfulfillment of German wishes, the overadaptation to German interests, and finally, the overzealous participation in mass murder in the form of a premature obedience.

The Jewish councils did not have these illusions — they were concerned with survival. No one who, by the grace of the SS, was able to play the role of a second-ranking ally in the Eastern sector of the new European order under German command held out the prospect of a Jewish satellite state. The Jewish councils did not have the strategy of Vichy France before them, and yet their collaboration and the logic of their behavior had a function similar to that of Pétain and Laval: The first step toward collaboration led with logical consistency to the next. The first decision for the lesser evil was not only an isolated decision, it was the decision for a certain logic. And this logic set into motion a series of events that progressed with the inexorability of a Greek tragedy.

The collaboration of the Jewish councils and the collaboration of the quislings in occupied Europe are comparable in their logic, but not in their moral underpinnings. The quislings were concerned with a part of the power on the second level just below that exercised by the German occupying forces. The Lavals and Pétains were prominent, and by no means replaceable cogs of the National Socialist machine of murder. They were meant for permanent privilege in Hitler-occupied Europe. The Rumkowskis, the Eppsteins and Murmelsteins on the other hand, could expect only death, even if they had succumbed to illusion for a time. They were the smallest cogs of the machine; their power was that of arbitrarily replaceable marionettes.

There was resistance, of course, especially Jewish resistance, to the quislings as well as to the Jewish councils. The resistance of the Jews in the ghettos and the death camps is a constitutive part of Jewish history (Langbein 1980, 193-206). This resistance has great significance for Jewish self-esteem and for the perception of the particularity of the Holocaust. But even the revolt in the Warsaw ghetto could not change the fact that this ghetto was liquidated and that the Holocaust was carried out. The fact that some were able to save themselves does nothing to change this: a few would have been able to save themselves even without the heroic gesture of the revolt. Considered in light of the actual influence on the Holocaust as it was taking place, the option of armed resistance had for the Jews the same efficacy as the option of collaboration for the Jewish councils: both variations of Jewish behavior were not significant for the events of the Holocaust.

In Israel, in one of the cases brought against a member of the Jewish police units that had been active in the ghettos and camps of central and eastern Europe, an Israeli court confronted the problems surrounding an action that bases itself on the ethics of a "lesser evil." The justification offered by the Jewish councils, to whom the Jewish police troops had reported, was that they had wanted to avoid the worst by collaborating with the organizations of the NS-regime. The Israeli court ruled that this justification had to be understood in the particular context and circumstances of the times (Trunk 1972, 565)

But a justification such as this one must be examined and differentiated vis-à-vis its juridically moral and political dimensions. It may be plausible in individual cases to believe that collaborators assumed their actions could indeed mitigate evil, aside from what the real consequences might have been. One has to assume here, of course, not only after the fact, but also in the concrete extreme situation of the Jewish councils themselves that the temptation was great to justify the saving of one's own life and the protection of one's own interests (family, property) by referring to the greater good for the community. One can strive for the differentiation into the individual and the political realm in concrete circumstances but it is certainly not always achieved convincingly in the final analysis. The historical record shows to too great a degree that various motivations lay at cross purposes and that in judging the collaboration of the Jewish councils, one cannot overlook the degree to which the members themselves were being persecuted in a manner hitherto unknown.

In Bert Brecht's "Caucasian Chalk Circle" the figure Azdak sets the example of this logic and tries at the same time to escape it and thus overcome it. Azdak is a collaborator in Schwejk's style. He plays the collaborator and in order to do this convincingly, he plays seriously again and again with the oppression, exploitation and even annihilation of people. His logic is this: If I do not serve the regime as judge, then someone else will; and that someone else will not look for the cracks in the system of terror, as I do and which I use to save people in individual cases. Azdak is the resistance fighter in the cloak of the collaborator who, in order to disguise himself, is also prepared to act accordingly. Azdak is Charles De Gaulle in the guise of Philippe Pétain.

Azdak is a literary attempt to solve a problem that perhaps cannot be solved in reality: to be a collaborator on the outside, but a resistance fighter on the inside above all with an unequivocal clarity, above all for history. Azdak is a dialectical-literary character who simply does not exist in political practice. What was the extent to which Jewish councils could go along with the (forced) participation in the Holocaust and still remain within the logical framework of the lesser evil, and which step made of them arbitrarily replaceable instruments without the least influence on the course of events? With which step in the development were they forced to recognize that their only room for maneuvering, that is to say, that their only possibility of conducting politics was the participation in deciding who would be transported more quickly, who less quickly to the death camps, without being able in the least to influence the capacity and rapidity of the machinery of death? Where was the exact threshold of development at which Philippe Pétain must have known beyond a doubt that he could do nothing more for the cause of France, as a democracy and a sovereign state, than to resign? When must he have known that the justification for his collaboration which had still been plausible in the early summer of 1940 could no longer stand up to geopolitical developments?

The Pétain of the year 1945 who turned himself in to the authorities of newly freed France is most certainly not the same Pétain of June 1940 who assumed the bitter duty of carrying out the apparent will of the majority of the French citizenry and the will of a clear majority of the parliament of the Third Republic, and of assuming responsibility for the step that had incurred the call "November criminals" to the social and centrist democrats of the German Reich nearly 22 years earlier, namely, to accept politically the military defeat that had already taken place. Between this last Prime Minister of the conquered Third Republic and the President (head of state) of the "état français" that had been conquered in a much different manner and far more clearly, lie the incremental gestures of premature obedience vis-à-vis the National Socialist machine of terror. Here lie also the French measures undertaken internally toward a revocation of human rights for French citizens of Jewish descent; here lies fascism à la française which especially in the dimension of its annihilation of Jews was more like fascism à la Pavelic than fascism à la Mussolini.

Pétain was no Azdak. He did not attempt to deceive and escape the machinery of National Socialism like a Schwejk; he was no servant Matti who used his Master Puntila's hours of drunken stupor to repair what the sober Master Puntila had wrought. Pétain lacked the dialectic of the borderliner between collaboration and resistance, and for that reason he remained a quisling whose overeager adaptation soon (but when exactly, when clearly?) ceased to permitted the justification that the fate of France and her citizens (including those defined as "Jewish") would have been worse without his collaboration.

In this case history pronounces — ex post facto — a clear judgment. But before the fact, in June 1940, none of this was so clear. And the Jewish councils that had to deal with the accusation that they had tainted the Holocaust with the odor of Jewish guilt, at what time was it clear to a Jewish council in Riga or in Lublin, at what point in time must it have been clear that it only supported the machinery of the Holocaust by making the business of the National Socialist mass murderers a little easier? When would the moment have been to rise up out of the inexorably advancing logic of collaboration and still be able to invoke the strategy of the lesser evil?

This moment did exist at one time, and many people in France and elsewhere in Nazi-occupied Europe found it for themselves and acted accordingly. One example for this is the Sudeten-German

National Socialist Oskar Schindler who came to occupied Poland to get rich quickly by means of cheap Jewish slave labor and who, at some point, inwardly changed sides. He went from being a parasite of the Holocaust to being one of its most bizarre infiltrators; from being one who wanted to profit from the misery of the Jews to one who saved hundreds of Jews from the annihilation long since recognizable as an end in itself, as the actual goal of the National Socialist regime.

Collaboration is often the attempt to escape from the paralysis of a defeat that excludes all politics; the attempt to become politically effective again; that is, to progress from a situation without prospects to one with options; to win back the possibility of choosing between different evils. With regard to Metternich-Austria's defeat by France in 1809, Henry Kissinger sings a veritable song of praise to collaboration as the reinstatement of politics: cooperation with the victor without losing one's own identity, one's own interests hidden behind a deceptive cloak of compliance. (Kissinger n.d., 19f.)

Collaboration in and of itself, then, cannot be judged unequivocally with regard to its substantive, moral meaning nor with regard to its functional and structural meaning. One will always have to consider with whom and with what intention, but also with what result cooperation with a victor, that is to say, collaboration, has taken place. One has to consider, then, whether a concrete instance of collaboration is truly a believable attempt to reestablish one's own political capacities by working together with the victor, to deploy the evil called collaboration in order to avoid still greater evils.

The root of the Jewish councils' collaboration has both general and existential as well as concrete and historical aspects. The first is the reasonable lack of understanding about the essence of National Socialism. The second stems from the experience that at least before the invasion of Poland, National Socialism actually conceded a political space for Jewish collaboration. When organizing Jewish emigration Adolf Eichmann's "Department of Jewish Affairs" in particular needed the cooperation of Zionist institutions that, at that time, felt connected to the National Socialist dictatorship with regard to one goal: to bring as many German Jews (and, beginning in March 1938 also Austrian and then Czechoslovakian Jews) as possible to Palestine.

The politics of Adolf Hitler was at first recognizable as directed toward what would later be called "ethnic cleansing": on the basis of their membership in a group defined externally (the Nürnberg laws), human beings were deprived of their rights, robbed of their belongings and driven out of the country. It is true that National Socialist politics was already full of murderous rhetoric (for example, Hitler's "Mein

Kampf," in which the image of the parasite is already present — the Jews as biological vermin to be destroyed). And the concrete politics of the NSDAP that had come to power was also in certain aspects a murderous one (such as the pogroms of the "Reichskristallnacht" or "night of broken glass" that were organized from above). But at first, it was not fundamentally different from well-known forms of historical anti-semitism, for example, the tsarist pogrom policy or the policy of murderous expulsion from Spain in 1492. What today appears as the logical development of racial social Darwinism or as a concretization of the parasite image was a new, historically unknown quality before 1939 and until 1941, hardly comprehensible since it had not yet been experienced.

The fact that German Jews and other Jews lulled themselves into a false sense of security (that with hindsight can only appear extremely naive), and the fact that they unsuspectingly made their way toward the dawning reality of the systematic "extermination" of the Jewish people were things the Jews shared in common with the governments of the Soviet Union and Great Britain and France and also with the one government that worked systematically to construct a global alliance against Hitler: that of the USA.

The Holocaust presented a new quality of eschatological anti-politics that made an absolute moral — that of "racial purity" and the "extermination of life unworthy of living" — the guideline for its own concrete measures. Precisely because of this, the Holocaust was not recognized in time. Not by the Jews, not by the Marxist-Leninists and, similarly, not by the liberal democrats. For that very reason, the Jewish councils in the ghettos and camps of central and eastern Europe were only the continuation of a historically explainable misunderstanding: The uniqueness of the Holocaust led to the mistaken belief that one could "prevent the worst" in one individual case or another by cooperating on certain issues.

The Jewish councils felt themselves confronted with the political choice between two evils: either to delay and thus prevent certain events through a willingness to cooperate; or to relinquish the chance to do this by refusing to cooperate. The Jewish councils themselves represented the desire to conduct politics; to choose between options; to recognize and accept the lesser evil. The new quality of the Holocaust meant that politics had literally come to an end and there were no more choices to be made. This was something that many people were not able to recognize, and many more were probably not able to recognize in time.

The politics of the Holocaust was in this sense no politics at all, and it permitted no politics. The answer lay only in submission and the acceptance of one's own death, or (military, violent) resistance. The National Socialists, at least Hitler, were not conducting politics "with the Jews." When Himmler recognized that defeat was unavoidable and tried to trade Jewish lives for military goods, that is, when he tried to conduct a reasonable, cost-effective military politics, he was acting without Hitler's approval; and when he offered to end the Holocaust as a military-political bargaining chip via connections to neutral Sweden, the entire murderous rage of his *Führer* was unleashed against him. Because Himmler had not understood with ultimate finality that Hitler was concerned not with politics, not with the choice between different evils and thus not with the political securing of military victories — Hitler was concerned with exterminating the Jews. He made his war policies subordinate to this goal. And when the opportunity to improve the military position of the German war machine competed with carrying out the Holocaust, then Hitler chose, and National Socialism chose, the Holocaust.

In the middle of the defense battle in the East, the *Wehrmacht* had to provide logistics, material and personnel for the transportation of hundreds of thousands of Jews from the Balkans to Auschwitz, only for them to be gassed there. And when the Red Army was already stationed at the Hungarian border, Hitler directed all his energy not toward resisting the military threat, but toward the extermination of Hungarian Jewry.

This refusal to conduct politics, inherent in National Socialism, went unrecognized, or was recognized too late by the Jewish councils. And the fact that it was the SS and the SD who cooperated with Zionist organizations until the beginning of the war in order to drive out Jews, not exterminate them, was an additional factor in explaining the phenomenon of Jewish collaboration. Until the war began, Eichmann worked seriously not on the extermination but on the deportation of the European Jewry and he assured himself of the cooperation (collaboration?) of Zionist activists to this end. There was also cooperation toward the realization of a common National Socialist interest and all of this certainly contributed toward keeping alive the notion that there was a political option in the Jewish councils that as of 1941 were made instruments of the Holocaust (without the National Socialists taking the possibility of illusion or self-deception). There was still an evil that was greater, against which collaboration could and did appear to be a lesser evil.

It was the illusion of being able to challenge the messianic execution of the National Socialist eschatology by means of a limited politics. The full insight into the futility of this undertaking would have required the full insight into the essence of National Socialism and thus into the Holocaust. National Socialism was not conducting politics in Auschwitz and Majdanek, Treblinka and Sobibor. It was realizing a *Weltanschauung*. And for that reason the collaboration of the Jewish councils was a mistake, if an understandable one. That is why, except for a limited number of individual cases (which in each of these cases would have been, or at least could have been a justification for collaboration) the collaboration of the Jewish councils had no effect and changed nothing. The evil remained as it was intended: unimaginably great and of a quality that overwhelmed the prevailing experience of human existence.

The situation in Vichy France was quite different, where it was not fundamentally an illusion to collaborate with the NS authorities in order to realize political choices. At least until the occupation of southern France in 1942, the French institutions had no small amount of latitude within which to maneuver. This space arose largely from the fact that France, reduced in its role as a super power, was certain to assume a secondary role in Hitler's new European order. Precisely for that reason, the use of this latitude by Laval and other politicians of the "overaccommodation" must be evaluated much differently than the collaboration of the Jewish councils: Hitler had plans for France — for the Jews he had none. For this reason, the fact that French collaboration increasingly took on the character of premature submission, an anticipatory execution of German wishes that were only suspected, must therefore be evaluated differently. For it was not only the fact that, compared with the situation of the Jews in the ghettos as of 1940, there were many more plausible choices for resistance and cooperation with French exile (De Gaulle); the main difference was that the German occupying forces themselves had given France political latitude. This is the essence of Hitler and Göring's meeting with Pétain and Laval's participation in discussions and organizational meetings in Germany.

France and its political structures certainly saw themselves in 1940 in the position of recognizing options and choosing between them, that is, of making politics. Between the complete submission to German (National Socialist) goals, to which only a small minority of French Fascists were inclined in 1940, and De Gaulle's choice to continue the struggle from the British isles, which, in 1940, only a few French could find themselves willing to do, there lay a certain space within which to maneuver which can be described with the conceptual terms "cooperation — collaboration."

Stanley Hoffman touches on this differentiation when he distinguishes between a "collaboration d'état" and a normal collaboration. The first, more a sort of cooperation out of technical necessity, emphasizes the political autonomy that the Vichy state (and other western European governments in the countries occupied by Germany) possessed. The French institutions, from the railroad administration to the police, had to cooperate with the German institutions if they wanted to continue the policy of capitulation that had been legitimated by the democratically elected constitutional organs of the Third Republic. The other, the "true" collaboration is based on a fundamental sympathy with the actual goals of the occupying powers, in the case of Vichy France most clearly expressed in the annihilation of the Jews. (Trunk 1972, 570-572)

The fact that reality in Vichy France was characterized increasingly by normal, actual collaboration and less and less by "collaboration d'état" speaks to the effect of a certain logic that points toward the loss of politics brought about by collaboration. The Vichy France of the summer of 1944 differed significantly from the Vichy France of the summer of 1940: collaboration for reasons of political sympathy had taken the upper hand and with that, the freedom of the French state to maneuver was decisively limited. Vichy France had not understood how to draw the line between a technically necessary cooperation, grounded in the defeat of 1940, and a collaboration, which went beyond it.

The fact that the Marshal of France withdrew toward Germany from the troops of Free France in a sort of German honorary arrest demonstrates his fall and that of his regime of collaboration: the political maneuverability had been wasted; Vichy France was no longer even a secondary political factor. Even before the Allies had freed France, the collaboration of Pétain and Laval had led to their having no more real decisions to make in France; they had lost every option. A collaboration that had been able to rely on the ability to choose between possible outcomes and that precisely for that reason had chosen collaboration as the lesser evil, had become sheer instrumentation through German interests. This was only reinforced by the fact that the fate of the French government in exile in Germany at the end of the war —the remnants of Vichy — was utterly insignificant for the future of France.

The Jaruzelski of 1981 was a collaborator. His politics corresponded to the logic of given dependence: Poland was a Soviet satellite. Jaruzelski's behavior showed that he was aware of his dependence on the central bureau in Moscow. But this dependence was not created by him, he was not responsible for it, and it could not be brought to an end by him. His justification was that of a collaborator: He did not choose the option of heroic resistance. He chose the "lesser evil." But, unlike the Jewish councils and unlike the Vichy regime as of 1940, his collaboration had a significant impact on Poland: Without his political action the fate of Poland would have been a markedly different one.

12 On the Presumption of Objectivity

Dirty Hands — The Script of World History — The Longing for Categories — All Orthodoxies are Alike

Jorge Semprun has his aging leftist revolutionaries remember that, as late as 1944, the defenders of the Communist party of France labeled Paul Nizan a traitor "objectively." This "objectively" was "an insidious adverb that spared them from having to make an objective analysis" (Semprun 1991, 228).

"Objectively," in the sense of fact, Paul Nizan had left the Communist party as a protest against the Hitler-Stalin pact. "Objectively," again, in the sense of fact, the French Communists, occupied at that time with categorizing the war of France, Britain and Poland against Hitler's Germany as "imperialist," had denounced Nizan as a police spy. Even after June, 1941, when the war had drastically changed and had become an armed resistance against Germany, a patriotic as well as an international duty for them, the Communists, they refused, "objectively," to rescind the denunciation of Nizan that had been based on nothing, that is, not on facts. This would have meant, of course, dealing "objectively" with one's own past and one's own involvement in a logic that was not to be understood in Marxist terms, namely, that the daily politics as defined by Stalin was the expression of "objective" necessity in the interest of the socialist revolution.

Nizan was no longer accused of actually (objectively?) working against his party in the service of the French government as a spy. Nizan was reproached with the fact that his departure from the party had been detrimental to the Communist cause and thus treasonous, regardless of his motives and regardless of his actual (objective?) actions.

The way that the Communist Party of France acted toward Nizan is significant. It expresses a specific logic of a specific approach to politics. "Guilt" is deprived of any subjective element: ultimately it does not matter what Nizan's motivations were; it does not matter why he protested Stalin's pact with Hitler. Furthermore, it is completely irrelevant (and this is most important) whether the changes in Stalin's politics justified Nizan's protest after the fact. The violation of the discipline of the law against thinking constitutes guilt. And if an additional guilt must be constructed in order to better propagate this guilt for the understanding of the outside world, such as spying, then this has little bearing on the matter, even if this construction is "objectively" a lie.

This logic of (Stalinist) communism turns any imaginable concept of objectivity into its opposite. It is of no interest whether Nizan really was a police agent; it is of no interest whether Nizan's attitude seems justified in light of the development of National Socialist politics of war. None of these questions, "objective" in the scientific sense, gets asked within the framework of Stalinist logic. For whatever reasons and with whatever justification, Nizan is "guilty" of betraying the party and that means doubting Stalin's "objectivity."

In "The Dirty Hands," Jean-Paul Sartre describes similar patterns of Stalinist logic when he has Hugo kill Hoederer on behalf of the party. Hoederer is a "traitor" like Nizan: He does not share the same concept of the "facts" as the Stalinist party leadership and for that reason, he is guilty, even when, shortly after his execution, which was made to look like a personally motivated murder, Hoederer's perception looks like that of his party. Both the party and Stalin say he is "right." The murder that is reinterpreted as an individual act makes this easier. Nevertheless, Hoederer is a traitor and remains a traitor because, "objectively," he has hurt the party.

The denunciation of Nizan did not end in 1941 and it did not end in 1945. Nizan remained a traitor, especially for Communist intellectuals like Luis Aragon (Beauvoir 1968, 213). The denunciation of Nizan could not come to an end because it protected the logic of Stalinist objectivity. Even when this objectivity let anti-fascist fighters be liquidated under the pretense of anti-fascism, the question of individual guilt had to be dismissed as a petty bourgeois concern. The question had to be one of objective guilt. And the answer was always determined by the party and that meant Stalin and the Soviet Union.

These are the experiences George Orwell had in the Spanish Civil War. He saw how bitterly the Communists in Spain fought against the anti-fascists who did not want to submit to the strategy dictated by Stalin. The P.O.U.M. was destroyed as an anti-Franco party, not by Franco, but by the Communists. Their leader was murdered, not by fascists, but by the Communists. Their guilt was "objective," like that of all "Trotskyites" labelled leftists: regardless of their subjective efforts to combat fascism with all their strength, they were guilty because they did not submit to the dictates of the Communist party and thus to Stalin's dictates (Slater 1985, 149-151, 168f.).

Orwell, who published his experiences in the Spanish Civil War in his "Homage to Catalonia," also offers an analytical explanation for the function of the Stalinist concept of objectivity. Beyond it lies a quasi-religious concept of orthodoxy. He draws parallels between the attraction that the Catholic Church had for intellectuals in the first half of the century, especially in Great Britain, and the attraction Communism held for the same group (Slater 1985, 158).

It is the attractiveness of a closed system that conveys a sense of home, a pattern of thinking that promises ultimate clarity. From the morass of social contradictions arises the "City of God." And suddenly the solution is clear to all who doubted in the face of social misery and the rise of fascism. There is the eschatological promise that all contradictions will be subsumed; not, like with Marx, abstractly and at some time in the distant future, but concretely, in reality: the home of all workers whose leadership, in secure possession of the script of world history, invites everyone to conform and subordinate themselves. The clarity of this order has a price. One's own thinking must become immanent to the system. It must accept the premises from which the doctrines of orthodoxy are deduced.

This orthodoxy, called objectivity in Stalinist jargon, has its quasi-theological logic. All politics is directed toward a goal. Its ethics and its morals are always deduced, inferred from this goal. Politics must not be judged on its own; neither the politics of the Hitler-Stalin pact, nor the show trials, nor the agricultural collectivization that was carried out with such force. Politics must be evaluated in terms of its dependent relations. It is, in this sense, neither "good" nor "bad." Politics is "good" if it is functional—for the goal Stalin defined in concrete terms for building socialism. Politics is "bad" when it is dysfunctional for this goal.

This is more or less what was meant by the Inquisitors of all Churches and all times. When what is at issue is the opening of the kingdom of God to lost souls, then it may be permitted, even called for, to cleanse these poor souls through torture and burning at the stake in order to impart to them eternal happiness. If the issue is access to the kingdom of God, then such values as freedom of belief and of conscience are illogical and inappropriate because they are dysfunctional. Or should an eternal soul be lost simply because it let itself be tempted during the short time of its earthly existence?

Stalinist objectivity and the orthodoxy of the Church destroy politics because they do not allow distinctions to be made in the evaluation of social action. An analysis of the relationship of political goals and means oriented in reality is impossible when the means, that is, the actual politics, can only be objectively correct or objectively false. Stalinist objectivity and the orthodoxy of the Church also destroy the possibility of analyzing political events. They reduce every form of social-scientific approach to either its useful or damaging effect. Politics becomes the execution of an a priori fixed goal and political analysis becomes the propagation of the necessity of events.

In this sense, the Jaruzelski of 1981 and 1989 was free of Stalinist orthodoxy. His leadership, oriented in the determination of the "lesser evil" was not directed toward any "objective" goal, except for reaching the decision that was least painful for Poland. The form of this approach to the decision of late autumn in 1981 was, as Jaruzelski describes it in his memoirs (Jaruzelski 1993), not the decision of a Stalinist, nor of a Leninist, nor a Marxist. Jaruzelski's decision was not directed by any recognizable orthodoxy. For this reason, its nature of personal responsibility was clearly discernible. For this reason, too, it stood as an example for openly recognizable and openly declared leadership.

Jaruzelski did not ground his decision by stating that he had to implement some sort of pre-determined "objectivity." Jaruzelski did not adhere to any scripts that were offered by orthodoxies as the key to world events. He did not act with reference to "Capital" or "What is to be done?" or to the Bible. He made politics and he accepted the fact that, in so doing, he had to get his hands dirty. The ethic of his actions was not an ethic of conviction, but a concrete ethic of responsibility. With that he ensured his capacity for action and thus his capacity for decision-making and for politics.

The keepers of the holy grail of Stalinist objectivity and the orthodoxy of the Church are pragmatics in their praxis. Stalin oriented himself to the formulation of "socialism in one state" which made the concrete state interests of the Soviet Union into the unconditional product of Marxism-Leninism. Whoever met Stalin's concrete steps with skepticism fought not against a certain policy but against "socialism." This person was therefore not an opponent but a traitor. When it seemed necessary to Stalin to stop along the way of what he described as socialism, then the advancing Bolsheviks of the left wing (Trotsky, Kamenev, Zinoviev) were traitors. If Stalin wanted to accelerate the development, then suddenly those on the right (Bukharin, Tomsky, Rykov) were the traitors. Any variation in political tactics or strategy was declared a theory with the end result of a thought structure highly stylized as Marxism-Leninism. Tactics and strategy dissolved into "truth" and "objectivity" no matter how short the notice or how spontaneous the "theory."

Making reference to some sort of "objectivity" even conveyed by such slogans as "Everyone knows that..." characterized the semantic aspect of Stalinism (Ulam 1989, esp. 10f.). Stalin gave the impression that his concrete decisions were the epitome of a higher, given wisdom. And in the "great terror" of the show trials the concrete delivery of evidence played hardly any role at all, at least not beyond the bizarre confessions. Arguments were made of "objective" damage, using the "objective" similarity between Trotskyism and fascism. In the show trials, the "objective" evidence that was not based on factual but only functional objectivity that could only be claimed and therefore not proved, played a special role, evidently also for the internal reasoning of the confessions of the accused (Conquest 1986, 177-210 and 496-573).

What caused so many intellectuals to applaud Stalinism for so many decades? What was the secret attraction of this theory whose essence was the refusal of theory? Why were so many theoreticians attracted to this anti-theory?

One of them, Ernst Fischer, tried to find an answer. After his experience in Damascus, that is, after his break with the Communist party which was closely related to the invasion of Czechoslovakia by the troops of the Warsaw pact countries, he pursued his own historical motivations. Finer had reported for the German-language media of the Comintern in Moscow on the show trials, completely in the sense of Stalinist interpretation. And Finer had believed this interpretation. Not because he had to believe it but because he wanted to. Finer wanted to be a part of the community of believers. He wanted to conform and submit.

Thirty years after writing about the "Great Terror" that which he now recognized as "objectively" false, Ernst Fischer reflected: "The ego who wrote these reports was in no way insincere ... It was a partisan, a party-oriented ego: the conscious negation of my individualism, that is, my former spontaneous, continually developing ego. This ego did not strive for identity with past conditions but rather for identity with a freely recognized 'super ego': with the cause, with the party ... A party that is proud of being 'monolithic' demands that each of its members also be monolithic ..." (Fischer 1969, 396).

Fischer and the others had decided on their own fundamental submission. Behind this stood the original intention to do everything in order to restrain the fascist wave. But this need to categorize and submit went further, otherwise most of the intellectuals would not have submitted between 1939 and 1941; they would not have helped to undermine the real anti-fascist struggles in France and Great Britain, as evident in the denunciation of Nizan.

Fischer and the others wanted to give up what they had taken into the concrete political responsibility: their own self-sufficient political ego. They submitted to the superego of Stalinist objectivity. And with that, they found the justification they evidently had sought for the flight from their own self-defined politics for which they had to take personal responsibility. They had satisfied their longing to conform and dissolve into the community of those who knew themselves to be in the safe and secure possession of the truth and objectivity of the script of world history. Fischer and the others did not actually want to know; they wanted to believe.

"The Marxism-Leninism of the Stalin-mythos was a pragmatism that proclaimed the respective state truths, whether reasonable or not, to be the unconditional truth and knowledge of Marxism-Leninism. Richard Wagner, for example, was praised after the German-Soviet pact of non-aggression and Hegel was exposed as reactionary after the attack on the Soviet Union" (Marek 1970, 159).

Stalinist objectivity and the orthodoxy of the Church make theory and theology into handmaidens of a politics of pragmatism. At the same time, they dissolve all politics by making politics into the handmaiden of an "objective" goal. Theory is instrumentalized and politics is made obsolete.

The social doctrines of the Catholic Church follow a pattern of development that can be traced historically. But this very historical context endangers the claim to theory that this form of theology makes. What the Popes and their social doctrines in the sense of an understanding of natural law have declared to be "true" reflects historical change and the interest of the Church to conform to the new conditions created by change. In slave-holding society, the Church was "neutral" with regard to slavery as an institution, only to confront the principle of slavery when it lost its social grounds and others went before the Popes to fight against the principle of slavery. In pre-capitalist society the Popes adhered tightly to the canonical doctrine that forbade interest only to accept interest themselves and thus establish themselves on the ground floor of the capitalist society that was already in control (Knoll 1962).

The principle criticism of this adaptational behavior is directed not toward the conforming itself but toward its detachment from the historical background and toward its absoluteness and the stylization of a Church pragmatism into a theology of natural law that can be declared and traced.

Stalin allowed the praise of Wagner when he made the pact with Hitler and he demanded that Hegel be condemned when German troops attacked the Soviet Union. The social doctrine of the Popes of the late nineteenth and early twentieth centuries is full of observations on estates and their respective forms of organization in politics and society. The Popes themselves are silent on the subjects of democracy or parliamentarianism and political parties. Not until Rome was freed and occupied by American troops did Pope Pius XII suddenly discover democracy. And in his Christmas radio address of 1944 the Pope, who, along with his predecessors had never had a thought about democracy, preached to the whole world about the "qualities ...., that (must) distinguish human beings ... who have the power in a democracy"; and about the necessity of distinguishing between the "people" and the "masses" (Texte 1975, 170).

The fiction of being free from concrete interests and historical conditions constitutes the parallel nature of Stalinist objectivity and the orthodoxy of the Church. Neither one confronts the strategy of the "lesser evil"; by declaring their concrete measures to be a timeless theory (or theology), neither one acknowledges them as such; each practices a systematic politics of de-politicization in order to immunize themselves against opposition and criticism.

This immunization shows only the intellectual effrontery of such processes. Stalin's pragmatic subterfuges were declared to be the climax of Marxist philosophy and the theological opportunism of the Popes was construed as the law of nature. But behind both of these cases lies a systematic, purposeful flight from politics or, rather, a refusal of politics: The "objectivization" of concrete politics should, and must, prevent the discourse on the connections between the end and the means from taking place, at least not immanently. Instead of a political discourse, judgments on "traitors" (or "heretics") were pronounced, precisely because deviation was not the beginning of such a discourse but, "objectively" speaking, treason.

The fact that Stalin had traitors murdered while the Popes of the twentieth century, unlike those of other centuries, did not or could not reach for this means made a significant difference to those involved. *Stalin's* ironically malicious question as to how many divisions the Pope had makes this difference obvious. But it was only a relative difference made clearer by the passage of time: The Pope had no divisions — any longer. The intellectual presumption of the Stalinist way of doing things and the Papist way must be seen as analog to one another.

Orthodoxies do not allow democracy. They allow only conformity. They forbid (and fear) open situations. The task of orthodoxy is to implement doctrine. The taboo of orthodoxy is to debate doctrine. But this also produces a clear dichotomy in the possibilities for politics. Politics is either Stalin's business or that of Pope Pius XII. They may, indeed, they must, weigh the evils in order to choose the lesser one. They are free, totally free, to conduct politics. Of course, those belonging to each orthodoxy are just as totally unfree to conduct politics. Entering orthodoxy is the same as the taboo on making politics within their (substitute) Church.

13 *On the Ambiguity of Difference*

The Stubbornness of Karl Kraus — Partial Fascism as a Lesser Evil — Between devil and Beelzebub — Churchill: Political Capability through Differentiation — Churchill: More than *Realpolitik* — Not every Appeasement is Alike

Karl Kraus has never been easy to categorize politically. As a critic of the politics of war of Austro-Hungary and of the First World War in general, and as an advocate of fundamental liberal rights, for instance in the sexual realm, he was considered a man of the left — until several years before his death when he came under suspicion of being a propagandist of Dollfuss' politics and thus of Austrian fascism.

In the 1920's , the Communist party had even courted Kraus because his literary rigor set him more and more apart from the Social Democrats. The radical nature of his thinking seemed to bring Kraus closer to the radical quality of Communist politics than to the relative pragmatism of the Social Democrats (Pfabigan 1976, 255-336).

Kraus heaped his political scorn on the politics of the established powers, for example, in "The Last Days of Humanity" when he castigated the Social Democrats in Germany for their tendency to ingratiate themselves with the German government regarding its expansionist foreign policy and authoritarian domestic policy; or when he criticized the politics of the bourgeois block in Austria with his attacks on Johann Schober. In "The Invincibles" he caricatured the corruption of bourgeois politics, especially the role of the press. This play provoked politically motivated censorship on the part of the Austrian government, a government that was a coalition of the united right and their common philosophy of anti-Marxism (Zohn 1971, 86-197; Pfabigan 1976, 255-287).

When Adolf Hitler "seized power" in Germany, it was clear to Kraus that a new dimension in European politics had been reached. In various studies for his posthumously published book, "The Third Walpurgis Night" that he published in his journal "The Torch" in 1933 and 1934, he demonstrated with the documentary collage technique he had employed in "The Last Days of Humanity," the violent character of the new type of regime. Everything that Kraus used as a foundation for this was in the public domain, especially in the form of newspaper articles from the foreign press.

With this, Kraus not only showed that for anyone who wanted to see, the particular character of the National Socialist regime had to be obvious as early as spring of 1933, and that the general theory of fascism, preferred by the Social Democrat and Communist leftists, did not offer an adequate means of describing the NS system. He also demonstrated that the contradictions of the past had to be relativized in the face of this new threat.

But in this he went against the grain of Austrian politics. Parallel to Hitler's "seizure of power," Dollfuss' government practiced a strategy of eliminating both the parliamentary system and the multi-party system and thus, above all, the largest opposition party, the Social Democrats. And when the party finally succeeded in doing this, after a brief civil war in February of 1934, in which the Social Democrats defended the republic and the constitution state, Dollfuss called for the "Christian state" while invoking "God the Almighty." This state can perhaps best be classified as "immature" or "partial" fascism (Talos, Neugebauer 1984).

Austrian social democracy saw itself (and democracy in general) as the victim of a specifically Austrian variant of European fascism. The conflict with the Austrian National Socialists and the NS government of Germany that was immanent to the authoritarian Dollfuss regime from the beginning (which concerned the independence of Austria from Germany) played no particular role in this assessment.

But for Kraus, not every fascism was alike. Dollfuss was not Hitler. And when Dollfuss became a victim of the failed National Socialist coup attempt in July of 1934, Kraus saw this failure as positive. Dollfuss and his successor Schuschnigg and the authoritarian form of government they represented was for him clearly the lesser evil over and against the only real alternative that the international constellation had to offer Austria: the "annexation" to National Socialist Germany, an alternative that was to prevail in 1938, after Kraus' death.

Kraus expressed his preference for the lesser evil of the Dollfuss-regime in literature — and in so doing, became, in the eyes of the left, a traitor. The Social Democratic and Communist left, active in the underground and in exile, insisted on equating the two types of fascism. Kraus' militant readiness to differentiate and accept political consequences as a result of this differentiation, namely the support of the "lesser evil," was harshly criticized propagandistically as Austro-fascist propaganda. The harshness of this confrontation was likely all the greater because the left had originally seen in Kraus one of their own and now attacked him as a rebel and thus coated their polemic with a particularly moralizing tone (Pfabigan 1976, 337-359).

In his intellectual argumentation, Kraus was a leftist version of the right-wing Churchill. For each of them, National Socialism was evil itself. In the struggle against it, each was prepared to join forces with all other possible evils if such an alliance would damage Hitler. Churchill, who had originally made no secret of a certain sympathy for Italian fascism, was prepared to join forces against Hitler with death and the devil and Bolshevism. Having left the inner circle of the Conservative party's leadership in 1931 because he considered it to be too yielding to the independence movement in India, Churchill, this conservative hard-liner with the lukewarm relationship to liberal democracy, who had continued to stylize himself as the keeper of the holy grail of British imperialism (Manchester 1984, 691-700), embraced his new ally in the summer of 1941 — Stalin (Charmley 1993, 453-458).

In so doing, Churchill had not only acted opportunistically. Since the fall of France in 1940, he had, as Prime Minister, counted almost desperately on rapprochement with the Soviet Union, just as he, while still a "backbencher," had openly criticized Chamberlain's government as early as the summer of 1939 because it had not played the "Soviet card" against Germany quickly or efficiently enough.

Naturally, Churchill's behavior was also a variation of the old political primitive rule that the enemy of my enemy is my friend. But the way in which Churchill pursued his alliance with Stalin demanded a deeper explanation: If Hitler had invaded hell, he, Churchill, would have made at least one friendly remark about the devil (Charmley 1993, 453). And Winston Churchill did not simply make a few friendly remarks about the Bolshevist dictator. He did everything possible to strengthen the resistance of the Red Army against the German military; he did everything he could to help the Soviet Union to victory because this victory would mean the defeat of Hitler's Germany.

Churchill broke with the Polish exile government when it became a hindrance to his arrangement with Stalin. He agreed to Soviet hegemony in Rumania and Bulgaria. As long as the war remained undecided, he was agreeable to any means to weaken Hitler, even if it meant making Stalin stronger. Was he, for this reason, a "useful idiot"?

Churchill's behavior toward Stalin and the Soviet Union was more differentiated than that of Roosevelt (Kissinger 1994, 410). He never forgot that the military goals of the Soviet Union and those of the British Empire were worlds apart, and he never put his relationship to

Roosevelt and the U.S. on the same level as his relationship to Stalin and the Soviet Union. But precisely because he, committed to *Realpolitik*, knew very well that he could never win over or even interest a Stalin for the goals of the Atlantic Charter he had solemnly agreed to with Roosevelt, he was able to cooperate with Stalin. A victory by National Socialist Germany was, for Churchill, clearly the greater evil over a victory by the Soviet Union. He believed himself able to come to an arrangement with Stalin because he believed to have recognized in him the same sense for *Realpolitik* despite all their differences. And he was not wrong in this. There was no making arrangements with Hitler, and Churchill did not need Munich to teach him this. The eschatological nature of National Socialism, expressed most starkly in the Holocaust, permitted no politics because in the end, National Socialism amounted to the denial of politics.

Churchill was able to differentiate between one dictatorship and another, between one threat and another, between one interest and another, between one evil and another. For his conception of foreign policy, Churchill needed no grand design in the sense of an all-encompassing philosophy à la Wilson. He compared and he made distinctions, then made a decision and acted on it. He compared interests in the sense of the traditional British doctrine that says that great powers have no friends, only interests.

This readiness to weigh things and decide, in the utilitarian sense, made Churchill politically viable. What was advantageous to the interests of the British Empire as he defined them, what was disadvantageous? Because he was committed not to a general idea of justice, but to a special weighing of interest, he was able to influence world politics in the decisive years of the 20th century. In the sense of this political viability he was the actual antithesis to Hitlerian idealism, which led logically to the lack of political viability and thus to defeat.

Karl Kraus' moral rigor and Winston Churchill's pragmatic *Realpolitik* point to a parallel: logic that demands action. For Kraus, the intellectual hermit, action naturally meant something different than for Churchill in whom all political and military threads of the British superpower intersected between 1940 and 1945.

Kraus called for action from the left that would align itself with the non-National Socialist right against the Nazi terror, even if it was itself (partly) fascist and he was also prepared to make an arrangement in the sense of this logic with the authoritarian Dollfuss regime as a writer and critic. The fact that the left did not follow him in this led to his isolation but also solidified the Austrian right's lack of political viability. After Kraus' death, the slogan of the People's Front of Comintern was, at times, to prove him right.

Kraus could not accept that the (Social Democratic and Communist) left did not want to see or understand that the dictatorship as it existed in Germany beginning in 1933 and the dictatorship that existed in Austria beginning in 1933/34 could be compared but not equated. Kraus recognized in the leftist theory of fascism an excuse for the denial of politics. As heroic as the individual actions of the resistance against the Dollfuss regime might be, the weakening of the regime that this resistance was at least partially in a position to bring about could be advantageous only to one interest in light of geopolitical realities, according to Kraus, and that was National Socialism. The only real alternative to the dictatorship of Dollfuss and Schuschnigg was, for Kraus, the dictatorship of Adolf Hitler.

And with that, Kraus had arrived at Churchill's analogy of hell from 1941. In order to avoid strengthening Hitler indirectly, the Austrian left would have had to make friendly gestures toward the devils Dollfuss and Schuschnigg. These gestures were made rather late, to be sure, not until hours before the militarily extorted "annexation" (Schausberger 1978).

Churchill was able to take action. After the attempts to practice *Realpolitik* with Hitler had failed miserably as a part of the politics of appeasement carried out by the ruling branch of the Conservative Party, that in turn claimed to see in Churchill a dangerous romantic, Churchill, the right-wing outsider, was carried by the trust of the Labour Party into the office of Prime Minister of a government comprised of all parties — against the resistance of the conservative establishment, including the King. The Socialists had realized now, in the spring of 1940, that the politics of appeasement that they had supported for so long did not only have to be given up, it had to be replaced by a radical reversal of politics if the war was not to be lost. The left hoisted the eccentric "imperialist" Churchill into the saddle (Charmley 1993, 394f.).

For Churchill, his unconditional willingness to act was the decisive quality. His opposition to Hitler legitimated him from the beginning as British version of the Prime Minister of the "People's Front." Precisely because he could differentiate and thus act, he was able to mobilize the entire British population to conspire with Roosevelt and support Stalin. Churchill's achievement was certainly not that of political conviction, or philosophy or perspective. His achievement lay in being able to recognize political realities, to deduce the corresponding options for action, to make the possible evaluations and then make the logically deduced decisions and carry them out.

Karl Kraus was misunderstood as an appeaser of Austro-fascism. Churchill was misunderstood as an appeaser of Stalinism. And even Jaruzelski was misunderstood as an appeaser of Soviet imperialism. Were they really misunderstood?

The British (and French) appeasement policy in 1938 was based on the same logic of differentiation as the journalistic position of Kraus and the concrete action of Churchill. Chamberlain and Daladier did not want to let their soldiers die in order to keep Czechoslovakia intact, an attitude that prevailed in September of 1938 in the public opinion of both democracies. And the "mourir pour Danzig?" became the slogan of the appeaser barely a year later. The appeaser of late summer 1939, like the official position of the Communists at that moment, estimated the military struggles and war victims of their own country as a greater evil, compared to the annexation of west Polish regions to Hitler's Germany.

Churchill's and Chamberlain's considerations in 1938 were not different in their logic of differentiation but in the estimation of interests and goals of German politics. And Kraus' analyses and those of the Austrian Social Democrats in exile differed not in the claim of having to differentiate, but in the perception of what constituted National Socialism. Jaruzelski in turn was not criticized by the democracy movement in 1981 because he had wanted to prevent a Soviet intervention but because he had all too willingly summoned the mere possibility of Soviet intervention in order to justify his dictatorship.

If the Chamberlain of September, 1938 had been right and Hitler had really been prepared to agree to the arrangement that the British and French governments had read into the Munich Agreement: Would Munich then not have been justified and would Chamberlain and Daladier not have received the Nobel Peace Prize? Because of the situation of the Jews in Germany before the "Night of Broken Glass" and because of the political repression against any internal German opposition, no leader and no public opinion would have seen peace as being threatened.

It is not the logic of appeasement that makes Munich a chiffre for a completely failed politics; it is the false perception of reality. It is not Churchill's constant willingness to fight that makes him one of the ruling figures of the 20th century; it is the correct understanding of National Socialism. Appeasement is not an anti-virtue in general, no more than the willingness to fight is always a virtue.

For that reason, the accusation toward Jaruzelski cannot be called appeasement. No one interested in politics and not some pure doctrine can doubt the fact that it was necessary in 1981 to differentiate and consider the Soviet interests. Who would want to deny the fact that a little brother cannot simply lay claim to morality and international law if the rest of the world leaves him to the fight with the big brother and that appeasement must be the formula which the little brother should employ? It is not that Jaruzelski can be accused of being an appeaser, for he was one. Rather, the accusation would have to be that he misjudged the willingness of the Soviets to use military force in Poland. But did he really misjudge?

The Churchill of the early 1930s who accused the British government of caving in to the Indian National Congress and made disparaging remarks about Mahatma Gandhi (Manchester 1984, 693), this Churchill who accused the governments of MacDonald and Baldwin of appeasement does not stand the test of history. In the case of India, he could not do justice to the actual conditions with his style that leaned toward "jingoism." It is not appeasement that is no good, but rather appeasement at the wrong time and toward the wrong opponent.

In order to make this distinction, however, between the wrong and the right time, between the wrong and the right opponent, an (empirical) instrument for the perception of reality and a (normative) means of sensing the evaluation of this very reality are needed. The fact that certain circles in British civil society enthusiastically supported Chamberlain's appeasement policy had to do not with a certain perception of reality, but with the evaluation of reality. In these circles of the Cliveden set whose mouthpiece for a long time was the "Times," Nazism was seen as the lesser evil as opposed to Communism (Kissinger 1994, 306-312).

Since the circles of power in the Church in Poland in 1981 approached the victims of martial law with pastoral sympathy (one example was the Pope's letter to Walesa [Walesa 1987, 313f.]) and avoided direct confrontation with the regime and always supported the moderate, not the confrontational forces within the opposition, we can make certain assumptions. The Church shared Jaruzelski's estimation of the decisiveness of the Soviet Union and more probably, the Church saw in the "purgatory" of martial law the lesser evil vis-à-vis any imaginable alternative, even if the Red Army was not the only real one. In other words, Jaruzelski's appeasement in 1981 was based on estimations that were evidently not so different from those of the Church. Jaruzelski's meaning was also that he understood how to use his policies to relativize the traditional prejudices that divided the Communist party and the Catholic Church by being able to convince the Church of the plausibility of his own estimation of the real options for action (Jaruzelski 1996, 427f.). In this regard, Jaruzelski the appeaser was successful.

Churchill's lasting meaning for Europe and for the world, then, is not only the result of his strategic ability to have recognized the lack of orientation on the part of National Socialism in the sense of *Realpolitik* and to have correspondingly excluded the possibility for an arrangement with the Nazi regime. Churchill's success was also the result of having met National Socialism not only with a tactical and strategic bias from the beginning. Churchill's anti-Nazi bias was stronger than his bias toward Stalinist Communism not only in 1941, but as early as 1939. His emotional rejection of Hitler's regime was the motor that kept the bundle of energy called Churchill in motion. This was what allowed him to build and propel his *Realpolitik*.

On closer inspection, the pragmatic Churchill was no pragmatic at all, just as the moralist Kraus was not simply a moralist and the dictator Jaruzelski was not only a dictator. The dialectical mixture of Churchill's vision and pragmatism and Kraus' strategy and moralism is what distinguishes each of them, both of whom recognized much earlier than most other observers, at least earlier than the "Realpoliticians" in the Kremlin, the fundamentally new quality of National Socialism.

The fact that one of them, Churchill, fell into isolation because of the way his clear-cut style was seen as stiffness but was then called from isolation to real power allowed him, who was much more an anti-Communist than an anti-Fascist, to play this real power against National Socialism. Due to his capacity for learning being seen as opportunism, Kraus was alienated from the leftist-intellectual milieu known best to him and thus powerless, a lonely caller whom those to whom he turned did not want to hear. For both of them, National Socialism was not "fascism," but a significantly different force. And in this estimation of reality, Churchill, who had at times viewed (Italian) fascism as a relatively lesser evil and Kraus, who had had a certain closeness to the Communist party in the 1920's, found common ground. This parallel estimation of Nazism made Churchill a partner for Stalin and Kraus a defender of Dollfuss.

Churchill had the luck of the corresponding privilege of birth. Born into the British upper classes, he could not, given the unfavorable conditions of 1939 and 1940, isolate himself in order to be recruited in turn for the decisive leadership position of the only power that stood between Hitler and a pan-European victory of National Socialism. In 1939, Chamberlain had no choice but to appoint Churchill to his cabinet; and in 1940, the King saw himself forced to make the unloved Churchill Prime Minister. Churchill's membership in the old ruling class as well as the social atmosphere around him and the connections he held as a result were an important condition for his entry into the corridors of power.

Kraus, on the other hand, the Jewish intellectual, was, from the beginning, too much the outsider to maintain the luxury of the visionary, even to maintain correctness vis-à-vis the Zeitgeist and his own milieu. For that reason he was isolated and politically broken.

In this regard, Jaruzelski was closer to Churchill. Through the contradictory combination of roles, the aristocrat, officer, and Communist combined the divisive forces in his own person. He was able to calm the Kremlin for he, the Communist, was still at the helm. And he, whose patriotism and personal asceticism were never in doubt, was, for parts of Polish society, a plausible "lesser evil." For this reason, Jaruzelski could act as "appeaser" toward the Kremlin, toward the bishops, and ultimately, toward Polish society.

Kraus, Churchill, and Jaruzelski: all three knew how to differentiate. Kraus between various types of fascism, Churchill between various types of totalitarianism, and Jaruzelski between national and foreign dictatorship. The political meaning of Churchill and Jaruzelski, like the intellectual meaning of Kraus, lay with their drive, as well as their ability to differentiate. They were driven by passion: one for the British Empire, for the community of English-speaking peoples, for (white) freedom; the second for the humanistic goal of liberating people from force; the third for the Poland caught between Germany and Russia. This drive alone explains why, despite all the expectations and constrictions of the respective *Zeitgeist*, they all insisted with the stubbornness of Don Quixote on their respective strategic insights.

14 On the Amorality of Foreign Policy

Wilson: Principles without Strategy — Roosevelt: Principles and Strategy — Johnson: No Principles and no Strategy — Nixon: Strategy without Principles

During the course of the First World War, a player stepped onto the stage of world politics that had, until then, rather fearfully kept its distance from international involvement: the United States.

The U.S. came with high moral claims. The Allies who had enticed their new partner into the World War used these claims to manipulate her. They let her play the morality game as harmless tomfoolery. Henry Kissinger describes how the British Foreign Minister Edward Grey was able to use the imputed idea of a League of Nations to lead into temptation an American President already viewed as an idealist (Kissinger 1994, 223). And Woodrow Wilson was only too eager to fall into the trap. He wanted to conduct a war that would make the world "safe for democracy," a war whose goal was to put an end to all war. *Realpolitik* for this emissary of the new world power was immoral. At stake was democracy as an international order, collective security and especially, the right of peoples to determine themselves.

Yet from the beginning, this concept, the rhetoric of which Wilson forced upon his Allies in the agreements, had a strange operational weakness. The noble wishes and goals were only loosely bound to concrete politics. Wilson knew what he wanted, but he had no idea how to achieve what he wanted.

The First World War in particular was, from the beginning, an antithesis to the notion of the American President. The participation of the European masses more or less used to democracy, their terrible sacrifices, and the propaganda necessary for legitimation on the domestic front had provided for a fundamental change in this primarily European war. It was no longer a nineteenth-century war of Cabinets, but a democratized war of the masses of the 20th century. But precisely for that reason, compromises, flexibility, and thus a relatively quick end to the war were not possible. The democratization of the European war of 1914 made of it an exhausting war that destroyed the masses, precisely because it wanted to and had to build on the approval of the masses (Kissinger 1994, 219).

The democratization of the war had greatly reduced its political maneuverability. The democratic war was latently totalitarian as early as 1914. It had to be defined and propagandized as a crusade against the powers of darkness in order to achieve the democratically necessary approval of the masses. The war had stopped being a means of politics that could be arbitrarily deployed by the political elite. Once set in motion, the democratic war could not be controlled, precisely because it was democratic.

Woodrow Wilson's successes, which ultimately ended in a gigantic failure, demonstrated the dilemma and the tendency toward the mutual incompatibility of democracy and leadership in foreign policy. Under Wilson's leadership, the victorious powers wrote moral goals like the self-determination of nations across their banners, with the result that one self-determination confronted another and that the high number of international players resulting from the self-determination of nations was also to increase the real danger of war. The moralization of the First World War bore within it the seeds of the Second.

The destruction of the multi-national empires that came about on the authority of moral values — Austro-Hungary and Turkey, but also Russia — demonstrated the same consequences that the destruction of the Soviet Union and Yugoslavia in 1991, similarly based on moral grounds, was to demonstrate: arbitrariness instead of predictability, a multiplicity of wars instead of a negative peace.

Yet Wilson failed through his inability to justify his foreign policy to his fellow Americans. The Senate rejected the ratification of the Peace Treaty of Versailles and thus the League of Nations that had its legal foundation in this agreement lost its logical leadership power, namely the U.S. Democracy had destroyed democratic foreign policy. The justification for messianic interventionism had been lost.

Nonetheless, foreign policy — or, what analysts such as Kissinger call "diplomacy" — remains a niche for the withdrawal of leadership. Driven from the routine of politics that, under the sign of democracy, makes individual leadership impossible, foreign policy and diplomacy remain the political arena in which leadership can demonstrate and maintain itself. For the interconnection of relationships toward which foreign policy is targeted is necessarily non-democratic — the relationship between sovereign entities that is controlled by no democratic order and is based on naked, unfiltered, unveiled power. Because foreign policy knows no higher sovereignty than that of states, that is, of the players, it is more independent of the strings of routine democracy, and it can also provide space for non-routine leadership (transforming leadership) within democracy.

This was also what had pushed the moralist Wilson into the World War — the vision of being able to prepare an end for this immoral state of affairs; being able to put a super sovereign state — the League of Nations — before those unpredictable sovereign states. But Wilson failed: he could not convince his own Congress of the conclusive nature of this missionary design. Foreign policy, in spite of its characteristic exceptions and niches, has a fundamental need for democratic legitimation under the conditions of a liberal democracy. And this Wilson had overlooked, or, rather, not been able to produce.

The President from the ranks of the Democratic party who was to follow him after three Republicans was smarter due to Wilson's experience. As a member of Wilson's administration, he had learned his lesson. And he practiced leadership in foreign policy by hiding his political ambitions, by conducting a dual politics of deception in order to preserve leadership.

The voters were deceived; the democratic superior was deceived. Kissinger of all people, who is exceedingly sympathetic toward Roosevelt, concedes: The masterly qualities of leadership that Roosevelt employed to bring the U.S. to war against Nazi Germany were close to being unconstitutional. "No contemporary President could resort to Roosevelt's methods and remain in office" (Kissinger 1994, 387).

In his attempt to lead the U.S. into the war that, until Pearl Harbor, had been European, Roosevelt had public opinion against him, or at least not for him. For that reason he kept his intentions hidden. He let the public see only as much as it could handle. Not until Japan's aggression and Germany's declaration of war forced this American public into the arms and undeclared policy of its President could he finally openly carry out what he had already set into motion — the alliance with Great Britain and the Soviet Union.

Roosevelt needed the approval of a public whose majority did not yet agree with his goals; and for that reason he fought for this approval using means for which the word "lie" is certainly justified (Kimball 1997: 7f.). When he had reason to fear losing ground to the Republican candidate during the 1940 election campaign, he formulated his promise to the voters who were against the entry into war that Roosevelt favored: "I have said this before, but I shall say it again and again and again: Your boys are not going to be sent into any foreign wars" (Miller 1983, 457).

Less than a year after Roosevelt's third inauguration he did indeed send the boys to an Asian and a European war. Thanks to Roosevelt's skill and thanks to the lack of skill on the part of Japan and Germany, these wars were suddenly not "foreign" any more.

One of the few who had seen through Roosevelt's tricks and felt betrayed by him was Joseph Kennedy. The appeaser par excellence who, as Roosevelt's ambassador in London, had seemed to represent more the interests of appeasement than those of his own government and who had tried everything to keep the U.S. away from any intervention, broke with Roosevelt after Pearl Harbor. Against the backdrop of the Democratic Convention of 1944, where Roosevelt was nominated once again and Truman was suggested as his running mate, Kennedy expressed his deep, hate-filled resentment of the President in a conversation with Truman: "Harry, what the hell are you doing campaigning for that crippled son-of-a-bitch that killed my son Joe?" (McCullough 1992, 328).

The eldest son of Joseph Kennedy had died in the war that Roosevelt had wanted and that Kennedy had tried to avoid. The ambitions of the Kennedys to make one of their own a President, rested all the more heavily on the shoulders of the second son. And he was to succeed during the lifetime of his father. John Kennedy would prove himself to be an avid pupil of the "son-of-a-bitch" Roosevelt.

Roosevelt's qualities of leadership that let him test and perhaps also overstep the limits of democracy as laid down in the Constitution gave western democracies what they had not had in the years prior to the Second World War: a strategy. Kissinger writes on the outbreak of the Second World War in Europe: "Stalin had a strategy but no principles; the democracies defended principle without ever developing a strategy" (Kissinger 1994, 348).

Roosevelt led the U.S. to the side of Great Britain and the Soviet Union. He gave the democracies a strategy and, in the spirit of competition, he confronted Stalin's strategy with a principle. Without Roosevelt's linkage, the anti-Hitler alliance would have been an alliance of theoretically irreconcilable differences; and, in this form, would not have been capable of victory geopolitically. With Roosevelt, the relationship between end and means was finally an issue again: he succeeded in hiding the degree to which he went against his own principles until success seemed to prove him right. But because he was also an idealist, he was able, ex post facto, to count on the democratic justification of his anti-democratic procedures.

Wilson's politics was a politics of political refusal: The international order and thus the political conceptions were perceived as an image of norms; whoever transgressed them could count on being punished. It was soon clear on the international stage that this line of thinking could not be implemented. And Wilson had had the painful experience of realizing that this moralizing understanding of politics could not be legitimated on the domestic front. Wilson's approach was one of political refusal because he avoided the problems and the dilemma associated with weighing the end and the means and choosing between the various evils. Roosevelt surrendered to the necessity of having to determine a lesser evil. In so doing, he surrendered to the condition of being able to conduct politics effectively. But for that reason he came into conflict with the fundamental principles of democracy.

Roosevelt's concept of leadership was copied with a recognizable catastrophic success by one of his successors. Lyndon B. Johnson manipulated the "Tongking" affair in order to obtain a blank check in 1965 from Congress for his policy in Vietnam, which had long been a militarized one, not least on the part of his predecessors since Truman (Kearns 1976, 263-299). He not only pushed the limits of the American Constitution, he pushed past them.

As Johnson's Secretary of Defense, Robert McNamara was one of those largely responsible for this policy. He tends to negate Johnson's intention to consciously deceive Congress and the public. He self-critically accuses the Vietnam policy of his administration of a lack of solid information and therefore false conclusions, that is, the lack of a consistent strategy. But even McNamara concedes that Johnson's Tongking Resolution was misused in order to escalate the U.S. military involvement in Vietnam. The Vietnam War only became a great war through this disguised, and thus, manipulated resolution (McNamara 1995, 128f.).

Like Roosevelt, Johnson wanted to force the enemy, as defined by him, into a role that was immediately recognizable for the American public. Tongking was Johnson's Pearl Harbor, not in the sense of the military consequences but in the sense of the political use of the event. The blank check of 1965 was equivalent to the declaration of war in 1941.

But while Roosevelt led an idealistically motivated, closed nation to war after Pearl Harbor, Johnson ultimately became the victim of domestic conflicts caused by his policy in Vietnam. Roosevelt created the consensus with which he could demonstrate his leadership; Johnson destroyed this consensus.

This showed the limitations of the recipe for demonstrating qualities of leadership: at first bypassing the rules of democracy, indirectly breaking those rules, and then obtaining democratic justification after the fact. The difference lay with the opponent: the enemy against whom Johnson wanted to lead the American nation was for many understandable reasons less threatening for the American public than the enemy against whom Roosevelt had mobilized. North Vietnam had not destroyed any U.S. Navy ships; no one could believe in 1965 or thereafter that the California coast was threatened; and world Communism was, in light of the open and ongoing conflict between Moscow and Peking no longer the mobilization factor it had once been.

Johnson and the Tongking Resolution also demonstrate how close the limits for leadership are in niches of foreign policy when a political system is stabilized with democratic rules. Truman's policy in Korea offers an interesting example for this, or, rather, the interpretation of wishful-thinking that Kissinger lends to this policy. Kissinger freely applauds Truman's decision in June of 1950 to send American troops to Korea. He sees this as an example of leadership. He creates a bridge between the idealistic values that determine American foreign policy and Truman's interventionist policy in Korea. But Kissinger mentions parenthetically the fact that in the summer of 1950 Truman was largely motivated by reasons of domestic policy, namely to head off criticism after the Communist victory in the Chinese civil war ("Who lost China?"): Truman's decision was by no means determined "only" by foreign policy considerations; rather, he was also forced to integrate the "China lobby" in the Senate into his policy (Kissinger 1994, 479).

Roosevelt's ability to combine Wilson's vision with a concrete strategy and his ruthless willingness to break the rules of democracy in order to save democratic principles is thus within the conditions of stable democratic relations, more the exception than the rule. Kissinger himself became a victim of Johnson's failed attempt to construct an enemy only to then fight against it with democratic support, after having manipulated the public. Precisely because both the American public and Congress had rescinded the carte blanche of the Tongking Resolution, Kissinger, entrusted with handling the Vietnam War, was no longer able to implement foreign policy options. He could only disguise the failure of the American policy in Vietnam with the misleading formulation of an "honorable peace" in Paris.

The lack of a democratic legitimation had destroyed leadership in foreign policy. Democracy, a sort of sensor of far-reaching notions of leadership, made of the obsessed players Nixon and Kissinger notarized executive organs of military and domestic defeat. Democracy prevailed in the end, in the face of foreign policy and its own peculiar dynamic, against its "amorality," against leadership.

Precisely because Johnson's politics of deception was not successful, leadership in Vietnam could not take place; precisely because
democracy did not let itself be deprived of power, U.S. involvement
in Vietnam ended in a debacle. It was not a military failure, but rather
the failure of a concept of leadership that was not compatible with
democracy.

In his foreword to the third volume of his biography of Nixon,
Stephen E. Ambrose quotes a perceptive comment by Hannah Arendt:
The U.S. President is, on the one hand, the most powerful man in the
world; on the other hand, the national leader with the least amount of
power. Nixon, according to Ambrose, was out to negate this contradiction (Ambrose 1991, 25).

Nixon wanted to overcome the restrictions of representative
democracy and of checks and balances; he wanted to free himself from
the controls that limited his leadership; he wanted to emancipate his
power in foreign policy from the Constitution and thus become a
leader legitimized by plebiscite, a leader beyond the constraints of
constitutional government.

Nixon failed in his attempt to transfer the techniques of power
typical of foreign policy, with its claims of "national security," to
politics in general: the illegal eavesdropping on unpopular persons, the
untruthful defamation of political opponents and the covering up of
crimes committed in the interest of the President. Everything that
became infamous under the name "Watergate" and that led to the
resignation of a President faced with the possibility of impeachment
was the attempted expansion of the usual and more or less accepted
relationship between the end and the means into politics in general.
The amorality of foreign policy, in which secret services are free from
the controls of the law even in democratic constitutional regimes,
would become amorality in general.

Nixon wanted to use the methods typical of foreign policy even
within a democracy to create politics in general. He wanted to break
free from the routine of politics that limits and even negates
leadership; he wanted to become a non-routine leader because he was
obsessed with the idea of creating politics and demonstrating an all-
encompassing leadership. He did not want to resignedly accept the
narrow playing field of options which he found before him. Instead,
he wanted to expand this playing field significantly with techniques
that went far beyond the deceptive maneuvering of Franklin D.
Roosevelt and Lyndon B. Johnson. He wanted to maximize personal
power, if needed by destroying the representative and democratic
checks and balances of the Constitution. While invoking the people,

the "silent majority," and his own election, he questioned whether democracy really must limit, narrow, and ultimately cancel out leadership, or whether leadership is able to reverse this trend.

With this idea, Nixon first came into conflict with the political elite, or rather, with those who did not identify with his ambitions but saw themselves endangered by them. Nixon's claims were directed toward the redistribution of personal power, above all at the expense of Congress. Therefore, the (Democratic) majority in Congress fought against his claims out of self-interest. But this resistance also makes clear where Nixon's notion of leadership would end up. In the face of every instance of congressional and judicial checks and balances, Nixon's closest colleagues insisted that the President stood above the basic laws ("executive privilege") and that for reasons of "national security," he was allowed to nullify any protective law that individuals could claim on constitutional grounds (Ambrose 1991, 381-385). Thus, break-ins would be "legitimated" just as much as the arbitrary eavesdropping on telephone conversations.

Nixon's hubris, his fantasy of omnipotence which broke through all boundaries and eventually destroyed him as well, was ultimately directed not toward some establishment that he viewed as competition for his personally defined power; not against the institutions of representative democracy that he attempted to push back while invoking his plebiscitary mandate. The final consequence of his style and his claims would have been the destruction of the fundamental principles of liberal democracy. The separation of presidential power from all connections represents a Caesaristic and Napoleonic principle of representative democracy that, if uncurbed, destroys its democratic basis. The unconditional desire to engineer society, i.e., to make politics, to make choices, is incompatible with democracy if it is not linked to conditions and limited by corresponding rules, by checks and balances.

Nixon's sin against the spirit of the American Constitution resulted in an injury to democracy stemming from the desire to create political options. What threw him from office was the fact that this destructive intention was not only viewed by society — the elite and by a decisive segment of the electorate — as a problem of constitutional checks and balances but was interpreted as a dangerous break with the fundamentals of democracy. The general reaction to this break limited his claim to leadership.

Like Roosevelt, Kennedy, and Johnson before him, Nixon had experienced the limits of his personal power as limits on politics. The fact that he failed in his attempt to overcome these limits demonstrates the strength of democracy, but also how consistently democracy works against leadership and thus against an expansion of politics in the sense of the playing field for decision-making. Throughout Watergate, democracy as the iron opponent of leadership had prevailed impressively.

15 On the Logic of Leninism

Just is the opposite of Just — Professional Revolutionaries and Leadership — Lenin and Stalin as Empiricists — Absolute Politics becomes Non-Politics

In his novel "Darkness at Noon," Arthur Koestler engages intensely with the consequences set out in Lenin's understanding of politics. The "hero" of the novel, Rubashov, a mixture of Bukharin and Kamenev, is so bound up with this logic that, in the end, he accepts his own death sentence. He knows that he is "innocent" in the sense of a "bourgeois" concept of law, in the sense of "subjectivism." And yet he knows that he must be sacrificed for "objective" reasons.

In one particularly impressive scene, Rubashov finds himself in a Belgian harbor city in order to explain to the Communist functionaries of the dock workers that, contrary to the customary boycott policy of the Soviet Union, the dock workers now have to unload goods from the Soviet Union for fascist Italy. The sanctions levied by the League of Nations would not, he explains, be taken seriously by the bourgeois, imperialist, reactionary powers. If the Soviet Union is the only power that keeps to the sanctions, then the Soviet Union would be the only country to carry the full burden of the boycott.

The Party Secretary of the local organization, "Little Loewy" radicalizes Rubashov's (and thus Lenin's and also Stalin's) logic: If the Soviet ships do not deliver the raw materials that fascist Italy needs for its war front in Africa, then someone else will (Koestler 1947, 64).

At first glance, Jaruzelski's argumentation in 1981 resembles the one radicalized by "Little Loewy": If he, the Polish General and Communist, had not seen to the business of suppressing the democracy movement, then the Soviet generals and Communists would have done it. But Jaruzelski's argument goes beyond that of "Little Loewy": The Polish dictatorship would have meant a significantly lesser repression compared with the Soviet dictatorship. Not the business advantages of the perpetrators (Soviet economic interests in breaking the boycott against fascist Italy), but the essential difference that the one dictatorship made for the victims in comparison with the other, is central for Jaruzelski's calculations. It is a calculation based on victims, not perpetrators.

The division of Russian Social Democracy into Bolsheviks and Mensheviks in 1903 made it possible for Lenin to refine his understanding of revolution and progress both theoretically and practically. In order to abolish the rule of people over their fellow human beings, the forces of progress, the proletariat, had to seize power themselves. This form of rule was meant to be the most extreme form of rule, namely dictatorship, all in keeping with Marx. Yet in order to inform the proletariat of its "objective" interests, of its own needs, and bring it to its rightful place in history, professional revolutionaries like Lenin and his closest comrades had to precede the working class. As long as the subjective needs of the proletariat are not at the level of objective needs, the professional revolutionaries have to act as the avant-garde in the interests of this proletariat and even erect a dictatorship in the name of the working class.

Everything that disturbs this path that is seen as objectively "correct," can and must be swept away: social structures as well as concrete individuals. The question of individual guilt is a bourgeois vestige, it smacks of a lack of revolutionary consciousness.

The professional revolutionaries practice leadership. And they are, in their self-understanding, only "objective" tools in the process of history. Their actions are an objective given. Their behavior follows clearly recognizable rules. If the interest of the existing rule of the proletariat, i.e., of the Party, of the Central Committee, i.e., the "Number One" demands it, then the Communists of the world must break through the boycott against fascist Italy. And if the interests of the Soviet Union demand it, then a pact of non-aggression must be signed with National Socialist Germany that divides Eastern Europe between Hitler and Stalin like booty.

This logic of the lesser evil as it becomes clear in the theory and practice of the Leninist interpretation of Marxism ultimately justifies the opposite of what was declared to be a principle. Concrete Leninism becomes its opposite: while invoking the "objective" abolition of the state, state terror is lifted to new levels of extremes; with the invocation of international revolution, the most brutal, anti-socialist, nationalistic, imperialistic dictatorships are supported; with the invocation of "democratic centralism," all revolutionaries deemed even potentially dangerous to the regime are murdered.

It is no accident that Koestler prefaces his novel with a passage from Machiavelli's "Discourses": "He who establishes a dictatorship and does not kill Brutus, or who founds a republic and does not kill the sons of Brutus, will reign for a short time only."

By killing Rubashov, Stalin killed the sons of Brutus. His rule, therefore, was long-lasting. But it was not the rule that abolished all rule; it was not the dictatorship that was to liberate humanity. The logic of the lesser evil transformed everything into its opposite. That which was conceived of as an instrument became the end in itself.

Koestler prefaced his novel with another motto, this one from Dostoyevsky's "Crime and Punishment": "Man, man, one cannot live quite without pity."

Is it really only this general moralizing protest that sounds highly non-obligatory and does not really lead anywhere analytically that confronts this logic of the lesser evil which, in turn, reverses everything?

In one of his conversations with Ivanov, the executor of the logic that is directed toward Rubashov, the latter rejects any sort of moralism: "The Jacobins were moralists; we were empirics" (Koestler 1947, 71).

The Leninists claimed to have recognized the laws of motion of society and history. With this thoroughly Marxist self-understanding they wanted not only to recognize, but to act. The Lenins, Rubashovs, Trotskys, and Stalins were, after all, not only scholars in the ivory tower of social science and analysis, they were human beings oriented toward action to an extraordinary degree. They wanted world revolution, but did not understand themselves as creators but as midwives. The norm which they invoked was not the Jacobin formula of any liberty or equality or fraternity. The formula was to bring forth what was "necessary."

This normative and also moralizing rejection of the normative and the moralistic closes the circle of theoretical rejection of theory. It is the end point of the reversal of all norms, all facts into their respective opposites. The equanimity with which Rubashov ultimately accepts his own death is, of course, not free from values. It is the consequence of a thoroughly value-laden acceptance of necessity.

Lenin and Rubashov opt for Machiavelli against Dostoyevsky. All of their actions were aimed toward the instrumentalization of politics. All the evils of this world were compared to one another, checked with regard to their relative usefulness and then correspondingly deployed or rejected.

But Lenin and Rubashov avoid the decisive question: When the last justification of this instrumental understanding of politics is supposed to be international revolution and the liberation from any rule, then this goal could not be separated from the morality that Rubashov attributes to the Jacobins with a certain scorn. The mere invocation of the necessity of international revolution can certainly not justify the Hitler-Stalin pact; and by no means the purges of the 1930's; nor the millions of human beings who died in the 1920's and 1930's as victims of the civil war labeled as class struggle; and finally, it cannot justify the October Revolution. If the justification of a radicalized logic of the lesser evil is the bringing forth of the historically necessary, then it collapses: If world revolution will occur anyway, why did the czar's family, including servants, have to be shot? If world revolution will occur anyway, why did the peasants as a class have to die? If world revolution will occur anyway, why were Zinoviev and Kamenev and Bukharin murdered, why did Trotsky have to die? Why did Rubashov get the final bullet that released him?

The fear of morality that exists within Leninism is revealing. If politics is only the recognition and realization of certain social events, then all persons and all concrete measures are interchangeable. Then there would have been no need for the gigantic struggles and the gigantic sacrifices of the October Revolution and the developments thereafter. The gigantic struggles and the gigantic sacrifices of the Jacobin Revolution are more easily understood: they were grounded in morality, in the morality derived from the central values of liberty and equality and fraternity.

This does not make the sacrifices any less terrible, of course; it only sets a more convincing theoretical limit to the to the dead-end of Leninist logic. Rubashov is fully aware of this consequence of his and Lenin's logic. In his prison diary he maintains: "The final truth is ultimately always a falsehood." And further: "Our only guiding principle is that of consistent logic ... which is the only thing that counts: who is objectively right" (Koestler 1947, 81f.).

The Leninist understanding of politics deduces and thus avoids the issue of subjectivity. The Leninist understanding of history is pseudo-objective. If the issue were really one of being objectively correct, then the functional task of the avant-garde would lie only in reading the developments that were present and necessarily transpiring in society in time.

Where is the leadership here, where is an option, where has there been a decision made between a greater and a lesser evil, where is politics in general? Leninism acts as if the question of individual freedom did not exist, nor the freedom to decide, as if there were no question of individual morality, separate from "objective" correctness. And there is probably no other political system than the one that invokes Lenin that has opened the door as widely to personal unpredictability in theory and praxis.

In accordance with their self-understanding as empiricists, the Lenins and Rubashovs, the Trotskys and Stalins extinguished personal responsibility and thus personal guilt as a category. Whatever the individual people in history and in the present wanted, was declared irrelevant. The only thing that mattered was whether they acted in accordance with the objective rules, with the logic of history and the present. There were no rules, of course, concerning what constituted this logic and who determined its material content. The process of making politics scientific in Lenin's sense opened the door to arbitrariness. The supposedly strictly ordered logic of the Leninist understanding of politics led finally to a chaos of Hobbesian dimensions. The logic invoked by Rubashov in his prison cell in the name of all who felt themselves to be in the tradition of Lenin became, in the end, its absolute opposite. In place of an ordered system of rules in which dependent variables can be calculated based on the knowledge of independent variables was complete anarchy — in the form of absolutist, personal arbitrary rule.

The logic on which Stalin's Leninism was based led, during the Great Terror, to the opposite of what Lenin's instrumental understanding of politics had claimed to represent. The victims of the show trials that, unlike Rubashov, did not experience the grace of the quick shot to the back of the neck, but rather were put on public display, were destroyed in the sense of a traditional individual morality. Vyshinsky, as district attorney, was caught up in primitive scolding; the defendants took on the most absurd crimes and the distracted public demanded the execution of these "mangy dogs" (Conquest 1968). Not Machiavelli, not even the Clausewitz so treasured by Lenin, but witch trials stood at the end of this development.

In Rubashov's closing dialogs with the district attorney, who, unlike Ivanov, no longer represented the old generation of revolutionaries but already the products of the revolution, Leninist politics are radicalized once more: The tactics of the party are determined by the principle, "the end justifies the means — all means, without exception" (Koestler 1947, 190).

The complete instrumentalization of politics in the interest of a single, all-encompassing political goal (policy) leads to the destruction of revolution. Rubashov accepts this principle and thus justifies the fact that his life's work, the Leninist Revolution, turns into its Stalinist opposite. And thus Rubashov accepts his own execution in the interest of the Leninist principle that leads, consistently and logically, to Stalinism.

The renunciation of differentiation, of weighing the choices and distinguishing between means and end, between an instrument and its purpose, makes leadership superfluous. The totalitarian dictatorship knows leadership just as little as the consistent democracy. The totalitarian dictatorship dissolves leadership by transferring all the forms and functions of leadership to the executor of iron necessity — to Stalin. The consistent democracy dissolves leadership by replacing it with the political marketplace and its mechanisms of self-navigation.

If all means are just, then the issue is no longer one of the greater or lesser evil. By willingly, indeed, greedily, taking on the role of scapegoat in the interest of the party, Rubashov clarifies the consequence of negating all notions of morality that are denounced as "bourgeois": the end of values, in the interest of whose attainment the instruments had supposedly been deployed; the end of everything Rubashov had lived for. The Revolution destroys itself and this self-destructive logic needs no leadership. Good and Evil, Right and Wrong become "objective" and the distinction between them is negated.

Directly before his execution Rubashov indulges in the fantastic vision of a revolutionary party after Stalinism has been overcome: Perhaps, Rubashov thinks, the members of this new party will wear monks' robes and preach that only the absolute purity of the means can justify the end. Perhaps they will teach that a human being is more than the product of a million divided by a million (Koestler 1947, 207). At the end of his life, Rubashov comes to individual morality, to the roots of Christianity and (or) bourgeois enlightenment.

The history of existing Leninism shows where the renunciation of weighing the end and the means leads to, what it finally means when everything, even if it is directed against the stated goal, is accepted as the instrument of politics. The political players of Leninism agree to anything that brings them a little closer to the "objective" goal, whether it is the Revolution, or socialism or the final Communist society. But because they do not distinguish between greater and lesser evils, because the end justifies any means, the result (policy) of their politics is the opposite of what they had once decided to do: Instead of the negation of human beings ruling over other human beings, under Lenin's attentive pupil, it comes down to the direct form of rule: totalitarian dictatorship.

The principle of Leninism put into practice clarifies the fact that the alternative to the principle of the "lesser evil" can take on two extreme forms: in addition to the renunciation of any instrumental thinking, the absolutism of this thinking is just as much a possible and practiced alternative. In addition to the rejection of politics, the limitlessness of politics as an instrument is set against the principle of the lesser evil.

The variation known as the rejection of politics keeps its distance from the instrumental behavior (of politics) in order not to influence the purity of the goal (policy). The result is that the possibility of reaching the goal is relinquished. The variation that sets politics as an absolute instrument ultimately means that the instrumental aspect covers over the goal and becomes the end in itself. Here, again, the goal is renounced.

The renunciation of politics and the making of politics into an absolute each have the same result: the political goal that serves as a justification of refusal or activity is surrendered.

The Jaruzelski of the years 1981 to 1989, the Communist party leader and military dictator of Poland, argued not only outside of this Leninist logic, he also acted fundamentally differently. He made politics and he had others make politics; he practiced leadership, but he also did not monopolize it because he could not have erected such a monopoly for himself in Poland given the actual, geopolitically conditioned dependence on the Soviet Union. Moscow was always also a player in Poland. Another reason Jaruzelski did not monopolize leadership was because he quite consciously let other Polish players act politically: the Bishops, without interruption even in December 1981; and soon those forces of the democracy movement who, like Walesa, did not disobey, who entered into a sort of oppositional collaboration with the Communist system; and finally, provoked by the new winds blowing in from Moscow beginning in 1985, all the forces of Polish society willing to articulate their political concerns.

Regarding his way of thinking and acting politically, Jaruzelski was no Leninist. He represented the precedence of an ethic of responsibility over an ethic of conviction. He not only got his hands dirty, he acknowledged the fact that they were dirty, unlike Stalin and his executioners. The Communist Jaruzelski had clearly already risen from the Leninist logic when he became the main player of Polish history.

Artur Koestler describes his own personal experience with the emergence of this logic. Koestler, the Communist, who was to write his novel about Rubashov from his own experience with the Soviet Union and with the Communist "world movement" of the 1930s came to Spain in the service of Komintern after the civil war broke out. Disguised as a Hungarian newspaper correspondent (Koestler had a real Hungarian passport), he was supposed to collect information from

General Franco's headquarters for Komintern. He was discovered and spent many months in prison under Franco's dictatorship. He was convinced that a simple execution without an "unpleasant prelude" was the best he could hope for. As a result of British intervention, however, he was released and was now a different man.

He had had a decisive experience that he summarized in his "Spanish Testament" and that he himself described as a collection of "commonplaces": "that man is a reality, mankind an abstraction; that men cannot be treated as units in operations of political arithmetic because they behave like the symbols for zero and the infinite, which dislocate all mathematical operations; that the end justifies the means only within very narrow limits; that ethics is not a function of social utility, and charity not a petty-bourgeois sentiment but the gravitational force which keeps civilization in its orbit" (Koestler in Crossman 1949, 68). In other words, Koestler had discovered Dostoyevsky whom he would then place opposite Machiavelli.

This Koestler whose experience in Spain was similar to that of George Orwell, on the other side of the civil war, of course, this Koestler then wrote his novel about the logic of Leninism. He was able to analyze this logic because he himself had been held in its bonds. And he could summarize the contradiction — that the impatient desire for excessive social engineering and the Leninist hubris of knowing the script of world history and thus being able to act in accordance with it had to become the justification of an unlimited arbitrariness disguised as necessity.

16 On the True Nature of Personal Leadership

Leadership as Mass Murder — Excessive Leadership — Distancing as Style — The Freedom from Having to Learn — The Question of Succession — To Chain or Unchain Leadership?

The Holocaust is written in Hitler's personal handwriting. Even in his last will and testament, written only hours before his death, he held to the murderous anti-Semitism that constituted his entire politics; and unlike his faithful servant, Heinrich Himmler, Hitler refused to make politics with the lives of Jews. Hitler would not agree to any arrangement with the Allies that would save the life of even one Jew. He was the person ultimately responsible for Auschwitz and the other death camps, for the special commandos (even those for which the *Wehrmacht* was responsible) and the other elements of the murder machine that brought people to their death because they had the wrong grandparents.

Similarly, the deaths of millions of people who died in the course of the collectivization of Soviet agriculture are the result of the personal actions of Stalin, as are the deaths of millions murdered during the great purges — either shot or put to death in the camps, either as Soviet officers in 1937, Polish officers in 1940, as enemies of the party, as Chinese, Crimean Tartars or people denounced for personal reasons. Stalin himself, in accordance with the Bolsheviks' program and thus with Lenin's, had set the course for the "war against the nation" and he carried personal responsibility particularly for the murderous "war against the Party" beginning in 1934 (Ulam 1989).

Millions paid with their lives for Mao's personal decisions to take the "Great Leap Forward" in 1958 and begin the Cultural Revolution several years later (Salisbury 1993). Even earlier, the Communist Party of China had begun the systematic murder of the landowners, but the famines that followed the "Great Leap" and the anarchic violence released by Mao through the Cultural Revolution were no longer the result of a policy of the party, they were the result of the politics of a single individual.

If there are examples in the 20th century for leadership, then they are these three. If the consequences of the effects of individuals in the history of this century are to be studied, then it will be the examples of Hitler, Stalin, and Mao. These three are the most impressive examples for the weight that can come to the "personality" factor. If there is longing for leadership, who could better satisfy that longing?

As leaders, Hitler, Stalin, and Mao have many things in common. This is not meant to hide the fact that their influence on the course of history is characterized by essential differences:

— Hitler's impact was in essence one of destruction from the beginning. The foreign policy of Nazi Germany did not follow a direction headed toward the self-preservation of its own system, unlike the two Communist dictators who, particularly in foreign policy, acted "realistically." From an outside perspective, Stalin and Mao conducted *Realpolitik*; Hitler, who invoked Bismarck at times, quite clearly did not. His politics was one of maximizing his enemies. Through a systematic destruction of all the options that politics might have offered him, he destroyed himself and his regime (Haffner 1978). Stalin and Mao had developed a good bit of the drive for self-preservation for themselves and their systems — the operatic staging of their own demise was utterly foreign to them.

— In light of this, a decisive difference in the destructive fury of totalitarian leadership emerges: Hitler's mass murders were directed externally against the Jews, "Gypsies" and Slavs defined as enemies, against the powers defined as hostile. Hitler's destructive fury needed war and was thus directed toward it. Even the Holocaust, which had nothing directly to do with the war, only became fully effective with the onset of Hitler's war. Stalin's and Mao's mass murders, on the other hand, were directed toward the inside. The reign of each needed civil war and the concomitant, never-ending flow of possible enemies, defined and invented over and over again. With the exception of Röhm, all of Hitler's loyal comrades remained unharmed by his bloodthirstiness, whereas no one in Stalin's or Mao's empires lived in more danger that those who served them most loyally.

— Hitler's followers could rest easy, unlike those of Stalin and Mao. Of the 1,966 delegates to the 17th Party Congress of the Communist Party of the Soviet Union in 1934, 1,108 were arrested and many of those were shot during the next several years. Of the 139 members and representatives of the Central Committee elected at this Party Congress, 98 were shot during the great purge (Ulam 1989, 373). In the course of the Cultural Revolution, some of Mao's closest comrades were murdered with his knowledge and approval (Liu Shaotshi, He Long), some died under unexplained circumstances (Lin Biao), some survived the torture of the Maoist terror (Deng Xiaoping) or died in connection with these persecutions (Peng Dehuai, Chen Yi). Those named were presidents, ministers and marshals of the People's Republic, by the grace of Mao, before he arranged for their violent deaths despite or because of their loyalty (Salisbury 1993, 467-474).

Yet the commonalities of these regimes are just as conspicuous as the differences. These commonalities point to an inner logic of their reign. In spite of the personal responsibility that these three dictators have and in spite of the consequences carried by the ideologies found, not invented by them (hatred of Jews, for example, or class hatred which can not be equated, but compared to it), the reigns of Hitler, Stalin, and Mao are characterized by the logic of excessive leadership. Individuality and ideology do not suffice for an explanation. What is needed is the insight into the specific logic of excessive personal leadership.

This logic results from the development of the regime of mass murder. All three were by no means directed toward the unlimited rule by a single person, not even Hitler's. While the Führer principle and the cult of personality within the NSDAP were already highly developed by the "take-over" in 1933, this development was not yet at an end, but progressed further: by the linking of the offices of the President and the Chancellor in 1934; by Hitler's takeover of the supreme command of the Wehrmacht in 1941; by the gradual binding of the justice department and the administration to the "Führer" personally. The Nazi regime was, in spite of the tendencies toward personal power already visible in 1933, at first still a dual state in which constitutional and totalitarian elements co-existed (Fraenkel 1974).

This is even more so the case for the reigns of Stalin and Mao. Until the late 1920s, Stalin had to take into account the majority in the Politburo and enter into intraparty coalitions. As late as the 15th Party Congress in 1927, Trotsky could criticize Stalin publicly, even if in vain (Ulam 1989, 270f.; Radzinsky 1996, 224-228). Khrushchev rightly pointed to the 20th Party Congress in 1956 and the contradiction between the personal rule of Stalin beginning in 1927 and the party structure desired and practiced by Lenin. Khrushchev, of course, did not even allow the question to arise of whether or not Stalin's personal reign was not already laid out in the logic of Leninism.

For decades, Mao was an equal among equals. As late as 1949, the year in which the People's Republic of China was founded, members of the innermost circle of leadership could contradict him. After the question of leadership had been clarified during the "Long March," Mao was indisputably Number One in the party. But until the mid-1950's, one could say: "Mao was not yet sacrosanct ... They (the members of the innermost circle of leadership, A.P.) had not — yet — suspended judgment on ordinary matters" (Salisbury 1993, 21). When this changed, "they" had to agree that Mao was right in each and every instance. But even that did not help in most cases — most fell into the maelstrom of the Cultural Revolution and many of "them" did not survive, not even the one who, in executing Mao's will, had used the Cultural Revolution to annihilate his comrades — Lin Biao. Yet, above the hysterical masses of the Cultural Revolution that praised a radical egalitarianism stood, god-like, as an unequal among equals — Mao Zedong.

The secret of the personal reign of Hitler, Stalin, and Mao lies not in the personality structure of these three dictators. The secret lies in the structure of a reign that, because it is devoid of controls and counterbalances, must lead to excessive leadership. None of the three were born as dictator, no matter how many elements of their socialization can be found as elements of their personal reigns. The secret is the absence of democracy and the elements of the constitutional state, the separation of powers, and the checks and balances associated with any form of democracy (Pauley 1997).

It may be useful to analyze the mother-father relationships of the three dictators, relationships that have certain things in common: the mothers who dominate indirectly through their goodness, the fathers who are forbidding and strict. It may be interesting to look more closely at the effect of baroque Catholicism on the young Hitler, of the priest's seminary on the young Stalin, and of religious thought, introduced by the mother, on the young Mao. It may be helpful to illuminate the three dictators' different attitudes toward women. But: the results of such comparative analyses are always rather insignificant, because nothing points logically to the fact that the Adolf Hitler who acted shy and rather repressed sexually would become a mass murderer; or that the sexually hyperactive Mao, with his love of classical Chinese poetry, was therefore predestined to become the

Führer-dictator of the largest population on earth; or that the "great Stalin" could have or even must have been recognizable in the everyday roughness of the young Georgian revolutionary with the codename Koba.

If the essence of Hitler's rule had already been present in the crude, paranoid anti-semitism of the Upper Austrian, how many Hitlers must there be! Would the combination of classical Chinese poetry and philosophy together with a superficial understanding of Marxism suffice to declare Maoism? How could China save itself from all the Maos? If the actionistic rebellion of the Georgian with his inability to keep stable friendships were the precondition for Stalinism, when would the next Stalin appear? Not the individual, but the structure helps to explain the essence of excessive leadership in all three cases. And this structure is expressed first of all in easily recognizable aspects of political style.

Hitler, Stalin, Mao — what are the commonalities of their leadership style? First, one notices apparent secondary issues. All three tended to make night into day. They all preferred to work at night and then sleep long into the day. All three avoided traveling abroad as much as possible. All three reduced the decision-making committees that still existed — the government of the Reich, the Party Congresses — to mere window-dressing (like the Party Congresses of the Communist Party of the Soviet Union and the Communist Party of China that were ritualized blessings of their own personal power, not so very different from the media spectacle of the Party Congresses in Nuremberg) or they simply refused to allow them to convene (for instance, the German government in the final years of Hitler's reign). All three tended toward the excessive transformation of their political leadership into art and architecture; all three worked as designers of cities and other spaces — Hitler more intensely than Mao and both of them more intensely than Stalin (Speer 1969, 166-175; Salisbury 1993, 187-191). The dictators expressed the excessive character of their leadership in their megalomaniacal architectural fantasies.

Until the war broke out, Hitler lived a Bohemian life (Fest 1973, 697-741). Irregular working hours and a generally recognizable, deep dislike of the routine of governing characterized the working style of the German Chancellor from 1933 to 1939. Mao disappeared for weeks and months at a time from the limited publicity of the party elite in Peking. These phases of absence would then be followed by phases of extremely hectic activity (Salisbury 1993, 286). This sort of disappearance is known of Stalin only for the period immediately following the German invasion of the Soviet Union in June of 1941. In the sense of routine leadership, he was surely the most constant of the three. But even Stalin was infamous for calling important meetings at midnight and asking foreign visitors, including Churchill, to the Kremlin during the night.

Stalin's nocturnal banquets, which were generally accessible only to men, as well as Hitler's nocturnal monologues that were often extremely exhausting for guests, were complemented by an interesting parallel: Stalin and Hitler loved to watch movies at night and the respective camarillas were charged with attending the nightly presentations. Mao was presumably the most intellectually demanding and interesting of the three, even in his nocturnal behavior, which included not only the tendency toward sex games with young female partners that only increased with his age, but also the attitude of the teacher, philosopher and poet, an attitude that was willingly accepted and appreciated in pre-totalitarian times.

The three leaders' working style is characterized by distance from the populace. A working style like this is simply not possible within a real democracy as it exists today. The necessity of a media presence and the schedule of public appearances, press conferences, etc., a schedule that must be synchronized with the day to day lifestyle of the consumers of media and politics, prevents political leadership from being a primarily nocturnal undertaking in today's democracy. In addition, a leader who slept past noon, a fact which, of course, could not easily be hidden from the media of a democracy, would not correspond to the expectations of a media-savvy public any more than the constant use of one's office for group sex games.

The pressure toward a public personal style in democracy has surely intensified since the deaths of the three dictators. But even during the first half of the 20th century, politicians in democracies had to submit to public controls on their "private lives" and had to respect the desire for access on the part of the media. Unlike Mao, Roosevelt could not have withdrawn for weeks and been inaccessible to the media. Truman could not have afforded the eccentric, nocturnal invitations to the White House à la Stalin without risking being scolded by the media. His attempt, for instance, to respond to the criticisms of his daughter's singing ended in a media disaster (McCullough 1992, 827-830). Jackson, Lincoln and other presidents of the 19th century had already discovered that there was no private sphere for them — a working style characterized by distance was not possible.

The dictators, on the other hand, could indeed afford such a working style. They were free from the pressure of having to market themselves constantly. They were free from the pressure of presenting themselves to the media and allowing the media access to every aspect of their private lives. They were also free from the pressure of having to undertake spectacular trips abroad to ensure photo opportunities with other leaders. They did not care for summit meetings, and when they did agree to them, they expected their partners in dialog to come to them; Chamberlain and Daladier to Munich, for instance, or Churchill to Moscow and both he and Roosevelt to Yalta. Mao, the avid swimmer, even forced Khrushchev, who did not swim, to join him in the swimming pool in Beijing in 1958 (Salisbury 1993, 156f.). For the Chinese dictator, this humiliation of the Soviet party leader and head of government must have seemed like compensation for his own humiliation by Stalin in Moscow in 1949/50. The dictators had a clear view of the home advantage: a trip abroad meant doing without humiliating others; and it also meant the danger that one would be humiliated instead.

Before the Revolution, Stalin was abroad on short trips as one of Lenin's second-ranked party soldiers. In 1906 he was a delegate to the Fourth Party Congress of Russian Social Democracy in Stockholm and in 1907 at the Fifth Party Congress in London. In 1912/13 he visited Lenin in Cracow and then Vienna in order to collect material for his study on the question of nationalities. As dictator he had a deep-seated dislike of traveling abroad. He left the Soviet Union only two times and both times he was under the protection of the Red Army: in 1943 in Teheran, which was at that time the capital of a Soviet-British protectorate; and in 1945 in Potsdam, which belonged to the Soviet sector in Germany. All other conferences had to either take place in the Soviet Union itself (Stalin forced the deathly ill Roosevelt to travel halfway around the world to Yalta), or Stalin sent Molotov, for example to Hitler in 1940 and to San Francisco for the founding of the United Nations in 1945.

Hitler also avoided traveling abroad. Disregarding his military excursions into occupied territories, during the First World War as a soldier and during the Second World War as Führer (for example his originally secret visit to Paris in the summer of 1940), there remain only the two official visits to Italy in 1934 and 1937, talks with Pétain and with Franco in 1940 under the protection of the German occupational forces in France, and the dialog with Mussolini in Italy in 1943. There remain only the crossings of the Austrian-German border when the unemployed artist went to Germany only to return to Austria as the victorious dictator who declared its fall. Hitler had Goebbels go to Geneva for the League of Nations and he sent Ribbentrop to Moscow.

Hitler's aversion to foreign countries corresponds with Stalin's aversion to the extent that both "actually" came from a sort of foreign country. Hitler was an Austrian citizen who had evaded military service in Austro-Hungary by fleeing to Germany; Stalin was in fact born a Russian citizen but ethnically and linguistically, he was a Georgian. The Austrian Hitler and the Georgian Stalin could not bring themselves to part with Germany or Russia, respectively: a particular form of overcompensation.

Mao had a similar barrier regarding foreign countries. His visits to the Soviet Union, in 1949/50 with Stalin and in 1957 with Khrushchev, were the only times Mao ventured beyond the Chinese border. He left the international stage to Zhou Enlai. He was Mao's Molotov.

The dictators were fond of their usual surroundings. Leaving them evidently released certain fears: foreign countries as a synonym for the loss of control. This was true for the control of their accustomed everyday life. Mao's dependence on sleeping tablets, a result of the working style developed during the guerilla years, a dependency that he shared with other party leaders of the Communist Party of China of his generation (Salisbury 1993, 287) is only one aspect of his lack of flexibility. In addition, there was the unspoken desire not to have the given images of the enemy disrupted through more complex knowledge, nor the other clichéed simplifications that are often the expression of the desire to simplify complex politics. The perfection of the dictatorships was expressed in the apparent liberation from the pressure to constantly be learning.

Hitler's disparaging opinion of the weight of the U.S. influenced his foreign policy — an opinion that he did not want to see disrupted by a more complex flow of information. Stalin's brief visit to London for the Fifth Party Congress of the Social Democratic Party of Russia in April, 1907 evidently left no recognizable impression on the representatives of the Bolshevik wing of the Party from the Caucasus. "Generalissimo Stalin never mentioned his visit to London to the man who at the time was Under-Secretary for Colonies in His Majesty's Government, Winston Churchill" (Ulam 1989, 92). And Mao, whose only personal information about foreign countries stemmed from his trip through Siberia in 1949 and 1950 and from Moscow, "never displayed real interest in the West" (Salisbury 1993, 147). The dictators had a certain, fixed image of the international factors that surrounded them. And if at all possible, nothing should disturb this image, certainly not one's own experience.

What a contrast to the behavior of Roosevelt and Churchill, De Gaulle and Adenauer and Nehru, but also Tito and Gorbachev and

Yeltsin: they all pushed and continue to push for talks at the highest level. No summit so high that it would be unsuitable for a meeting; no calendar so full that it would not allow for a short stay abroad, as media-friendly as possible. This tendency of democratic, or rather, non-totalitarian leaders does not, of course, mean that a trip abroad alone has to contribute to a significant increase in the flow of information. This tendency contrasts noticeably with the behavior of Hitler, Stalin, and Mao, who did not even want to expose themselves to the risk of seeing their fixed image confronted with a reality that they could not personally control.

The separation of the three totalitarian dictators from the bases that first gave them legitimation — party, movement, and institutions, is most clear in the inability of these systems to solve the problem of succession. In all three systems, the death of the dictator brought about significant breaks in the system; in the case of Germany, this was intensified by military defeat. But Stalin's and Mao's deaths also led consistently to the end of the systems that both dictators had stood for. Neither Khrushchev nor Brezhnev was able to (or wanted to) continue Stalin's form of personal rule. And the China for which the name Deng Xiaoping stands is certainly not Mao's China. In each case, the system of personal rule could not survive its representative. In the case of Germany, the intervention of the Allies brought forth the production of the mechanisms of democracy that would stand in the way of the reproduction of excessive personal leadership. In the USSR and China, this task fell to the surviving party elites who had brought about non-democratic mechanisms of control during the violent struggles for power, whose most prominent victims were Lavrenti P. Beria and Jiang Qing, respectively.

In light of the fate of the USSR and as a generalization for all transitions that lead away from excessive totalitarian systems, it can be assumed that these post-Stalinist and post-Maoist systems were transitional ones that, unlike the totalitarian systems of their predecessors, were and are not typologically original. Between the unfettering of leadership in totalitarian systems and the shackling of this same leadership in democratic systems there lies a gray area of authoritarian systems of many kinds. But this gray area allows no stability. This can be seen most clearly in the fact that choosing a successor in this gray area is not possible: the old men in Brezhnev's or Deng's Politburo, the flight into the family clan in dictatorships à la Duvalier or Suharto, the instability of all forms of modern military rule confirm this. There is no stable middle ground between the shackling of leadership and its unshackled excesses. Leadership sways between the extremes contained in its conception, between its innate predilection toward excess and the mechanisms raised against this predilection that are always on the verge of extinguishing it. Unstable ground lies in between — an uneven plain.

On this unstable ground, in this gray area, Wojciech Jaruzelski had to be a leader and make decisions. And he confronted the challenge; he decided. No matter which motives might have played a role in the decision of December 1981, Jaruzelski caused the uneven plain of this gray area to slant not in the direction of the unshackling, but of the shackling of leadership. The martial law for which Jaruzelski was responsible was an example of minimal excess, that is, of limitations in repression. And this martial law created the conditions (or rather left the conditions intact) for the transition to the general shackling of leadership. Jaruzelski set a counter-example against the excessive, totalitarian leaders of his century. The dissolution of his own leadership role in 1989 was the final step in the logic of self-limitation which he had set into motion.

Political leadership tends toward excess. This tendency is a distinguishing characteristic of leadership, not a secondary, arbitrary hallmark. From the outset, excess is part and parcel of the notion of leadership. Hitler, Stalin, and Mao are the incarnations of leadership; examples of what happens and what must happen when leadership is not suffocated in routine, suffocated the way that excessive emperors in China and Rome were literally suffocated. The suffocation of the threatening conception of personal leadership that bears the excessive within it is the actual task of democracy. The democratization of leadership, its transformation into the routine of roles and functions, is the only guarantee against the excesses that are an integral part of the concept of personal leadership.

Political leadership also means viewing the formation of society as a task for politics — social engineering is the planned linking between the end and the means of politics. The examples that Hitler, Stalin, and Mao offer for excessive, uncontrolled and completely unfettered political leadership are also examples of excessive social engineering. Hitler's fantasy of an ethnically "pure" Germany and a Europe "free" of Jews, adolescent images of a primitive Darwinist fixed on conspiracy theories, were able to be translated into action because these delusions, widely held in Hitler's time, were unleashed on society through the possibility of excessive leadership. Stalin's and Mao's fantasy of a classless society, naive rewritings of what Marx had formulated theoretically and what Lenin had held to be concretely practicable, and what millions of people had also wished for, was able to be realized because the power relations suddenly allowed it, because leadership was unfettered, and because society seemed infinitely malleable.

The hubris of a such a technological way of dealing with society, which is simply a catch-all term for human beings, becomes abundantly clear with these examples. This hubris is also evident in the assumption that someone "forms" society, as if society had need of social engineers who would form it, the sum of human beings, as if society had need of elite leaders that would bring society into a certain type of future: a future without Jews and without kulaks and without people who seem indebted to the "Four Olds," the enemy images of the Maoist Cultural Revolution — old thinking, old culture, old customs, old habits (Salisbury 1993, 242). The excessive fantasies of practicability are released through excessive leadership — to the horror of humankind.

Whoever calls for leadership calls for the Hitlers, the Stalins and the Maos.

17 On the Necessity of Limiting Evil

The Category of Evil — The Function of Utopia — The "Lesser Evil" as Justification — Franz Jägerstätter

In Aldous Huxley's novel "Ape and Essence," an expedition from New Zealand comes to California in order to study what remains of nature and civilization a century and a half after the destruction of the North American continent by a nuclear war. The researchers experience a culture that understands itself as the rule of Belial, as the rule of evil.

The representatives of this cult who also rule politically have kept the memory of pre-nuclear culture alive and define their new culture as a counterculture, a thoroughly rational, viable antithesis to enlightenment, modernity and scientific, technological civilization. Civilization is held responsible for the destruction of the fundamentals of human existence. But it is not a Rousseauean, pre-technological, bucolic idyll of the ecologically sensitive, noble savage that characterizes this post-nuclear anti-civilization. Rather, it is the strict rule of enlightened priest-politicians over the masses who are consciously kept in ignorance. The vicar explains the background of this rule to the New Zealanders — the rejection of the modern concept of progress. The belief in progress and nationalism had set a development in motion whose dynamics could no longer be controlled and whose inability to be politically controlled had led to nuclear catastrophe in the Third World War (Huxley 1985, 87-97).

The rule of evil is the reproduction of the political control of society at the price of excluding the masses from politics. The enlightened elite of the priest-politicians holds society in a state of extreme superstition in order to prevent the repetition of the dynamics of progress. The perfect non-democracy of the rule of Belial allows politics and a clear leadership — for the caste of priests, and only for them. In the following stanza, the "narrator" summarizes the theoretical basis of this rule:

> Conscience, custom — the first makes cowards,
> Makes saints of us sometimes, makes human beings.
> The other makes Patriots, Papists, Protestants,
> Makes Babbits, Sadists, Swedes or Slovaks,
> Makes killers of Kulaks, chlorinators of Jews,

Makes all who mangle, for lofty motives,
Quivering flesh, without qualm or question
To mar their certainty of Supreme Service. (Huxley 1985, 96)

Conscience and custom, that is, culture, is made responsible for scientific, technological civilization and its logic that destroys everything. The recipe is the prohibition of conscience and custom. The recipe is absolute control from above, unlimited political power. In order for this recipe to work, all conditions for democracy must be eliminated. In order to make leadership possible in the sense of preserving the fundamentals necessary for human society, the thought of democracy cannot be allowed to surface.

The novel Huxley wrote in 1948, the same year that George Orwell wrote "1984," reveals a sense of helplessness. If progress brings democracy, but democracy ends in a destructive logic that can no longer be corrected, then, in the interest of those concerned, i.e., of society, progress, and thus democracy, must be prohibited. For the sake of humanity, people must be saved from themselves; leadership means allowing no self-determination, no emancipation.

It is a strange system that Huxley portrays, a pedagogically motivated system of the prohibition of politics from above. The potential for violence that has already been experienced historically in the form of nuclear mass destruction is met with a prohibition of civilization. In order to ensure survival, freedom is denied. Knowledge of the possibilities for technological development is restricted. The elite, the caste of priests, conducts politics in order keep the masses away from politics for reasons that lie in the interests of the masses — a Hobbesian form of rule that is not driven by self-interest but by the concern for those being ruled. This is the antithesis to existing, self-destructive democracy.

Huxley does not sympathize with this system, but he also does not confront it with the same clear, enlightened, critical position as he did before the Second World War in "Brave New World." At that time he warned of the loss of freedom; in "Ape and Essence" he warns of the dangers of freedom. Between these two positions lies a process of increasing helplessness and skepticism vis-à-vis a linear optimism of democracy.

And Huxley's helplessness would have likely continued had he been able to observe what progress and nationalism brought about after the collapse of the Communist dictatorships in the Soviet Union and Yugoslavia. The democratization of Azerbaijan and Armenia meant the battle for Nagorny-Karabach; the democratization of

Yugoslavia was the beginning of the wars in that region. The release of self-determination was the release of the human capacity for destruction. Can the rule of evil, the rule of Belial be justified in order to prevent this evil?

Evil is a moral category. As long as there is human consciousness, as long as there is society, there will be attempts to replace evil with good. The attempt to do good is immanent in every culture, the result of conscience and custom that Huxley's Belial cult struggles against for that very reason. The fact that what counts as good varies from one culture to the next does nothing to change this immanence. The fact that those in power and all forms of rule make the claim to the good; in other words, that the claim to the good is always already an instrument of rule does little to confront this. The instrumental quality of the good constitutes its cultural permanence. Through constant political use, the good becomes indispensable, a cultural asset belonging to the essence of every culture.

The good lives from the existence of evil, and vice versa. To not appreciate this connection of mutual determination is to be politically naive. To want to overcome this connection of mutual determination is the theme of political utopia.

Utopia is not simply any fantasy of something that should or should not exist. Utopia is also a function to be described with the term "transcendence of being" (Mannheim 1978, 170f.). This function fulfills all concepts that point beyond a given reality and qualitatively transcend reality. If these notions are formulated with an eschatological or timeless perfection, they fulfill the task of a utopia: to confront reality with a perfect reflection, that is, to hold up to the reality that is imperfect due to the connection of mutual determination between good and evil a perfect counter-reality — a perfectly good or perfectly evil one.

From this opposition between imperfection (real) and perfection (imaginary) arises (or at least, is supposed to arise) the synthesis of political dynamics. The fascination with that which is either positively or negatively perfect should provoke action-directing interests that should, in the case of a positive utopia, move a given political reality toward perfection or, in the case of a negative utopia, away from perfection.

The eschatological character is especially visible with the type that Mannheim calls the "orgiastic chiliasmus of the Baptist" (Mannheim 1978, 184-191) — the attempt to produce the Kingdom of God in reality. But even the variant of the "Socialist-Communist utopia"

(Mannheim 1978, 207-213) is oriented toward the end of history. The perfect, Communist society is the omega of human development.

In this form, utopia claims to destroy imperfection and establish perfection for eternity. This radical, extreme consequence was not so typical of the "inventor" of the concept "utopia". Thomas More did not want to portray his Utopia, his nowhere as paradise but as the best of all possible non-paradises. The inhabitants of Utopia know crime, they know slavery, even as punishment. And the obvious advantages of Utopian society in no way lead to other states copying the examples of Utopia, nor to the Utopians acting like missionaries and forcing their model on others. The Utopians are also conceived of as imperfect, as carriers of original sin, which for More, prevents absolute perfection (Marius 1984, 166-170). More's claim to perfection was, then, a relative one.

What makes Utopia so attractive for More, that is, "good," is the difference between it and the defects of European society at the dawn of modernity. More does not tire of setting the advantages of Utopia against the flaws of Europe. Not coincidentally written at the beginning of the age of discoveries, Utopia is the "New World," held up like a mirror to the old. Even if much of what constitutes Utopia was foreign to a concrete realization in the England of Henry VIII, like, for instance, the Communist organization of property, More uses Utopia to criticize England and the other states of the European Renaissance — for instance, the rapacious crusades, to which he holds up the politics of Utopia which made wars superfluous or at least shortened them by murdering the enemy leaders in time or by bribing traitors.

It is remarkable that the political structure of Utopia is republican and lacks an individual who stands above the others, a leader. No one in Utopia, with the exception of the legendary founder, King Utopus, is called by name (Marius 19484, 160). What has been criticized in this book and what conveys the impression of a gray "socialist" patina, from the pen of the future Lord High Chancellor of England, is the surprising characteristic of a self-regulating political order of social equals. Thomas More's Utopia is a kind of imaginary democracy without a structure of personal leadership.

Thomas More practiced power and he worked in particular for a very concrete ruler. He played an important role in a system that he tried very much to reverse in his literary fantasy. But this divided More found the strength to resist. When Henry VIII, the monarch whose absolutist desires did not disturb More, began proceedings to break with the Catholic Church, More was no longer willing to be the true servant of his master. The moralist who had hidden his critical spirit behind a literary façade, took the place of the court adviser. The dissolution of leadership perfected in Utopia was concretized in sharp protest against the leader, the Prince. And he, in turn, saw to it that this resistance did not go unpunished.

More leaves the concrete questions about the actual political process in his Utopia unanswered. The analyses of the political structures that characterize his positive utopia remain inchoate. Positive utopias are evidently marked by a lack of concrete politics in utopian society, unlike negative utopias. In her positive, feminist utopia "Herland," written in 1915, Charlotte Perkins Gilman avoids giving concrete information about the way decisions are made, just as *More* does. Dealing too closely with the reality of diverging interests and their controversial realization in decisions is for both authors evidently disturbing, too "dirty" for the pure picture they paint. We also never find out how Rousseau's "volonté générale" works, at least not from the author. The constructed perfection makes this super-fluous.

The function of a positive utopia becomes clear using Gilman's "Herland" as an example (Gilman 1979). In a faraway land there exists a society consisting only of women. They reproduce parthenogeneti-cally and have simply done away with conflicting interests: hate, envy, greed, money, and religious faith have all disappeared. In this purely female paradise there are no recognizable political structures; they are also not necessary because there are no social contradictions. Politics has fled from this paradise, a sort of perfect democracy of equal women. The removal of one contradiction, that between the sexes, has dissolved all others. The result is the final society.

This longing for the end of politics framed in the context of utopian literature serves as a motor for political dynamics, for a political movement. Ideas like those in Gilman's utopia were and are motivating forces for the women's movement, just as the workers' movement was driven by idealistic images of a future perhaps not so far away. The good that is perfectly constructed and free of politics becomes an instrument of politics dedicated to the eradication of evil.

Margaret Atwood's "The Handmaid's Tale," written in 1985, is the functional pendant. In its negative formulation, this utopia tries to be politically effective. In a fundamentalist Christian dictatorship in the Northeastern United States, the "Moral Majority" has come to power at the end of the twentieth century. The postulated equality between the sexes has given way to an open rule by men. Non-Christians are repressed just as much as non-whites. Unlike the positive utopias of More, Rousseau, and Gilman, Atwood is very concrete when it comes to the analysis of concrete politics. Religious intolerance is the vehicle for political rule (Atwood 1987).

This almost perfectly constructed negative utopia tries to produces a dynamics of repulsion. Atwood takes certain tendencies of fundamentalism to their logical conclusion. The extreme result of this extrapolation functions as a shock that can and should motivate people just as much as Gilman's positive utopia.

As a genre, utopias function as a corrective to the tendencies toward the relativization of social differences inherent in the politics of the lesser evil. With their crass portrayal of positive utopia, More, Rousseau, and Gilman gain a distance from the morass of everyday politics and thus strengthened, tolerate distinctions in this politics. For example, when Gilman describes the harmonious workings of raising children almost without authority in Herland (Gilman 1979, 84-95) she calls on the critical potential of her readers in light of her own era's very different, confrontational and authoritarian style of raising children.

The negative utopias of Huxley, Orwell, and Atwood are analog correctives: their image of a world full of evil serves as a warning that intends to demonstrate real tendencies. The constant re-writing of history, for example, that is part of everyday government in Orwell's "1984" is an undisguised indication of the constant new versions of the history of the October Revolution and the Soviet Union in the era of Stalinism. Orwell's criticism must therefore be unpleasant for those who wanted to downplay the Stalinist mechanisms of repression using the argument of the "lesser evil."

The struggle of the intellectual left against the leftist intellectual Orwell was the struggle for survival of those who saw their justification of the politics of the lesser evil being endangered. With the "Homage to Catalonia" Orwell had described Stalinism as it existed. With "Animal Farm" he had analyzed the rise of Stalinism and with "1984" its establishment. In the time of the struggle of the non-Communist left against the politics of appeasement, prior to August 1939 he was just as annoying to the western European leftists as he was to public opinion in Great Britain and the U.S. starting in 1941.

Orwell's fable and his utopia are examples for the corrective that radical literary formulations can embody regarding political capriciousness and intellectual corruption, the very capriciousness and corruption that are inherent in the dangerously logical and thus dangerously complacent argument of the lesser evil. Orwell emphasized convincingly again and again that in the alleged *Realpolitik* of the lesser evil the Manichean tendency toward categorization and submission can be hidden in alleged good (Slater 1985, 158, 187, 240).

Orwell's position is aimed at a flight mechanism inherent in the formulation of the "lesser evil." It is the constant temptation to make the "lesser" evil seem harmless and tolerable in the face of the "greater" and thus to negate it. The engaged Internationalists of the Spanish Civil War who, in the face of the "greater evil," namely the Fascist International, ignored the murderous purges within the left, thereby justified these purges indirectly. The Communist and other Interbrigadists who were able to see the same thing that Orwell had experienced in Barcelona and, unlike him (Slater 1985, 117-173), were silent on the matter, these leftists made politics. They helped to make a non-evil of the "lesser evil," to rid the world of it, but thus also helped perpetuate it.

In Brecht's political figure of discourse, Herr Keuner, the result of this mechanism becomes visible. Keuner has clear insight, but his analysis always serves him as a justification to do nothing. He is a "yes and no" man who is similar to Bert Brecht in many respects, whose silence vis-à-vis Stalinism contradicted his pronounced wisdom (Fuegi 1995, 612).

Politics always stands before the dilemma that the thought pattern of the "lesser evil" leads to a logical chain of consequences that, left unbroken, becomes a justification of this evil. Politics has to choose, on the one hand, between options, positions, and alternatives of action. It must set priorities, must categorize the conditions recognized as evil; it must evaluate the one evil as "greater," the other as "lesser." On the other hand, politics thus stands before the problem of having to come to terms with the part of reality evaluated as evil and negative, the "lesser evil," even if only for a short time, for reasons of limited practicability. But this "coming to terms with" can potentially become the temptation to transform it into a permanent acceptance.

Roosevelt acceptance of racial segregation makes sense in light of the consistent priority given to the victory over Hitler for which the internal alliance with the Democrats of the South could not be risked. Brecht's silence regarding Stalinism makes sense in light of the just as consistent priority given to the mobilization of all intellectual forces against fascism. This "necessity" can, however, all too easily become an arbitrary acceptance of self-limitation, an excuse for adaptation due to complacency. The "lesser evil" ceases to be viewed as an evil at all because it is accepted.

However his motivations may have changed between 1981 and 1989, Jaruzelski did not let the "lesser evil" defined and implemented in 1981 become a permanent situation. Martial law was lifted and Solidarity, along with the Polish democracy movement, progressed from being a repressed oppositional force to a half-legal one, to a fully sanctioned one, with which Jaruzelski held talks toward compromise in order to transform the system. Jaruzelski did not try to make the evil he practiced, dictatorship, permanent. He did not fall prey to the temptation to define the lesser evil as non-evil. Jaruzelski does not deny the evil of martial law and the quasi-Napoleonic variant of Communist dictatorship, or Communist dictatorship in general. Instead, he did away with it.

This removal of evil assumes the corresponding space for action. Jaruzelski had this beginning in 1985, and increasingly as time went on. What if, on the other hand, this space is lacking? What remains when there is not even minimal freedom for politics?

The Upper Austrian farmer Franz Jägerstätter found an exemplary response to this dilemma. In the sense of a martyr, he made a mark. In his decisive objection to the evil he recognized, National Socialist rule, he became a conscientious objector, although he knew that this would cause his immediate execution. And he held to this decision even against the counsel of his Church. The Church, that is, the Bishops who had come to an arrangement with this evil, saw themselves shamed by this willingness to be a martyr that came from a Christian motivation. The Church was caught having resigned in the face of evil and for that reason Jägerstätter would be prevented from his mark by the Church (Zahn 1964).

Jägerstätter was beheaded. The rule of National Socialism suffered no recognizable consequences for this sign. But Jägerstätter could also not have influenced this rule in any other way. The totalitarian system had removed any possibility for political action on his part. But through his decision not to come to an arrangement, unlike the Bishops, he forced an analytical reflectiveness. He became an annoyance for those who had come to an arrangement. The analysis of his decision made obvious the corruption that is the unavoidable result of a certain unbroken chain of deductions from the concept of the "lesser evil." At some point when an evil is categorized again and again as lesser, the dimension of "lesser" becomes an excuse for the resigned acceptance of this evil. If it makes no sense to take action against National Socialism, when one's own arrangement for survival is declared and perpetuated as the lesser evil, then one is playing the game of totalitarian dictatorship.

Not that Jägerstätter's behavior can serve as an example to all those living under dictatorship. But Jägerstätter demonstrates that there can be something besides resigned acceptance in the face of absolute evil. And Jägerstätter demonstrated what can clearly be called moral leadership.

18 On the Longing for William Tells and Robin Hoods

Italy, Japan, and Switzerland as Exceptions — The Invention of Heroes — Leadership as Spectacle — Real Functions of Monarchies

In his memoirs, Henry Kissinger describes many personal meetings from his years as National Security Adviser (1969-1973) and Secretary of State (1973-1977) during which he helped form the politics of the U.S. as superpower and thus world politics. Helmut Schmidt surfaces here, as do Valery Giscard d'Estaing, Edward Heath, Andrei Gromyko, Mao Zedong, Zhou Enlai: individuals who, like Metternich or Bismarck or Palmerston before them, made history.

Kissinger's portrayals of the representatives of two major U.S. allies are pale in comparison — those of Japan and Italy. He even makes fun of the Italians a bit when he writes that when in Rome, he was never sure whether Mssrs. Moro, Rumor, Colombo and Andreotti were meeting with him in their momentary capacities as Foreign Minister or Prime Minister, so interchangeable were the roles and individuals.

Of Moro, Kissinger remembers primarily that he tended to fall asleep during conversations with him, Kissinger: "... so that I considered it a success to keep him awake" (Kissinger 1979, 101).

Kissinger tried to understand the political culture of Italy: Italian Prime Ministers were not leaders or men with far-reaching executive powers. Their interest, like that of the respective Foreign Minister, was directed almost solely toward Italian domestic policy because it had to be in order to keep their basis of legitimation. "Decisions were made by a consensus that included many people not in the government" (ibid.).

Regarding Japan, Kissinger recalled the alacrity with which changes in the personnel of the Japanese political elite were effected. Hardly had he become accustomed to the name of the Japanese Prime Minister when he was replaced by another from the depths of the governing Liberal Democratic Party.

Japan's political culture is a mixture of Emperor-mythos and real, political anonymity, that is, of de-personalization often difficult to understand for those accustomed to the European tradition of orientation toward individuals. "The hardest thing for us to grasp was that the extraordinary Japanese decisions were produced by leaders who prided themselves on their anonymous style. To be sure, there were great prime ministers. But they worked unobtrusively, conveying in their bearing that their policies reflected the consensus of a society, not the idiosyncrasy of an individual" (Kissinger 1979, 324).

In other words, Japan's politicians presented themselves as the ideal democrats whose decisions reflected not their own personal interests, but those of the society they represented. In light of such a political culture it is, of course, difficult for those who think in terms of "great men," not to be astounded at such deep cultural differences.

Japan and Italy are the success stories of democracy. As delayed empires with pretensions to being superpowers in the first half of the century, they slid into a phase of expansionist foreign policy and were, after their defeat in World War II, democratized from top to bottom, like Germany. During the time in which Kissinger did not know quite what to do with the political elite of Japan and Italy, due to the lack of a central figure such as Adenauer or De Gaulle, Japan was already the second-ranked economic power and, according to most of the economic indicators, Italy had surpassed Great Britain. For decades, both countries had been ruled by a hegemonic party: the Democrazia Cristiana in Italy ruled in permanent coalition with other smaller parties and in Japan, the Liberal Democrats ruled. Both parties in Italy and Japan consisted of an alliance of cliques — fractions or "correnti" in Italy — and the primary interest of the party and thus of the government was the security of a balance within the party (La Palombara 1987, 122-125; Richardson, Flanagan 1984, 100-106).

This sort of political thinking in terms of balance had its price and led then to the almost simultaneous fall of both ruling parties in Japan in 1993 and in Italy in 1994. What they had in common was the structure of balance, quite similar to that of Switzerland. Contrary to the founding myth of William Tell, Switzerland had found its way to a unique stability characterized by de-personalization. A democracy without a central role for a head of government or other leader, with a collective decision-making process in which every participant in the Federal Council stands and acts not only for him- or herself, not only for his or her party, but in the sense of a complex "amicabilis compositio," also for his or her linguistic group, his or her religious community, and his or her canton (Lehmbruch 1967, Steiner 1974).

Political cultures and systems with this sort of orientation to balance tend toward a largely de-personalized political viewpoint. Most attentive observers of current events know that in 1960 the

Chancellor of the Federal Republic of Germany was Konrad Adenauer and the President of the French Republic was Charles De Gaulle; also that John F. Kennedy was elected President of the United States that same year. But who knows the names of the Japanese or the Italian Prime Minister in 1960, or the Federal President of Switzerland for that matter?

During Secretary of State Kissinger's era, Japan and Italy were, like Switzerland, exceptions to the rule of democracy. In the rule, personality dominates, not de-personalization. The hallmark of concrete political systems is not the lack but the presence of central political persons, of leaders.

Such a de-personalization works against the trend analyzed under the rubric "New Politics" (Polsby 1983; Plasser 1987, 73f.). Individuals practice leadership, particularly as transmitted by the mass media, separated from "old politics," that is, from parties and parliaments, bureaucracies and organized interest groups. Ross Perot and Silvio Berlusconi stand for this trend to reconstruct the quality of leadership that has been lost by democracy.

The demands hidden behind this trend are characterized by the use, even the exploitation of a certain naiveté. A democratically elected leader who communicates with his "people" via the media and who thereby obtains confirmation for his policies conveys an unrealistically limited conception of politics.

Leadership as a marketing strategy is reduced, by and large, to a symbol. New Politics creates a type of leader who removes himself from Max Weber's categories of "bureaucratic" and "charismatic" leadership. The leader of New Politics is not a political producer but is himself a product; no creator of history but a personalized function in order to produce political legitimation.

Murray Edelman describes the necessity of developing new concepts in light of this new leader who acts symbolically, having himself become a symbol. Such a conception of leadership would no longer describe the capacities and potential of a single individual to choose freely between political options; leadership is rather the product of plebiscitary applause: "the willingness of followers to follow" defines the leader of New Politics (Edelman 1985, 73).

In other words, charisma as the quality attributed to and demanded of the leader is what the addressees of the charismatic leader think it is; leadership is determined not by the individual but by the people's approval of him. It is not the political substance of leadership that determines its quality but rather the ability to represent such a quality in a credible manner. Charisma and leadership become qualities of representation. Leadership is a spectacle that is not recognized as such.

Leadership in democracy is thus a product of a need and must, for that reason, be considered accordingly by a political system that must satisfy needs since it is a democracy. This need can be so pre-adolescent as to demand a person on whom to project fears and desires. It is a real need and therefore constitutive.

This need misses the point of the reality of complex politics, but it exists, and for that reason, must be "subjectively" fulfilled, if it cannot be "objectively" satisfied. Leadership thus becomes a surrogate for what it cannot give; an opiate that deceives with a situation that cannot correspond to reality. Leadership becomes a political drug whose effectiveness is found in its entertainment value.

Not far into his presidency, John F. Kennedy had to learn that the space within which he had to make decisions (which, as a political insider before the election, he had believed to have correctly estimated) was much more limited than he had expected. Restrictions on foreign policy, domestic considerations and particularly the constant attention to opinion polls in the interests of re-election limited the options available to the President. And so he fell deeper into the Vietnam debacle (Halberstam 1972), worked rather timidly on civil rights legislation and, above all, monitored his own popularity. In addition there were, of course, the checks and balances of Congress provided for in the Constitution that further limited his power, but above all, the informal power of the economic decision-making centers that were not vulnerable to the vagaries of direct democratic election.

Not even New Politics can change the constitutionality of checks and balances or the connection to the political market. But New Politics propagates the illusion of the democratically elected politician's personal freedom to act. And evidently the propagation of this illusion confronts a deep-seated need: a collective memory of the sagas of the heroic Robin Hood and the brave William Tell.

With these limitations, the loss of politics veiled but also cemented by New Politics become clear. The loss of politics in the sense of the removal of options is, after all, with regard to the possibilities for decision-making on the part of the political elite, inherent in democracy: The leaders interested in re-election orient themselves toward the givens of the political marketplace. This reduction of politics is, however, not only conceded, but also optically reversed. Leaders who are steered by opinion polls and transmitted electronically to the electorate are stylized and sold as lonely heroes, as individuals who make important decisions that influence history and who have to perform Herculean tasks that the very welfare of their electorate depends upon.

Through its longing for individualized heroism, the "people" falls into the anti-democratic trap. For the loss of politics that is inherent in democracy with regard to the elite, is, of course, structurally and fundamentally, not really a loss as regards voters. According to the model of liberal democracy, they can make decisions regarding content and personnel, they can act politically in the sense of the logic of the lesser evil. But the illusory aspect of the longing for heroes robs them of this possibility and they delegate their political role, that is, the role in which they make decisions, to a ghostly image.

It matter little that, in times of developed democracy, neither the electoral basis of a Robin Hood nor the philosophy of a William Tell ("The strong man is most powerful when alone") enjoys any sort of justification. "The people" wants to see power personalized and it wants to see heroes: John F. Kennedy as Sir Lancelot embodies this projection; John F. Kennedy as the man hopelessly entangled in the drama of Vietnam, as a man driven by his own strategy for re-election, is the opposite reality.

With its longing for heroes, "the people" accepts politics as façade. It demands leadership and thus, in democracy, is served leadership. It matters little that this form of leadership is a construct of symbolic politics. Yet the façade-like quality that accompanies New Politics' tendency toward personality reduces the possibilities for recognizing real politics. The complex division of labor within political decision-making processes is overly demanding of the possibilities for perception and control on the part of those called to participate in a democracy. Thus, they ask for simpler fare: they ask for a leader. He shows them that political decisions are made, and the very course of history determined, by a few great men.

But because very different acts of heroism are expected and demanded of the fictive heroes, since they have to address very different interests, the heroes of New Politics tend to promise all things to all people. The American Presidency, in which monarchal and thus pre-democratic myths are concentrated, suffers from the overly demanding role of the publicly elected mock heroes: "All Things to All Men" (Hodgson 1980). These myths contrast sharply with the inability of the non-hero living in the White House to conduct politics due to the limitations placed on him by the system of checks and balances. The result of this discrepancy is that the heroes are forced into theatrical gestures that simulate leadership when leadership cannot really take place.

The Constitution of Japan offers a partial remedy to the dilemma of existing democracy in which leadership is constantly demanded but which democracy itself cannot allow. The Japanese Constitution defined by the U.S., that is, by Douglas MacArthur, indirectly continued the abstract concept of "kokutai," the thought of a highly symbolic authority personified in the Emperor. Unlike the Meiji Constitution of 1889, the Constitution of 1946 gives the Emperor only such powers as accrue to a monarch in a parliamentary system. In the sense of Walter Bagehot, the Emperor has no longer to be efficient, but only dignified. The power to control the government is invested in the parliament.

But in political praxis, nothing much has changed vis-à-vis the Meiji Constitution (Richardson/Flanagan 1984, 36-39; Katzenstein 1996, 11-14). The Emperor did not create concrete governmental policy even under the Meiji Constitution. Feudal cliques ruled de facto in the name of the Emperor. Since the Constitution of 1946, democratically elected cliques rule in Japan. Both before and after 1946 in Japan, the Emperor had the task of functioning as an integral symbol of the Japanese nation ("kokutai") and in this sense, lending the democratically elected government an additional sort of pre-democratic legitimation.

The Emperor takes on the mystical, pre-democratic expectations that weigh upon the American President since the Constitution was adopted. The Japanese Constitution is therefore characterized by a particular sort of division of labor. The need for non-routine leadership and for heroism does not have to be satisfied by the parliament and by the parties because the Emperor is there to do this. Those who are actually governing need not trouble themselves with the paralyzing political spectacle of simulated leadership. They can dedicate themselves to the actual tasks at hand — political management and routine leadership. This is what disturbed Kissinger, the admirer of Metternich and Bismarck: the fact that the Japanese head of government and the foreign minister with whom he met, could not even demonstrate the theatrical gesture of simulated leadership. This burden was and is lifted from the Japanese political elite by the Emperor and the monarchy.

Common to both Emperor Hirohito and General Jaruzelski is that each, through his own doing, had to and wanted to surrender the authority he had acquired non-democratically. In August, 1945, the Emperor of Japan prevailed against the formidable resistance of the old, feudal cliques in order to bring about capitulation after Hiroshima and Nagasaki. He did this although it was clear to him that his role according to the Meiji Constitution would be over and that the monarchy as such was in danger. In early 1989, Jaruzelski began with the democratization of Poland, also against formidable resistance within his own party and within the Warsaw Pact countries, although he knew that this was the beginning of the end, not only of his dictatorship but of his power in general. Nevertheless, Hirohito preserved the monarchy and thus the symbolic function that distracts from the need for pre-modern and pre-democratic political patterns from those who govern. Jaruzelski preserved nothing from the old system.

In a Republic, such a division of labor cannot take hold, and in non-traditional monarchies, in newly created monarchies, such a division of labor would be unlikely to develop. It needs mythos, and mythos needs tradition. Japan is the exception to the rule — an exception that can still find a certain, partial correspondence in other monarchies that are simultaneously traditional and parliamentary. Without such a division of labor, however, the political class is left with the task of satisfying the atavistic needs of its voters.

Still today, under the sign of New Politics, politicians act in the manner of the man who brings freedom to his people through the arrow in Gessler's heart, who restores "justice" in Sherwood Forest through a clever redistribution policy (read: robbery). Still today (or better: now more than ever), the Teflon heroes ride the electronic pony of political acting and when they do it well, the audience does not notice that everything is happening only on screen.

This works until some naive outcry destroys the fictions. The fact that the Emperor has no clothes must be acknowledged while invoking reality and against the professionally transmitted deceptions. To acknowledge that the Robin Hoods and William Tells are not real persons but projections requires a view of politics that is free from the archaic need to submit and project.

As long as this liberated view of politics does not exist, the p.r. industry will produce heroes and the mask of one hero will compete with the mask of another hero to be the voice of the sovereign. He may not have the real opportunity to choose the "lesser evil" among the evils existing in his social realm, but he will entertain.

19 On the Necessity of Becoming a Parvenu

The Identities forced on Rosa Luxemburg — Pariah against One's Will, Parvenu as a Necessity — The Function of Zionism — "Black" and "White" — Benjamin Disraeli

Rosa Luxemburg made history: as a member of the leftist, anti-war wing of the German Social Democrats, as one of the founders of the Communist Party of Germany, and as a victim of the soldierly terror that restored "order" in a pre-fascist manner in early 1919.

To the men in uniform who murdered Luxemburg on January 16, 1919, she was not only a revolutionary, but also a woman, a Jew, and a Slav. The motivation of those uniformed men who fought against all manner of revolutionaries at the end of the First World War in Germany was characterized by misogynistic male fantasies, anti-Semitism, and anti-Slavicism (Theweleit 1980).

These identities — woman, Jew, Pole — were for the political consciousness that Luxemburg presented publicly either secondary considerations or components of a world of which she wanted no part. Her international credo opposed a specific Jewish sensibility. And so in 1917, she wrote to a friend, "What do you want with the specifically Jewish pains? The poor victims of the rubber plantations are just as close to me" (Nettl 1967, 827). She disregarded the fact that she was viewed and evaluated as a Jew by her environment: she refused a specifically Jewish identity.

She also struggled against her Slavic identity. Within the International she rejected any support of a Polish claim to national self-determination. At the Party Congress of the SPD in Munich in 1902, she was the most radical speaker of the party wing who, under no circumstances, wanted autonomy for the Poles within the Social Democratic Party (Nettl 1967, 180f.).

This Internationalist so unwilling to accept any sort of nationalism was born into a bourgeois Jewish family in Zamosc near Lublin in the Russian part of Galicia (West Ukraine) in 1870 or 1871. The national language of her country of birth was Russian; the inhabitants of the area in which she spent her childhood spoke Ukrainian, Polish, or Yiddish. But Luxemburg wanted to be international and for that reason she became a German. Under no circumstances did she want to be a Jew; was she not a Marxist?

As a Marxist, she saw in the problematic of an identity defined in religious or ethnic-national terms nothing but a distraction from the class struggle that had to be fought on an international level. And as a Marxist, she saw only a "secondary contradiction" in the contradiction between men and women. The fact that she was vulnerable to three forms of discrimination — as a woman, as a Jew, and as a Slav, and the fact that these externally assigned identities would accompany her to her violent death, only seemed to strengthen her resolve.

The identities that Luxemburg repressed were closely connected with "lesser evils": The national, linguistic, and cultural repression of Poles in Germany and in Russia had to remain in the background of her political engagement because it was less important; it was a lesser evil than the repression of the proletariat. The problem of the secondary status of women in the state and in society would have to wait until the victory of socialism could bring a solution, more or less on its own. She answered the denial of German (or Russian or Polish) identity for Jews for reasons of anti-Semitism by claiming a German identity for herself, not by attempting to recognize and fight the root cause of anti-Semitism.

By categorizing "evils," even those that comprised her own identity, Rosa Luxemburg made herself free for politics. She could not struggle against all the evils of the world simultaneously. And for that reason she could not identify with all the roles as victim that she could potentially assume. She had to set political priorities, and thus also personal priorities. For that reason, the Slavic and Jewish elements in her had to be repressed; the feminine had to step back. Or was it the reverse? Because she set aside the feminine, the Jewish, and the Slavic, she could fight for the international proletariat.

In her discussions with Eduard Bernstein, Rosa Luxemburg showed herself not the least bit enamored of his evolutionary and reformatory ideas. She polemically rejected Bernstein's revisionism, which was a pleading for entering the institutions of the existing state and a gradual change of capitalism through social reforms; that is, a pleading for a politics of the lesser evil and thus for politics generally. For her, Bernstein's theory was "a bogged down social theory, bogged down by the vulgar economic theory of capitalism" (Luxemburg 1970, 36). But one could also describe Luxemburg's repression of her own Slavic and Jewish identity and her lack of sensitivity for the "women's question" as vulgar and economic. Once she had chosen a political orientation, she did not perceive what might have distracted her from it. She did not want to see what might have precluded her economic fixation on what would later be called the "main contradiction."

Luxemburg's and Bernstein's theories were related to one another. Each had to set priorities and neglect possibilities for social perception and political strategies in order to be free for a certain, concrete politics. Each had to start from a necessarily simplified categorization. They each unavoidably helped to achieve legitimation for existing evils. Luxemburg's almost aggressive ignoring of Polish interests, for instance, helped German Social Democracy to conform to and thus strengthen, the dominant German nationalism. By rejecting Polish nationalism, the internationalist indirectly and unintentionally aided and abetted German nationalism. The fact that Wilhelm II was able to recognize only Germans and no parties, particularly not the Social Democrats, was therefore the indirect result of this internationalist position that, de facto, benefited German nationalism. It was to be Rosa Luxemburg's particular tragedy to be one of the victims of this Wilhelmine, and especially post-Wilhelmine, German nationalism.

Hannah Arendt did not define herself as a Marxist. As a woman born in Germany, whose mother tongue was German, she possessed a self-defined Jewish identity from which she developed a critical position vis-à-vis Zionism (Arendt 1989). A generation after Luxemburg, she had to come to terms with what was naively and insensitively termed the "Jewish question" before the Holocaust, as well as with what, in turn, was naively and insensitively termed the "women's question."

Hannah Arendt studied Rosa Luxemburg with critical sympathy. And she studied the woman who absolutely did not want to see a problem in being a woman: "Her distaste for the women's emancipation movement ... was significant ... She was an outsider, not only because she was and remained a Polish Jew in a country she disliked and a party she came soon to despise, but also because she was a woman" (Arendt 1968, 44f.).

Not although, but because she was an outsider, Rosa Luxemburg ignored — in her theories, in her demands, in the justifications of her concrete politics — precisely those factors that made her an outsider. She did not want to accept the fact that her arguments would be judged on that basis and that as far as her environment was concerned, she was a Jew, a Pole, and a woman. She did not want to accept what she was burdened with — being and remaining a pariah.

What wounds must this ascent from the existence as pariah have brought; how much must Rosa Luxemburg have felt and suffered in the knowledge that for others, she never stopped being a woman, a

Jew, and a Pole; that her environment forced her to take on certain identities from which she wanted to escape. But she evidently saw no other way to act politically. She did not want to be a pariah in order to be political.

Hannah Arendt places her protagonist Rahel Varnhagen "between pariah and parvenu" (Arendt 1995, 186-200). The temptation to be a parvenu, to which Rahel Varnhagen also felt vulnerable, is the temptation to please and to conform; to be acceptable to the status quo and, above all, to those in power. For the Jew Varnhagen, this temptation is nothing other than assimilation: to leave behind her particularity, her uniqueness as a Jew, to change from one identity to another.

Arendt characterized this tendency as follows: "Whoever has the decisive will to reach the top, to arrive, must, early on, become accustomed to anticipating the level to be reached in the dizziness of voluntary recognition; must, early on, take care to satisfy with the blind obedience that is demanded; must always act as if he were willingly achieving as master what is expected of servants and subordinates" (Arendt 1995, 186).

In other words, the fate of the parvenu is that of the social climber. In order to deceive others, he must first deceive himself. In order to complete the leap to the top, he needs the illusion of having already arrived there. He cannot admit, especially not to himself, the crass inequality he is trying to overcome individually.

Succumbing to the temptation of the parvenu is a prerequisite for the individual capability to engage in politics. This is particularly clear when the alternative to the parvenu become evident — the pariah. The parvenu must lie in order to enter into and ascend within society, particularly when one has the almost insurmountable flaw of being Jewish (not only in Varnhagen's era). The rejection of the role as parvenu, that is, the resistance against this temptation means remaining an outsider, not integrated into, but excluded from society as a pariah. The pariah is free from the desire to be a social climber. And for that reason, the pariah can be "honest."

In order to practice leadership, conformity is more or less demanded of a politician; he must be, more or less, a parvenu; he cannot allow himself to be pariah and nothing else. This is, of course, not necessarily the case for "transforming leadership" because a revolutionary can begin as an extreme outsider. But it is absolutely the case for "transactional leadership," for the sort of political leadership possible in stable democracies (Burns 1978, 257-397). The leader cannot bypass the development of interests, cannot disregard the considerations and needs that he purports to represent. He must respect what exists, at least the part of the political demand that he wants to fulfill with his supply. He must see to it that he is respected. And yet he cannot allow the suspicion to arise that he is only a parvenu. He needs the appearance of distance or else he does not do justice to the need for charisma. He can have no charisma that makes him appear too different from the others with regard to his political substance, particularly his own constituency. But he must have charisma in order to differentiate himself from the style of the others who offer political representation. Thus, he cannot cut off all possibilities of withdrawal and escape into a pariah existence.

With his decision on December, 1981, Jaruzelski became a pariah in Poland, the country whose dominant attitude was expressed by the democracy movement that Jaruzelski then violently suppressed. Jaruzelski's reference system in 1981 was, however, not that of Polish society and the Polish democracy movement, but of the Soviet Union and the Warsaw Pact in which Poland was inextricably bound up during the Cold War era. In the face of this system, Jaruzelski was a parvenu. He acted within the framework that the Brezhnevs, the Honeckers, and Husaks had allotted him. As changes occurred within this system, beginning with Gorbachev's reforms, Jaruzelski as General Dictator was able to infuse his actions with a different political content. Being a parvenu during the Brezhnev era was different from being a parvenu during the Gorbachev era. And for that reason, Jaruzelski could not avoid introducing democracy in Poland. For that reason, he was able to break out of his role as pariah in Poland. Because he was successful here as the initiator of the round table discussions of 1989 he made himself superfluous.

For a large segment of the Polish population, Jaruzelski remains a pariah, the suppresser of the democracy movement. For her environment, too, Rahel Varnhagen remained a pariah because she remained a Jew. She could not leave her identity behind because the anti-Jewish surroundings did not allow it. The attempts to conform are always limited by the degree to which those to whom conformity refers are willing to accept integration. The parvenu, who as such is not accepted as one of the group, attempts in vain to conform. He remains a pariah and remains incapable of politics.

This is the actual theme of Zionism: that a specifically Jewish reference system would have to be created as a response to the refusal of the anti-Semitic environment to accept Jews who are prepared to assimilate and integrate: the Jewish state or the longing for it. To this end, Jews were and are able to secure their individual capacity for political action, they may become parvenus and also be accepted as such. The Jewish state is a reaction to the rejection of a general human willingness to enter into and ascend within society. The Jewish state gave and gives those who have not been allowed to and thus do not wish to escape from their Jewish identity the possibility to leave behind the role of the pariah.

The anti-Semitism of modern times gave the Jews no possibility to "opt out"; no chance to leave behind their Jewish identity and, for instance, through baptism, stop being Jews. Anti-Semitism forced Jews to their Jewishness: "We have seen that it is not the character of the Jew that makes anti-Semitism, but the anti-Semite who creates the Jew" (Sartre 1960, 184). Anti-Semitism took from the Jews the chance to define themselves through conformity, as parvenus. Driven back to their existence as pariahs, they developed the solution to their identity problems: Zionism. It became the reference system of those who identified as Jews. As Zionists or non-Zionists Jews could now determine their own identity. And within this self-created system, they could choose between the role of the parvenu and the role of the pariah.

In this way, Zionism opened the door to politics. As the sovereign player of Jewish politics, the state of Israel gave the political strivings of people who identified as Jewish a purpose and a frame of reference — whether in attraction or rejection.

Hannah Arendt, who argues with such understanding for the difficult position between parvenu and pariah, accused Zionism of working with simplifications. In an article published in 1945, she turned against the definition of Zionism as a sovereign Jewish state. Zionism should rethink "all of its obsolete doctrines." Further, "It will not be easy to save the Jews or to save Palestine in the 20th century ... If the Zionists hold onto their sectarian ideology and continue in their short-sighted 'realism' they will ruin the small chance that small peoples have in this world" (Arendt 1989, 59).

The option for the Jewish state was, for the consciously Jewish Arendt, too oriented toward an either-or situation and was not dialectical enough. She saw in this option an all too clear and thus simplistic decision: for the acceptance of the pariah position in the Diaspora and thus for the rejection of the parvenu position in an environment whose majority was not Jewish. In order to achieve for Jews the capacity to act politically, Zionism wanted to renounce the capability to act politically in a primarily non-Jewish society; it wanted to literally move out of this society.

It is the dialectical tension between the roles of pariah and parvenu that constitute this capability to act politically. If all people are not only allowed to be parvenus, but really are; if no one sees him- or herself in a pariah role any longer, then the capacity for politics is destroyed. It is the "longing for the Brave New World" that stands for the negation of this dialectic (Büchele 1993). In Aldous Huxley's negative utopia, people are distinguished from one another in social terms, but through the corresponding programming, the consciousness that their differences could have something to do with pariah status is taken from them. For that reason, there are no potential parvenus who want to break free from their pariah status. Yet for the same reason, the actual hallmark of this "end of history" is the freedom from politics. With the destruction of the pariah role on the level of consciousness, the parvenu role dies as well.

The essence of utopias is the destruction of and the renunciation of politics. In Hobbes' chaotic original society there is only the struggle of everyone against everyone else — there is neither system nor rule. In Rousseau's idyllic original society the lamb lies down next to the lion; conflicts do not exist, nor does politics. In Marx' Communist final society, all people can live according to their needs; there is no shortage of goods and no problem of distribution and therefore no need for politics.

The utopias are the idea of the absence of politics — sometimes, as with Rousseau and Marx, in a positive sense and sometimes, as with Hobbes and Huxley, in a negative sense. They are fantasies about overcoming social difference and the social division of labor. In their positive or negative perfection, they take one's possibility to opt for this or that: The people of the "Brave New World" do not believe that they could choose between alternatives, between several evils. In this way, the utopias are also fantasies of overcoming the tension between the roles of the pariah and the parvenu.

The transition from pariah to parvenu is the beginning of politics. This was and is true for all those who, within the framework of the American civil rights movement, worked for legal, then political and social equality for blacks in a society dominated by white Americans.

As editor of the Pittsburgh Courier, Robert L. Vann, an Afro-American who worked for a time in the administration of Franklin D. Roosevelt as an adviser in the Attorney General's office (Franklin 1980, 391), began a campaign in 1938 for the introduction of black troops into all branches of the U.S. Armed Forces, although this would have to be achieved at the price of segregation, that is, at the price of increasing the separation of the races within the Armed Forces. The

NAACP, the most prominent and, at least at the time, the most influential civil rights organization, spoke out against these plans. For the NAACP, racial segregation was a greater evil than the exclusion of all black Americans from all somewhat attractive military positions.

The position that Vann took prevailed. In the time preceding the Second World War, the U.S. Armed Forces began recruiting blacks more aggressively and also gave them more interesting tasks. This policy was continued after the introduction of the draft in 1940. But racial segregation continued to exist in the Army and in the Navy. Black units led a ghetto existence: black officers were only there to command black soldiers.

Perhaps the most spectacular example of the results of this policy were the black graduates of the Army's Flight School in Tuskegee, Alabama. Black pilots were trained in a closed unit that flew successful missions on the front and fought for a democracy that continued to deny them civil rights. Not until 1948 did President Truman end racial segregation in the American Armed Forces.

The pilots of Tuskegee stand for a strategic dilemma: in order to take a step in the direction of respecting their civil rights, the Afro-Americans had to decide whether they wanted to make politics on the ground of the existing society that was unfair or whether, while respecting (or rather, accepting) certain rules of racism in the framework of a racist society, they wanted to take a step in the direction they recognized as right. Should they become parvenus and conform somewhat to racist society in order to build a lever with which to overcome some of the most burning forms of discrimination?

The politics of small steps in a society recognized as unfair legitimates it, on the one hand: whoever begins such politics engages with this society as a parvenu and becomes a part of it, even a part of its contradictions. Whoever renounces such politics and insists instead on his or her existence as a pariah prevents the hostile, discriminatory society and its political order from achieving legitimation from the behavior of those discriminated against, but he or she also renounces the chances to approach those levers that make politics possible in the first place, even a politics of change.

Robert L. Vann could also have cited Karl Popper. The politics of seizing the moment, which also risks corruption by the order being challenged, corresponds to the piecemeal engineering, the step-by-step changing of society through a pragmatic approach to politics. Popper holds up this pattern as a strategic model against the deterministic designs from Plato to *Marx* that endanger freedom (Popper 1970). It is a recommendation for taking the risk of the parvenu instead of remaining in the prophetic self-righteousness of the pariah.

Both are needed, however: the parvenu concretizes what the principal contradiction of the pariah thematizes. It is the contradiction and the resistance that actualize the problem and the consciousness bound up with it that the parvenu can use for his pragmatic politics of change through conformity. The U.S. civil rights movement needed the politics of a W.E.B. Du Bois, who represented the principle of moral accusation against racism; it needed the politics of a Booker T. Washington, who engaged with this extremely unfair, segregated and openly discriminatory society. It needed the pariah Du Bois and the parvenu Washington. It needed the objector and the one who had to let himself be called "Uncle Tom" (Aptheker, vol. IV, 1951-1974).

Benjamin Disraeli, who came from a prominent family of Sephardic Jews, became a key figure of British imperialism in the 19th century. He is the prototype of the parvenu. His father, Isaac, was a recognized literary scholar. Benjamin Disraeli was not only to become a successful politician, but also a successful novelist. In 1832, at the age of 28, he began his political career with the Tories, the Conservative Party, which he was to recreate as a socially engaged party. But one impediment would have stood in his way if his father had not known how to get rid of it. "Disraeli suffered from a potentially fatal handicap. He was a Jew" (Blake 1969, 10).

His father had taken care of things in time. In 1817, he had had his children baptized and accepted into the Anglican Church. The anti-Semitism which was, at that time, primarily religious in nature, no longer stood in the way of his son's career. In 1837 he was elected to the House of Commons. In his novels and in his politics he stood for the opening of the establishment to the "social question" and succeeded in changing the image of the Conservative Party as solely for the nobility. In 1868 he was, for a short time, Prime Minister, only to have to yield to his liberal opponent William Gladstone. In 1874 Disraeli returned to the head of government for six years.

During these six years he secured British hegemony over Egypt and the Suez Canal and expanded various social laws. In 1876 he was responsible for Queen Victoria receiving the title "Empress of India." In the following year he, in turn, received the title "Earl of Beaconsfield." Great Britain had forgiven him for being, originally, a Jew. And he had successfully made politics for Britain's sovereignty over the seas. But the parvenu Disraeli was never totally free from his memories as a pariah. His advocacy of an aristocratic world view, expanded by social components, made the social climber Disraeli acceptable in the eyes of the ruling class, but the mistrust remained. For Gladstone, for example, he was a man "influenced by Judaic sympathies" whose hate was directed toward "Christian liberty" (Blake 1969, 600f.).

Disraeli himself had never been able to overcome the thinking that characterized British (and European) imperialism as well as Nazism and thus the biologically-based anti-Semitism, the thinking in categories of "natural" origin, in categories of racism. Houston Stewart Chamberlain, a native Briton, a German for reasons of a strange desire, a predecessor of Hitlerian thought, thus referred to Disraeli: One should "learn from Disraeli that the entire meaning of Jewry lies in the purity of its race, this alone affords it strength and longevity ..." (Chamberlain 1922, 297).

The parvenu was thrown back to his pariah role and made a star witness for the fact that there could be no real successful escape from this role. The parvenu could achieve as much as he wanted for British imperialism, he would still remain a pariah, at least for those who were determined to hold fast at all costs to the division of people into "natural" groups, that is, races, with the result of Auschwitz already visible with Chamberlain. Ultimately, the parvenu was denied that which he had striven for with all his energy: to be able to define himself and liberate himself from the definitions of others.

20 An Impossible Encounter — The Second

"What is the subject of our thought? Experience! Nothing else!"

(Hannah Arendt in Hill 1979, 308)

"With all due respect, that is a very flat statement. Either I have to evaluate it as banal school wisdom along the lines of counting the number of angels who can fit on the head of a pin, or as a challenge to everything that will bring us further in the direction of human dignity, in the direction of socialism — yes, I maintain it in spite of everything. By almost fearfully emphasizing that all certain knowledge comes from experience, you are doing the business of those seeking the holy grail of the status quo. Should the statement that Coca Cola is the beverage most often drunk today — something which we can easily call a fact of experience — really have any other value than to raise the stock value of Coca Cola?"

"You are simplifying, Rosa, and you know it, of course. But in one thing you are right. I am cautious, very cautious with statements that promise us everything under the protective cloak of scientific procedure. I am distrustful of promises with the window trimmings of science. I distance myself from the danger of ideologization more decisively than you, of course. And I prefer to accept being suddenly called a 'conservative.' I prefer the behaviorists' statements often rightly dismissed as banal to the flaming prognoses of secularized prophets, even if they decorate their prophecies with footnotes. When an angel-counting colleague determines that in 1972 the average U.S. Senator made 11.75 phone calls daily, that may be banal but luckily it is also harmless. If someone, on the other hand — perhaps under the protection of that foolish academic freedom — proclaims that capitalism will soon collapse, then this is perhaps not banal, but by no means harmless because, under certain circumstances, it produces 'false consciousness.' And you must have some understanding for this category, besides the fact that every statement about the imminent collapse of the capitalist system, which has, after all, shown itself to be particularly long-lived, is utter nonsense."

"All due respect to your cautiousness, Hannah. I understand that you have developed sympathy for the criticism of ideologies in the post-fascist and post-Stalinist era. I am in agreement with you that all statements must be tested for their groundedness in experience. I detest idle talk that pretends that statements of belief are really statements of experience. But this methodological code cannot be everything, however important it may be. It is the foundation, like a semantic basis. Creativity has to be able to build on it

— *social creativity that can and should stem not only from experience, but from emotion. You yourself said somewhere that you are particularly critical toward capitalism precisely because you are not a Marxist. Now then, what is the result? Spartacus did not analyze the world, he tried to change it. And Spartacus is not some bigwig's ideological mouthpiece. He has rightly become the prototype of the social Prometheus. You reject all of that when you insist on your 'experience and nothing but experience.'"*

"I will ignore for a moment the fact that regimes that misused you, dear Rosa, as an ideological mouthpiece, likewise used Spartacus. And perhaps you are not personally guilty, or rather, you did not participate in the functionalization of Spartacus. But Spartacus as an historical figure and Prometheus as a mythological figure are each, of course, a part of knowledge stemming from experience, and it is just as true that the emotion of social protest and the, well, yes, the experience of suffering and pity are a part of what I mean by the concept of Spartacus. Experiential knowledge refers not only to counting the frequency of Senators' phone calls, but it also includes the economically and politically determined mass deaths in Ethiopia or Rwanda, like the terror that the shadows of our century's systems based on belief are still spreading. Yes, of course I take the sphere of belief seriously, but not in the intellectually dishonest mixture with the sphere of knowledge."

"Do you know what I really regret? That a sharp thinker such as yourself is stuck in the end, in academia, in the ivory tower with books. Just a short while before your death you, such a politically thinking person, were able to define yourself politically only in a negative way: You were never a socialist, you said, never a Communist, never a liberal. And then you added proudly and defiantly that you would never believe in progress ..."

"Yes, that was the conversation with Mary McCarthy and the others ..."

"In my view, you were already at that point when you reported on the Eichmann trial. Your criticism of the Jewish councils, of the corruptibility even of the victims — the next step is not far off and that can only be the challenge to direct action. When you accuse the Jewish collaborators of wanting to submit, then you are also saying what you actually had expected of them, namely, direct resistance. Otherwise your criticism makes no sense."

"That conclusion is by no means the only one. My criticism referred to the concrete situation, the fact that the politics of the Jewish councils in many cases caused people to ignore the possibilities for escape. The Jewish councils were only too often responsible for the victims behaving like lambs, and I'm not talking about the heroic gesture but about the possible variant of going underground, of evasion, of disappearing. Since I was not in this situation, I could not act. My personal rejection of direct political engagement the way you lived it, Rosa, is dependent on the situation, dependent on one's own *biography and is in no way a rejection of political engagement in general. On the contrary ..."*

"But that is probably the real difference between us: You backed off from direct involvement. And if it had been at the price of failure — a woman like you belonged in real praxis."

"I don't know whether I should feel honored, Rosa. But I am surprised. You are the woman who, more than anyone else, got directly 'involved' and you —excuse my directness — failed. For me, at least, you failed in a way that is very sympathetic. But you failed: The German Workers' Movement became even more fragmented through Spartacus and the Communist Party of Germany, the Republic became even weaker than it had to be, and the Leninist experiment, to which you were attracted but toward which you were not uncritical, thanks to your analytical capabilities, ultimately ended with Stalin. Your failure is naturally blurred by the heroism of your, I'd almost like to say, 'timely' death. And so none of us knows how you would have acted toward the Stalinization of the party you founded and what role you might have played in the final phase of the Weimar Republic. You were spared Stalinism and the business with Hitler, but I was not."

"Yet: I would not want to live without my praxis. We both know, of course, that our different backgrounds, even the age difference were decisive factors in our taking separate paths. For me, as a woman, the academic path was never a possibility, and for that reason, it was never a temptation for me. How would I have decided, if I had been born a generation later, with you? I don't know, but I can't imagine getting anything out of that Heideggerian bloatedness. And did I really fail so clearly in praxis? Did I not leave behind a piece of consciousness that remains? I am far from wanting to deny your books any effectiveness, and I know that you could probably say the same of me. But I had no other possibility as a Pole who did not want to be one, as a Jew who likewise tried to escape this designation, and as a Bolshevik who viewed the Communists who followed with less than full trust, as a woman who held that the class question was more important than the 'women's question.' With my praxis, which is difficult to survey even decades later, with my protest, with my imprisonment, my revolutionary pathos, and my revolutionary acts, I gave those in power enough to think about so that even the following generations of the oppressed profit from it."

"You were denied an academic career, or rather, you did not begin one against the resistance of your time. A political career was impossible for me and by that I mean political in the narrowest sense. How was I supposed to do that? Should I, as a student, have mounted the barricades for the Republic and against its enemies? Fundamentally speaking, I did just that — Günther Stern and I were at home in the Marxist milieu. But the time for legal participation was over quickly in Germany; and in exile the sectarian battles

*in the ditches were too repulsive. You know, I was soon influenced by
Koestler's image of the commissar ..."*

*"Oh, the one with the overzealousness of the convert, whom Franco's
prisons made into a propagandist for anti-Communism ..."*

*"Rosa, that borders on Comintern polemics. Koestler had a better sense
of real, existing socialism than you did ..."*

" ... which is really not too difficult!"

*" ... and the commissar whom he opposes to the yogi, this commissar
with his strategic dilemma says something about what I wanted to avoid.
Either this practitioner of revolution must subordinate his means to the end
— then his path will lead directly to Stalinism; or he sees his means as a part
of the end — but then he stops being effective as a revolutionary. That is why
I fail to see, even in hindsight, how any engagement for any groups in exile,
with the SAP or the Trotskyites or anyone else, had any effect whatsoever.
But that probably has to do with my personal situation. I felt like a
philosopher and for me, Jaspers was more a role model than, yes, who else?
Not even now can I think of a 'practitioner' as an alternative to Jaspers. Is
it coincidence that not one of the Germans in exile really stands up to critical
analysis? Or maybe one, Willy Brandt. But he was a true 'proletarian,' a
politician, a doer. That was simply not given to me. And the left was soon
burdened by what came to us from Moscow. Whoever says one couldn't have
seen what was coming, what was brewing there should read George Orwell's
'Homage to Catalonia.' Everything is there that, by 1938 at the latest, even
before that unholy alliance of those two who were so valuable to each other,
was obvious to all who wanted to see and not simply believe. That may be one
of the lasting differences between us: the ability to believe, which was clearly
possible for you, was foreign to me from the very beginning. And without
your Marxist beliefs, which you of course would never have described as such,
you would not have been able to survive being in custody in the Empire the
way you did. That was not given to me and at least in hindsight, I don't
regret it — with all due respect and yes, with love for your ability to achieve
this measure of political energy out of conviction."*

*"Of course, I don't know either how I would have acted. But I doubt
that the struggle in exile, whether in Spain or in the Soviet Union, can really
be dismissed in that way. I would presumably have ended up in the Hotel
Lux. No one can say whether my future path would have led to a Stalinist
camp, as it did for Margarete Buber. But I surely would have tried to
struggle against the fascist insanity. Your political effectiveness was bound
up with the years of relative peace. Your way of making politics by conveying
theoretical insights and thus by influencing people's thinking, would have
stood no chance under the sign of the international fight against fascism,
Hannah. And in spite of everything we know today, and perhaps always have*

known, beginning in 1939 the necessity of participating in the struggle would have been clear for me. No skepticism toward the terrible Georgian would have kept me from it."

"But Rosa, now you really disappoint me. Not that I have anything against your willingness to fight, but you simplify when you connect the year 1939 with an international front against fascism. In 1939, Stalin was more than prepared to applaud the spread of fascism. He was interested in the two imperialist empires being constantly at each others' throats. During the time of the 'imperialist war,' you would not have been able to call for the fight against the fascists without being excluded from the Communist Party in exile, being branded as a Trotskyite and, if you were within the domain of the Stalinist blood-hounds, being liquidated. As a founding member of the Communist Party of Germany you would, presumably, have been purged even earlier. You would scarcely have been offered an honorable grave in the Kremlin wall, as Clara Zetkin was. All due honor to anti-fascism, but it cannot be equipped with blindness."

"Admittedly, the period from 1939 to 1941 would have been difficult for me. But in 1941 at the latest, I would have had to choose, and I would have been able to. And for me, the choice would have been self-evident. Until the victory over fascism, I would have had to accept what had developed under Lenin's protection. In the face of the evils of this world, one must be able to make distinctions. At first, I could have accepted British colonialism temporarily, if I had been active in the anti-fascist alliance beginning in 1939 or 1941. In order to act politically we need a hierarchy — one of ends and one of evils."

"That is precisely why I am surprised that you advocate such an undifferentiated concept of fascism. Rosa, if you emphasize the necessity of weighing the various evils of society differently, then you cannot speak of fascism and mean National Socialism. That is the diction of the Seventh International Congress of Comintern. And today we know that its decisions were only reflections of Stalin's strategic interests; we know, too, that the rule of the NSDAP had a different dimension, one that was foreign to both Italian and Spanish fascism."

"Hannah, I know, of course, that you are talking about the Holocaust. I am aware that the historical facts have a specific language here. Only one element of the fascist regime progressed to the specific quality of mass murder of people whose only 'fault' was the coincidence of their birth — the Croatian and the Slovakian elements in addition to the German. I do not want to disregard this particularity. But what all forms of fascism, including the German, have in common is that a both inwardly and outwardly aggressive system based on the crisis of capitalism openly declared war against the Republic and particularly against the workers' movement."

"Well, what you say about outwardly directed aggression is, for example, something quite different for Franco's Spain. But what really disturbs me is the economics you still propound, which I am tempted to call vulgar. The fact that economic interests played a not insignificant role in the rise of Mussolini and Hitler is one point; the other is that the Marxist bad-weather theory falls short. If a capitalism stuck in crisis brings forth fascism with a certain logic, if, then, capitalism bears fascism within it, then the question remains: How did Franklin D. Roosevelt come to power with his more or less social democratic New Deal at the moment of deepest crisis for American capitalism?"

"Of course economics is not everything and I admit that the concept of political culture, a conception that came into being after my time, can surely say something about why the Anglo-Saxon democracies survived the crises of capitalism after 1929 without falling victim to the fascism inherent in them. But excuse me, Hannah: you act as if we were at the end of history, as if the results you used for your analysis of totalitarianism during the middle of the 20th century were the final conclusion of historical development. Are you really so certain that the U.S. will be immune to the temptation of fascism even in the future?"

"No, no, of course you're right, Rosa. The fact that we have no experience in it does not mean that we can exclude something — on the contrary. But I am not concerned with granting immunity to the liberal democracies of the West. I am concerned with spreading the methodology of our approach to explaining things. And in that regard I would like to return to Comintern's conception of fascism. If fascism is only one variant, the most aggressive one, of capitalism, then such a viewpoint negates the specific dynamics of the non-economic. This is exactly what is addressed in the concept of political culture. Social consciousness is more than just reflex, more than a superstructure of the dominant economic conditions. If we can't agree on that ..."

"Presumably we can. I also do not believe that the difference between a stable democratic system and a blindly fascist system is secondary simply because both build on a capitalist economy. But I am somewhat concerned that we are obstructing our desire for differentiated action due to our desire for differentiated analysis. And that's where my criticism of Western democracies begins — also, by the way, of theories in your tradition, Hannah. The entire attention is directed toward the course of political progress and toward its emergence; everything is 'politics.' But what the result of this procedure means for the men and women exposed to it — the policy — remains out of focus. Castro's Cuba is seen as an evil dictatorship because only one party exists. The fact that Castro's Cuba eliminated illiteracy within

the space of a few years and raised life expectancy to the highest in all of Latin America remains out of the picture."

"Here you have to distinguish between the opinion of the mass media and the analyses of political science. Of course you are right, Rosa, that, particularly during the Cold War, although not only in this period, liberal democracy was and is propagandistically simplified. And I agree with you completely when it is a matter of requiring that the theory of politics must always also include a theory of the effectiveness of politics. But, on the other hand, in their fixation on results and on their goals, the Leninists sacrificed every sensitivity for the means, that is, for the political process. A direct path leads from Lenin's impatience to act to dictatorship. I don't need to tell you of all people that: that was the first point of dissent between you and Lenin."

"And the reaction made great use of this criticism that I had not formulated for the public. But aside from Lenin: I do not see these relations as necessary, but we can probably both agree that we need a differentiated analysis of the result as well as of the process of politics; or, in other, scholastic terms, the analysis of the end as well as the means."

"Fine. I once said with reference to you, Rosa, that there is a connection between personal involvement and political action. You were very concerned with the world and not with your personal matters. If the latter had been the case, you would have remained in Zurich, written your dissertation, and perhaps pursued an academic career. But you simply could not accept the unfairness in the world."

"You're right that anger over the way things were was the driving motivation for me and for everyone who did not simply want to accept merely understanding them. But how was it with you, Hannah, were you really always so academic, so satisfied with observing, describing, and understanding?"

"There is a passage in Artur Schnitzler's 'The Road to the Open' that impresses me very much. Theresa, the socialist intellectual in turn-of-the-century Vienna says in a debate over anti-Semitism: ' ... the Jewish bankers are just as repulsive to me as the feudal landowners and orthodox Rabbis just as repulsive as those Catholic priests. But when someone feels superior to me because he belongs to a different religion or race than me and makes me feel this superiority in the awareness of his own power, I would ... well, I don't know what I would do to such a person.' That is the way I have always felt, but it is, of course, an actionism out of anger, out of feeling hurt and insulted."

"You curbed and sublimated your anger intellectually and tried to conquer it like an illness, Hannah. That was not possible for me. But I would like to touch you with your own approach. In your treatise on revolution you portrayed the American Revolution so positively as opposed to the French and

Russian Revolutions because it was 'only' political and not, like the others, primarily social. That is why you think, if I understand you correctly, the product of the American Revolution is stable and has had an exemplary influence throughout the centuries and the continents ..."

"... yes, because this revolution created a form and did not try to set the content for everyone. It is the form that lasts ..."

"... whereas the Jacobins' and Bolsheviks' zeal for social change would not have allowed such a lasting form. So far, so good. But even behind the American Revolution there was action, even that was revolution. Wouldn't you have wanted to participate in that?"

"Aside from the fact that it would not have been allowed me as a woman, I don't think I would like to have taken part in the Boston Tea Part, Rosa. I can't imagine myself disguised as an Indian, anyway. But of course I would gladly have taken part in the discussion of the Constitution with the Federalists and with Jefferson. And I have to admit, I could have developed a passionate antipathy toward Aaron Burr."

"... of Heideggerian dimensions?"

"Oh, leave that be. I can't believe this relationship is being put on stage now ..."

"But I am not interested in gossip, Hannah. I am interested in discovering the political in your private life. The fact that you fell for the 'last great Romantic' — those were your own words — after 1945 again is so hard to believe. The fact that you, such a self-confident woman, could subordinate yourself intellectually to that prattling Black Forest Nazi makes me reflect on the tendency of women to give up their own sovereignty. We women have got to stop bringing this romantic suffering on ourselves!"

"You are quoting Elzbieta Ettinger — I would prefer it if this side of my life had not become so public. But that can't be so difficult for you to understand, Rosa. I'm thinking of Leo Jogiches ..."

"But that is really such a poor comparison. First of all, Leo and I shared the same revolutionary perspective, and second, I did not subordinate myself, never made myself his or anyone else's life-long student ... But our, that is, my point was the element of praxis in our thinking. And I regret that, with regard to the degree of clarity I would like to see, I find that lacking in you."

"No, praxis is not a fundamentally negative concept for me. But I have always been deterred by the degree to which you accepted a mentality of blinders in your praxis, which I find heroic, tragic, and great. The fact that you repressed knowledge for the sake of praxis is not exactly a model for me precisely because it is so understandable."

"You'll have to explain what you mean, Hannah ..."

"That you let yourself be blinded for the variety of factors that move society! That with regard to the Polish question you were more German than

the Germans, that you never really wanted to perceive anti-Semitism because it would have complicated your analysis which was so oriented toward action! At the Munich Party Congress you were so German that even Bebel had to back off from you!"

"Well, I was an internationalist. And those gossips from Poland, especially those sectarians from the Bund, they would have defended the shtetl against world revolution! Don't you see the terrible mess the nationalism that replaced Leninism has gotten us into? When I criticized Polish nationalism I meant what sets the Azerbaijanis and Armenians off against each other today, and the Serbs and Croatians. It may be that, from today's perspective, I did not always argue in distinctions. But you cannot forget that the Munich Party Congress was in 1902 and what sort of experience we have gathered in the meantime."

"You are right there, Rosa. It would be too simple to act as if a hundred years of experience were simply being skipped. But I am concerned with methodology again: If one is so animated by an energy oriented toward action, as you were, then one tends unavoidably toward analytical shortcuts; one sacrifices distinctions and complexities because they could stand in the way of action. And I have trouble with that, the fact that action has at least the tendency to curtail knowledge."

"And I have problems with the fact that the orientation toward knowledge threatens to suffocate any orientation toward action. But we agree on that, Hannah, that it cannot be about an either-or situation."

21 On the Democratic Dissolution of Politics in General

Inner- or Other-Directed Leadership — Public versus Private — Politics as Knowledge of Climate — Autopoiesis: No one Rules — The Fiction of the "People"

To occupy oneself with politics means to occupy oneself with conflict. The theory of politics is not one of harmony. And that repulses people because politics is perceived as a struggle and seen as "dirty" due to its combative techniques. The withdrawal from politics is the result of all notions of the possibility of perfect harmony. The dualism characteristic of late antiquity that, in light of the imminent Kingdom of God, recommended avoiding the realm of politics, the "City of the World," is an expression of this tendency that stems from the need for harmony.

Politics always has something to do with contradictions, with the conflict of interests. The actual task of a political system is to regulate this conflict. Likewise, the function of the political process, that is, of politics, is to bring about binding decisions between the opposing interests.

The organizational competition of parties is deduced from this perspective on politics. The organization of opposing interests in "parties" is the logical result because what constitutes "the commonweal" is not clearly written and because the good of all is defined by a process based on a competition that must be decided anew each time. The fact that democracy has no use for the fiction that the common good is an absolute, i.e., that democracy must, rather, leave open the concrete notion of what is best for all, results from the contradiction between "the commonweal a priori" and "the commonweal a posteriori." If that which is useful to everyone is an absolute to begin with, then the political process, particularly the complex pluralism of democracy, must appear as an avoidable luxury. If the representatives of the commonweal are not to have a monopoly, if, then, they are to be committed to democracy, then the openness of the system is necessary (Fraenkel 1964, 59-62).

In stable democracies, however, this openness leads increasingly to neutrality toward interests and values, not only of political institutions in democracy, but also of the democratic players. According to the marketing model that constitutes the essence of existing democracy, they are open to all demands made of them. They see themselves as vendors of services that, in principle, must adapt to all demands. Democratic politics becomes a mechanism whereby the market is observed and satisfied. The motivating force for the political players is not the realization of certain ideals; their motive is self-interest: the interest to prevail on the political market, that is, to achieve and maintain political power.

This mechanism is inherent in democracy. To confront its results with a critical but nostalgic sadness is to question the tenets of democracy. Jean-Marie Guéhenno demonstrates the consequences of the mechanism of democracy with the examples of the U.S. and Japan and then poses the decisive question: "The politician imagined by enlightenment thinkers was supposed to be the midwife of truth in society. With the gifts of speech and reason, he was supposed to make social transcendence visible in parliamentary ceremony" (Guéhenno 1994, 56f.).

The politician imagined by enlightenment thinkers is first and foremost a leader, led by reason and directing others to the land of truth. This politician has nothing at all to do with democracy, for truth is not a category compatible with democracy, and reason is always relative.

The politician in democracy gets his impulses from organized interests who come together as associations or lobbies; his truth is that of market strategy, his reason that of the technological transformation of his demand-oriented messages into successful elections. The politician in democracy is the one who, in the public, political realm, has renounced his personal truth. What he himself thinks, what constitutes his conscience, what he thinks of as the best of all possible societies, is his highly personal private affair having nothing to do with his politics.

However, this is closely tied to the refusal of leadership in the sense of "transforming leadership," non-routine leadership, because this politician does not distinguish between various contents and goals. Rather, he differentiates between different strategies and instruments. The means becomes the end. The inner-directed politician who determines his politics according to his own impulses, who lets his highly personal private business be the guiding principle for his actions, is not compatible with democracy. The politician of democracy is the other-directed politician whose impulses for action come from the needs of society (Riesman 1950, esp. 261-267).

With the dissolution of truth and reason, however, the tendency is for politics itself to be dissolved. If the ideal type of politician is interchangeable, if his personality can only be effective as a marketing tool, then he is interchangeable — not necessarily his image, his commercially styled appearance, but certainly his unmistakable, specific, non-interchangeable person. Charisma as content is out — charisma as styling as in.

Jaruzelski was committed to a truth. It was, of course, his own, and not "objective" in that sense, but it could be appreciated intersubjectively: the truth that if the dual authority between Solidarity and the Communist Party continued, the Red Army would one day intervene in Poland. And Jaruzelski was committed to reason. Confronted with the alternatives of allowing a direct dictatorship by the Soviet Union, brought about by its troops and bound up with an unquantifiable loss of Polish life, or, on the other hand, becoming a (qualitatively and quantitatively "milder") dictator himself, he chose the second alternative.

Jaruzelski made a political decision as a politician and without being bound to democratic rules. If he had had to decide within the restriction of a stable democracy in Poland, if he had had to decide democratically, he probably could not have made that decision. The declaration of martial law was not legitimate in terms of an opinion poll — the overwhelming majority of Poles would not have agreed to the suppression of Solidarity, nor would it have been possible to implement martial law within a functional parliamentary system. Because Poland constituted a unique, specific transition between dictatorship and democracy between August, 1980 and December, 1981, the partial dictator Jaruzelski was able to become a full-fledged dictator and thus demonstrate leadership.

How far removed from the playing field encountered by a politician in an existing democracy of the European welfare zone at the end of the twentieth century is from Jaruzelski's playing field! This can be seen most clearly in matters relating to style: "Social veneer replaces politics. It is no longer the final touch with which one polishes social reality, it is itself this reality" (Guéhenno 1994, 57).

What Johannes Agnoli realized in the watershed year of 1968 is true today more than ever: "The parties compete against one another for political power and nevertheless build a symbiotic unit within whose closed circle the abstract conflict of leadership can be fought out" (Agnoli 1968, 38). The "conflict of leadership" is "abstract" — that is, the interchangeability of the parties willing to govern and thus dependent on the majority and on the market leads to the abstraction even of "political power." It is not political power that can set the course for society. It is, to be sure, personal power that influences a great number of people via a system of clientelism and is thus so attractive. But the "symbiotic unit" of the competing powers, wrung from the political market of stable democracy, removes the socially-engineered character of power from the democratic process of choice.

What Western neo-Marxist critics of existing democracy in 1968 and thereafter still considered to be a dimension to be moralized must be seen as a logical consequence of democracy and must be accepted if democracy is to be accepted: the dissolution of rule in the sense of Locke, Montesquieu, and the Federalists, as power in political forms, in institutions, in a constitutional political system. This rule is rationalized away by democracy. Here the advocates of identificatory and elite democratic theories, otherwise so antagonistic, agree; Jean Jacques Rousseau and Joseph Schumpeter converge: democracy means the negation of rule, politically defined in the narrow sense.

It is telling that this balance does not please everyone who lays claim to democracy. Instead of attributing the end of rule and the negation of politics in the narrow sense to the success of existing democracy, this end of politics is not labeled the victory of democracy, but its end (Guéhenno 1994).

A certain neediness can be assumed here: It may well be that the "ideal of this world is not institutionalized conflict but the stillness of the wind disturbed by nothing" (Guéhenno 1994, 113). But it is just as much the ideal of this world to expect the struggle of the powers of good and darkness and to hope that some Hercules or Siegfried or St. George will destroy the dark monster. The dualistic, Manichean tendency toward the simplistic good-against-evil dichotomy cannot be satisfied by the insight into a transition adequate to democracy from a heroic politics into a self-directing form of non-rule.

But beyond the lack of a democratic triumphalism lies also the knowledge that what is known as politics in the narrow, traditional sense encompasses only a part of society. The negation of politics in this — democratized — segment of society does nothing to change the fact that politics lives on in the non-democratic domains: unregulated (or scarcely regulated), often disguised as "administrative pressures" but always recognizable as politics due to its hallmarks: the presence of power relations and the rule of certain human beings over others.

Johannes Agnoli and the advocates of critical democratic theory (Bachrach 1967, Narr/Naschold 1971, Pelinka 1974) have shown that the tendency of politics to be negated in the actual, narrow realm of politics cannot mean the negation of power relations, of socially transmitted and, especially, economically caused forms of rule. The postulates stemming from this recognition concern society beyond the political system, in particular beyond the economy. The democratization of the economy — but not the strengthening of the fiction of rule by officeholders and institutionalized leaders — is the logical result of critical democratic theory. But even this understanding of democracy, which does not want to accept the status quo of Western reality, cannot simply negate the reduction of rule within the political while simultaneously maintaining rule within the non-political. Even a critical democratic theory cannot disregard the reality of the dissolution of politics through democracy.

This dissolution of politics through democracy makes a "technical" process of the political processes in the narrow sense — elections, parliaments, governments, parties, associations. Since a stable political market forces the suppliers into a strategic conformism, the political decision-makers have nothing more to decide. An "empire without rulers" emerges that can be described with concepts from meteorology: "In ... (its) world everything is completely rational and yet not predictable; the tiny change in a variable can release the storm such that it blocks all observation despite the progress made in the observation of weather phenomena. In this sense, it has become meaningless to want to control the political system and to compare the one who is politically responsible with a sort of watchmaker of society who sits in the center of the workings and regulates the entire mechanism by controlling and balancing the weights. One cannot control the realm of politics any more than the climate" (Guéhenno 1994, 112).

But the watchmaker is the leader. In this self-regulating system of stable democracy, he can still awaken the appearance of being competent to direct matters — in the most extreme case through an improvement of the social techniques of prognosis (quasi-meteorological early warning systems) that he cannot develop, but whose development he can encourage and whose use he can initiate. In light of these conditions, the expectations of leadership are nothing but the insistence on a nostalgic mythos that reaches from the early phases of social development into its later stages.

To want to make this accusation of stable democracy would be to misunderstand its intention and its logic. This is, after all, what all democrats, especially the radicals among them, have always wanted. This is the dissolution of the rule of human beings over each other. It is what Abraham Lincoln propagandistically reclaimed for the banners of democracy in his Gettysburg Address: "Government of the people, by the people, for the people."

This is true, of course, for government, that is, for the institutionalized realms of politics, for the state and for the political system. It is not true for society as a whole. The misleading fascination with leadership in politics distracts from the fact that globally, regionally, and nationally eminent social inequities reflect a noteworthy social imbalance of power; it detracts from the fact that the legitimation of this existing democracy can be traced to the terrible failure of experiments that wanted to confront this challenge and from the fact that it is not so much that Western democracy won, but that Marxism-Leninism lost.

The terrible failure of Marxism-Leninism must make us cautious. But that does little to change the basic problem. The stable democracies build on an historically coincidental, politically arbitrary, intellectually inconsistent division of society into the public and private sphere. In the public sphere there is and should be democracy; in the private sphere there can be no democracy. There are good arguments for such a division; there are no arguments for drawing the dividing line between the two sectors precisely where it is drawn in this stage of social development.

History is also the history of the constant readjustment of this line between public and private. The political order of antiquity, of the Attic polis and the Roman Empire, was built on the notion that the relations within the family and the house belonged to the private sphere, and the family and house ("oikos" — Hennis 1973, 38f.) were the sole responsibility of the "pater familias." Thus, slaves, women, and children were the private property of the master of the house.

This becomes outdated in modern times. The boundary between "private" and "public" has changed significantly. But the boundary has not reached its final resting place. As long as there is history, this boundary will be readjusted and there will be a struggle to readjust it. There will be a discussion about what the terms "private" and "public" mean — a discussion in the direction of ambiguity. Even in the "private" sphere, forms of participation are imaginable — for instance in business that, according to the understanding currently dominant in liberal systems, are to be ascribed to the private sphere, for instance in the family, which is considered the private sphere par excellence. There is consensus in the workplace and thus in "private" business and there are partnership models for the family.

This readjustment in modern times has not followed any single direction. What is private has, at times, been made public, but has also been removed from the public realm by legal guarantees and prohibitions on arbitrariness. The boundary has become more diffuse and porous. Politics takes place in many sectors: the outcome of decision-making in the workplace and at school is politics. Politics is becoming far-reaching and all-encompassing.

But for that very reason, politics is also more diffuse: by seeping into all social realms, by becoming omnipresent, it tends to negate itself. Politics is trickling away. Politics in the narrow sense, in the state chancelleries and parliaments, is less and less a matter of formation and more and more the technique of conformity. And at the same time, politics in the broader sense is taking place everywhere. The socialization of politics establishes and accompanies the loss and dissolution of politics.

In his essay on theoretical approaches toward explaining the fall of existing socialism, Klaus von Beyme mentions the tendency of systems theory (connected with names such as Parsons, Luhmann, Maturana) to understand political systems as self-directed (autopoiesis) (von Beyme 1994, 33f.). According to this view, the growing integration of all partial systems into a world system has failed to allow a deviation that defines itself in a socialist sense, no matter in what directions the concrete political attempts to navigate may have led.

This view of a self-directing evolution, consistently enough, removes autonomy from national subsystems, even those that conform in terms of capitalism and democracy. There is no conspiracy behind this, no Elder of Zion, no Wall Street experts, no Freemason secrets. There is, however, the de-personalization of politics with the end result of the de-politicization of politics.

Democracy only highlights this tendency. Its doctrine is, after all, either that the people rules or that an elite closely tied to the people carries out the business of government. In this way, the de-personalization of politics is openly addressed by democracy. The fact that de-politicization follows is only the next step.

Democracy gives the "people" the rights of the "sovereign," that is, the rights that in early or pre-modern times were accorded individual rulers while invoking God's grace or the needs of the subjects. These rulers were concrete and if not literally tangible then certainly individually perceptible, Louis XIV just as much as Joseph II. The concept of the "people," however, is abstract and fits perfectly into the extremely abstract conceptions of systems theory. There is no "people" — at least not in the sense of something more than the highly heterogeneous sum of groups and interests. It is therefore illusory to count on the re-politicization of democracy from within. The strengthening of the political content of society can only come from where there is no democracy, but where there is, correspondingly, politics, leadership, and open contradictions, where power is still personalized and tangible and perceptible — beyond politics in the narrow sense.

The pressure that is the precondition for any change in the status quo can only have its roots outside the system — in society, where there is no politics in the narrow, traditional sense. And this pressure can only come from contradiction, above all from the opposition between what is claimed and what is real. And contradictions are also clear in the existing democracy that directs itself so successfully — between "political" power (power that is democratized and thus deprived of power) and "unpolitical" power (non-democratized and thus powerful); but above all between the "people" and people.

The real people, not the "people" of the constitutional fiction, are the sum of those affected. In national (and thus in existing) democracy, the gulf between those affected and the "people" becomes increasingly larger; more and more of those affected are not "the people": for example, foreigners, aliens, and those not yet born, whose interests are greatly influenced by current politics.

The expansion of democracy has always conflicted with the interest of the "people" not to include all those who are affected, not to allow them membership in the "people." Women's right to vote had to be wrested from men just as the rights of blacks had to be wrested from the whites in South Africa. The actual motor behind the development of democracy comes from this contradiction between "the people" and people.

Politics really happens along this line of tension when what is at stake is the entry of previously excluded individuals into democracy. This is why the question of accepting those who, because of their citizenship are not allowed to be the "people" although they are people, is so important for economically advanced democracies at the turn of the millenium (Dahl 1989, 119-131). The great politicizing topics and conflicts are the efforts on the part of those previously excluded to push their way into democracy and the efforts to include in democracy those realms previously excluded as "unpolitical." It is a push from the unregulated into the regulated, from the unprotected into the protected sector of society.

Democracy has won. In accordance with its program it is dissolving politics. Politics no longer takes place — in democracy. The political system ruled by democracy is apolitical. Interchangeable persons make a pretense of leadership and the volume of the applause of the entertained public — labeled "sovereign" — is presented as reality. But the other partial systems not dominated by democracy — economy, education, culture, that is, the "unpolitical" elements of society — are the spheres that actually are political. Here, where there is no democracy, is where the really relevant politics takes place.

22 On the Transformation of the People into the Marketplace

The People or "One People" — McNamara's Management — The Market as Anti-Utopia — Fulbright's Logical Contradictions — "People" means Exclusion — The Stubbornness of the Woodworms

"We, the people of the United States": the beginning of the American Declaration of Independence, which is also a declaration of basic rights, is the beginning of a fiction — the fiction of the people. Since then, the notion of the people as sovereign entity serves to justify the actions of all possible rulers.

"We are the people," the demonstrators in Leipzig and elsewhere cried out in the fall of 1989 in the GDR. This soon became: "We are one people!" And thus the sovereign entity of the Workers' and Peasants' State transformed the meaning of populist philosophy into its opposite. "We are the people": the Vietnamese guest worker could locate himself in this expression as well as the student from Angola, both of them actively participating in the demonstrations in Leipzig. "We are one people": with these words, these two were no longer included but excluded. Suddenly, the people as the sum of all those affected became the people as the sum of all Germans. And then, even in Leipzig, the German from Cologne and the German from Heidelberg were included but the Vietnamese worker and the woman from Angola were excluded, although the political power toward — or against — which the political slogan was directed concerned the Vietnamese guest worker and the student from Angola concretely but not the German from Cologne or the German from Heidelberg.

The (one, my, our) "people" is, since it is arbitrarily definable, ideally suited to justifying every imaginable form of concrete rule. The (one, my, our) "people" is clear in only two respects:

— The "people" is the historical (and current) antithesis to the single closed, alternative ideology of justification of rule — God's grace in all its variations from the monarchy to religious or secondarily religious fundamentalism.

— The "people" always includes and therefore always excludes. It is never self-evident who belongs to the people; belonging varies in history and is thus achieved politically and can be removed by political means. Nothing is less "natural" than the people.

Politics in democracy must be grounded by invoking the "people." This cannot be avoided. But what this means in concrete terms and what the consequences are for those who invoke this term is at first highly unclear. What does the term the "people" mean for those who invoke it during the decision-making process?

When Robert McNamara, the President of the Ford Corporation, began his tenure in the administration of John F. Kennedy as Secretary of Defense, he, the rising star among American entrepreneurs, announced to the media his conception of his new role as master of the world's largest defense budget and largest machinery of destruction:

"The role of public manager is very similar to the role of a private manager; in each case he has the option of following one of two major alternative courses of action. He can either act as a judge or a leader... I have always believed in and endeavored to follow the active leadership role as opposed to the passive judicial role" (McNamara 1995, 23).

The leadership role of a manager, then, public or private, is the definition of political leadership. Actively making decisions and not passively weighing the choices; taking sides and not distancing oneself — this is leadership. What role do the people play here, what does all of this have to do with calling on the sovereign? McNamara referred to his experience in the world of a multinational corporation. And thus he included in his definition of leadership the harsh controls to which a "private" manager is vulnerable: his quality must prove itself in the marketplace. Whether Robert McNamara was a successful leader of Ford Motor Company was decided ultimately by the world of buying and selling; it could always be read in the segments of the market that Ford had taken over or lost.

If this is true also for the "public" manager, for the politician, what are the controls that evaluate the quality of leadership just as clearly and consistently? Again we must apply the analogy of the business world: it is the market that decides — the political market.

McNamara's definition of the leader as "public manager," only apparently far removed from the notion of democracy, has, in fact, considerable implications for democracy. The public manager is subordinate to the analogous criteria of success that are applied to any management tied to the marketplace, whether it is private or public, economic or political. And the "people" guard these criteria; or, to avoid mythological conceptions, it guards the political marketplace. Only the results of this public management legitimated after the fact by the market stand the test; other results lead to the removal of management and to change in politics. In anticipation of this market mechanism, however, the managers orient themselves to the market, or, in mythological terms, the "leaders" orient themselves to the "people."

The political marketplace is the coming together of demand, articulated in electoral behavior, and supply, for which individuals and parties are responsible; that is, routine leadership or public management in McNamara's terms. This market tends toward "populist" behavior, to the regret of liberal theoreticians in the tradition of Madison (Riker 1982). No longer do voters tend to determine merely the leading personnel, the public managers who then, in relative freedom, practice leadership; rather, in the logic of the market, they tend to force the public managers into a predictable and thus interchangeable behavior that is no longer personally distinguishable — they take from leadership the freedom to lead.

Thus the essence of the (democratic and only the democratic) *homo politicus* corresponds fully to that of the *homo oeconomicus*. The politician in democracy must create the optimum cost and effect with regard to an existing market; he must satisfy needs over which he has only limited control; he is caught up in the delicate balance of a market logic that forces him into an adaptive behavior.

In its objectivity in which nothing is "holy," in which only interests dominate, the market is the contradiction to the emotionality that is characteristic of all latently totalitarian movements and all latent forms of fundamentalism. The insight into this logic takes from the leaders of all times and all regions the means of emotionalizing the behavior of others and of stylizing their own behavior: of ideologizing interests. A leader whose motivation for leadership is obviously self-interest and who acknowledges the fact that he is a market leader will not, like Mao or Khomeini, be able to set loose the "masses" onto any chosen enemy. Such a leader will also not be able to convince Serbs or Azerbaijanis in great numbers that it is worth dying for a Serb Amselfeld or for an Azerbaijani Mt. Karabach. The market cannot convey the moral outrage that a dichotomous understanding of politics signifies vis-à-vis the "City of the World" any more than the unreflected acceptance of the "City of God."

The market does not need to be propagated. As a system of regulations of society and politics, it needs no advertisement. It must only be recognized as an existing logic to which axioms can be subordinated or not; to which both advantages and disadvantages can be attributed; which can be described and analyzed. The objectivity of the market whose effectiveness as a political market and thus as a democracy has often been described (Downs 1957), the results of whose actions have often been analyzed (Olson 1965, Frey 1983) is its great advantage, as well as its great disadvantage.

The objectivity of the market, its instrumental and thus non-intrinsic character, allows us to test the control mechanisms inherent in its system of checks and balances. Within the framework of its logic, the market can be improved, and it must be tested constantly, also within the framework of its logic. The political market is never finished: making sure that political cartels are not formed is a constant task, as are the controls with regard to possible exclusionary effects. The political market, which, according to the dominant understanding of democracy, is built on the principle of equal power among those who demand, is, after all, inserted into a society of real inequality. From this social milieu come the unavoidable impulses that clash with the postulate of equality that stems from democracy and thus from the political market.

The history of the political market demonstrates this dynamics of change: access to the market, i.e., political rights, particularly the right to vote has shifted and can and will shift in the future in the direction that corresponds to the axiom of democracy (in the direction of equal treatment for all those affected) or in the opposite direction. Since it is never finished, the market is a paradigmatic anti-utopia.

This constitutes its weakness. A democracy consistently described as a market scarcely motivates people. A people declared to be a market does not release these identifications, it does not lend the sort of identity that the "people" as mythos can convey. The people used to images, fairy tales and archaic patterns evidently prefers to be the "people" instead of viewing itself as a market. In this way, of course, the view of real social processes is skewed.

The victory of the people is a victory through and of the market. A "people" that can not organize as a market, that does not know how to bring its interests, in the form of political demand, into the mechanism of a competitive democracy has abdicated as a people. It may be cited as a justification of political rule, but it is politically irrelevant. A "people" that cannot become a market can be ignored politically.

Yet not everything that is politics is also traded on the market. The real "political person" is different from the fictitious "ideological person" by dint of the political interest that is present, but only in a limited fashion (Lipset 1960). Without such interest, however, there would be no political market. If there is no relevant — i.e., no potentially decisive — interest given for certain spheres of politics, then the political market simply cannot function in this particular sphere. This sphere forms a niche in which decisions are made without regard to the navigating logic of the market. There is no democracy here. But for that very reason there is leadership — non-routine, transforming leadership.

J. William Fulbright's contradictions reveal the complexity of such a political niche. The intellectual from Arkansas, a U.S. Senator from 1944 to 1974, Chair of the Senate Committee on Foreign Affairs for 15 years, was the spearhead of the American foreign policy described as liberal. The scientific exchange program that, not incidentally, carries his name, demonstrates the international openness of this politics and of this politician. As a critic of the U.S. policy in Vietnam, the Democrat Fuegi disagreed vehemently with President Johnson, what made him an identificatory figure of the American left.

But Fulbright's politics had two sides. As Dr. Jekyll he represented a consistent opposition to the militarization of foreign policy, to the power of the military industrial complex, to the anti-Communist paranoia that had led to the morass of the policy in Vietnam. But as Mr. Hyde he fought against the civil rights legislation advocated by Lyndon B. Johnson, against whose foreign policy Fuegi also fought. Fuegi was an advocate of segregation; he wanted to insure the old order for the South (and thus for his home state) that divided people into two categories according to the color of their skin. In domestic policy Fuegi was a bigoted, racist reactionary (Woods 1995).

The contradictory nature of this behavior can only be explained by the political market. In the 1940's, 50's, and 60's, when the voters of Arkansas sent Fuegi to the Senate, the most important political topic in the South was the question of race. And since the blacks in the South were prevented from exercising their right to vote due to a policy of open discrimination, there was only a single dominant interest in the voter market in Arkansas: to preserve white privilege at all cost. No one whose politics did not conform to that market could have been elected Senator in a traditional Southern state. Fuegi was elected again and again because he fulfilled the mandate of his electorate — to prevent civil rights laws that would take privilege away from whites.

In light of this interest that completely preoccupied Fulbright's constituency, his foreign policy ranked a distant third. It was the hobby of an intellectual who could afford it because he simultaneously fulfilled his duty as an elected official. Fulbright's foreign policy cannot be explained in terms of the existing market of his time. His domestic policy, however, can only be understand in those terms.

In domestic politics, Fuegi was the manager who attentively observed the market segment of his product and was able to hold up these segments successfully for decades. In foreign policy, on the other hand, Fuegi really was a leader who made politics not according to the market, but according to his own knowledge and conscience. And this leadership was possible only because there was in Arkansas neither a positive nor a negative demand for his pet project of liberal foreign policy. He was not elected because of or in spite of his liberal foreign policy — he was elected fully independently of his foreign policy because of his reactionary domestic policy. Fulbright's leadership was possible because the market did not function in his sphere of foreign policy, since the "people" had no interest and therefore no say.

Fulbright's people was, to be sure, a "people" in development, from a (white) people that excluded on ethnic and racial grounds to a people (which Fuegi resisted) that comprised both blacks and whites. Fulbright's "people" were overcome by history, in accordance with the principles proclaimed and simultaneously infringed upon by the white, male Founding Fathers. And with the inclusion of blacks into the market and into the people, the direction of market logic changed also. It is a significant aspect of this change that this people of Arkansas which now included blacks no longer wanted to send J. William Fulbright to the Senate — in 1974 he suffered his first defeat during his fifth re-election campaign.

The market creates its non-leaders. When Ross Perot became the star of the American political stage in 1992, his message was that the two-party system was not in a position to produce leadership. And by using the electronic media, he succeeded in offering himself as leader and was to influence the Presidential election significantly. The message was by no means one of substance. Perot did not criticize George Bush's policy in Iraq and he did not debate Bill Clinton on his ideas for healthcare reform. But his role as a non-leader was that of an indicator: he demonstrated the voters' dissatisfaction regarding the results of the market, paradoxically by using the techniques of the market (Goldman 1994, 424-435).

The "Perot factor" demonstrates that the market also transmits illusions on the market, that certain ideas are effective on the market, e.g., the idea that democracy is not "only" a process, that the people are more than the market, and that leadership is what voters truly need; but also that the content of this longed-for leadership is diffuse to the point of controversy. The market shows reliably that its reality does not satisfy needs. But it also does satisfy them, simply not all expectations that are made of it. But it fulfills its function as a mechanism of rule in which all those affected (the real "people") can participate.

The "Perot factor" also demonstrates the stubbornness of the capability to grieve for illusions not yet lost. To grieve for the "people" and to defend the notion of the "people" leads to the trap of *völkisch* ideology, because the emphasis on inclusion and exclusion is imma-nent to any definition of the people who see in it more than the sum of those participating in the market. Identity must be attributed to such a "people", usually a national identity, or even an ethnic identity. And this identity has the effect not only of the desired inclusion but also, unavoidably, the effect of exclusion. Certain individuals must remain outside the concretely figured "people" because they cannot prove they had the right grandparents (Nuremberg Race Laws); because they have the wrong mother tongue, because they belong to the wrong religious community, because they have the wrong skin color, because they do not possess the right papers — of citizenship.

The right to be part of the "people" is not viewed as a consequen-ce of one's mere presence on the market, of one's existence in a concrete society. Rather, markers that differentiate between one' s own people and the other are sought and constructed with a quasi-biological consistency. Ethnicity is the name of this trap — as a result of this *völkisch* thinking there is violence in the form of post-Commu-nist wars in Europe and ethnic "cleansing" throughout the world.

In correspondence with the claims of the bourgeois revolution, the willingness to let anyone be a member of the "people" is expressed in the notion of "ius soli" which remains not coincidentally the governing principle of American and French legislation regarding citizenship. This position, which is fundamentally opposed to the *völkisch* trap, has of course been superseded particularly in the U.S. by the toleration of "additional qualifications." Schumpeter justified the exclusion of outsiders who were members of U.S. society and who, despite the citizenship promised by "ius soli," were prevented from making political use of it, through a demonstrative indifference toward the racist exclusion of black Americans from the right to vote, as was the case in the Southern states until the 1960s. This apparently value-free indifference toward the rules governing access to the political market is, of course, a heavily value-laden steering mechanism that brings a *völkisch* element into the market mechanism that is, in essence, supposedly blind to color, sex, religious creed and ethnicity. It is not the equating of those affected with those who have rights, i.e., it is not the value judgment inherent in the equating of all who live in a given society that harms the logic of the market; rather, it is the value-laden criteria of exclusion that prevent those affected by political power from controlling this power over the market (Dahl 1989, 121-130).

The political market called democracy has an axiom: not to accept any markers of sex, race, ethnicity, or religion as an axiomatic reason for exclusion. Being affected is the single criterion for the right to take part actively in the market to whose mechanism one is vulnerable. To this end, the representatives of the bourgeois revolution proclaimed natural rights. This is the immutable core of all declarations of these rights — on the part of the United Nations and on the part of the Council of Europe.

The people in democracy is not a "people;" it is not defined in terms of ethnicity. Any ethnocentric definition of the people has results that can be observed en masse: discrimination according to arbitrarily chosen categories, justification of racism and xenophobia, populist legitimation of nationalist wars and ethnic "cleansings." If democracy does not lead to the dissolution of the "people" on the market, and if the axiom of the market as blind to ethnicity and other categories is not a given, then even Auschwitz can be interpreted as a democratic process: with a final consistency, human beings who did not belong to the German "people" were removed from the German "body of the people."

If one considers history and the history of theories of modernity, the "people" is well on its way to becoming people, that is, the market, instead of a social segment recognizable and defined by its inclusionary and exclusionary effects becoming a whole that increasingly includes all those concerned and thus excludes no one. The expansion of the right to vote was and remains an important indicator for this transition; the acceptance of natural rights at least as a program is the corresponding direction.

There are steps backwards in this development. For instance, the rebirth of ethnocentric nationalism that once again enthrones "the people." The myth of the Serbian or the Croatian or the "X.Y." people triumphs, at least for a time, over the possible and desirable reality of a market that is not primarily exclusionary but inclusionary. This rebirth also signifies the return of the Führer who, in a grand gesture, can invoke the real and to be sure, increasingly exclusionary market in terms of ethnicity, whose first reference is to myth, not of the people but of "their people"; not that of all those affected, but of an arbitrary selection from the circle of those affected.

The return of the Führer is not coincidentally connected with the return of the "people," of *völkisch* ideology. The atavistic figure of the Führer and the atavistic understanding of the "people" are memories from pre-democratic times that, in part, reveal themselves as resisting democracy and the metamorphosis inherent in it of the "people" into the market and of the Führers into managers.

In his novel "A History of the World in 10 1/2 Chapters," Julian Barnes writes of the burning question about how the woodworms could survive the flood. If it is true that all the fauna that exist today have been preserved from prehistoric times by Noah's Ark, how did the woodworms, the mortal enemies of the lifesaving ship, survive to the present day? (Barnes 1990, 1-30).

This question about the explanation of a paradox is like the question why democracy, despite its victory, carries around with it certain myths that endanger democracy: the myth of the "people" and the myth of leadership. Barnes answers the question posed to him by pointing to the woodworms' will to survive that makes them creep secretly onto the ark and also prevents them from eating the entire ark during its journey. The question remains whether the supposition of an analogous self-interest suffices to explain the stubborn, anachronistic existence of myths.

23 *The Cockpit*

Once there was a man who was both curious and smart. Having flown very frequently, he had always wanted to enter the cockpit of one of the planes he always flew in: Boeings, Airbuses, and DC 10s. He had already screwed up his courage a few times and asked a stewardess if he could observe the pilots at their work for at least a few brief moments since he was such a loyal customer. But the answer was always: "In principle, yes, but not right now; not so soon after takeoff; so soon before landing; with this particular flight ...; there's turbulence at the moment ..." There was always something that stood in the way of making his wish, acceptable in principle, come true.

For years our frequent flier flew throughout the world. He had gradually given up hope of seeing his wish come true. But suddenly he had the chance to reach his goal, which was, after all, quite modest.

He flew with Democratic Airways, flight number one from Athens to Florence. It was by no means a full flight and he was about to enter one of the restrooms located in the front of the aircraft when a stewardess exited the cockpit right in front of him. She must have been a rather inattentive flight attendant because she paid him no attention and shut the door to the cockpit so carelessly that it did not close entirely but was left slightly ajar.

Since the stewardess had already left for the middle of the cabin, our frequent flier suddenly found himself in front of the partially open door. Behind it he saw with an "inner eye" a scene he had often observed in the movies: pilot and co-pilot exchanging brief messages in English with air traffic controllers while more or less attentively observing the numerous electronic instruments. And then he simply could not resist. He did not want to see it in his imagination, he wanted to see it for real. And so, making sure no one was watching him, he firmly pushed open the door to the cockpit.

Then he saw it. The cockpit was empty. Flight number one of Democratic Airways had no pilot whatsoever. The plane was underway from Athens to Florence on automatic.

And he began to understand.

24 On the Possibility of Intellectual and Moral Leadership

Mahatma Gandhi and Martin Luther King, Jr. — The "Guilty Conscience" — The Refusal to Take Office as a Prerequisite of leadership — The Impatience of the Bolsheviks — Angelo Guiseppe Roncalli

One might think that Albert Einstein was an objective person. And yet he once wrote, full of pathos: "Generations to come, it may be, will scarce believe that such a one as this ever in flesh and blood walked upon this earth" (Shirer 1982, 11).

The person to whom perhaps the most famous scientist of the 20th century dedicated this quasi-religious formulation was Mahatma Gandhi. Gandhi's influence on humanity was not grounded in revolution, and not even directly in reform. Gandhi's effect was not primarily of his politics. He faced no general elections. He never held an "office." No masses of soldiers paraded before him; his books were not prescribed reading for students, recruits, or prisoners.

No one can doubt his influence on humanity, nor his effect on history. He influenced the history of India in the 1920s, 30s and 40s, but he also influenced the history of Africa, Europe, and North America. European policies, particularly Britain's, toward the colonies were also indirectly traceable to Gandhi. The civil rights movement in the U.S. referred to him in its strategy and in its goals.

Adolf Hitler had only one recommendation for Lord Halifax in 1937 regarding the British policy in India: "Shoot Gandhi!" (Manchester 1989, 241). Churchill would not have accepted Hitler's method but in rejecting Gandhi he was not so far from Hitler's position. When Gandhi came to London in 1931 (alone except for the goat that gave him milk every day) in order to speak for the future of India in a conference with the British government, the ruling class in Britain fell over itself to meet Gandhi, to be seen and photographed with him. Only Churchill remained demonstratively distant from Gandhi, whom he had called an "evil and subversive fanatic" a few months earlier (Manchester 1984, 698-700, 693).

In Gandhi's writings, Martin Luther King, Jr. found the bridge between a Christianity hitherto perceived as oriented toward an individual ethic and the political will to change society: Gandhi gave him the hope to "lift the love ethic of Jesus" and to make of it "a powerful and effective social force" (Weisbrot 1991, 15). Gandhi's ethic was political. It was ideally suited to politicizing individual conceptions of morality and motivating to political action those who were resigned due to their oppression. Gandhi was the message that could be used by the American civil rights movement to mobilize the majority of blacks and a minority of whites.

The brands of leadership practiced by Gandhi and Kimball were characterized by a combination of teaching and action. As teachers, both were moralists first. But their activism was a part of their message — political action was not only the supplement and concretization of morality; rather, political action was a part of morality. Gandhi and Kimball succeeded in negating for themselves the division between ethics and politics. Shortly before his death, when Gandhi moved to the miserably poor neighborhood where the West Bengal Moslem minority lived, this action was part of his message of the necessity to overcome religious intolerance. When Kimball demonstratively let himself be arrested in the Southern states, this activism was not only a vehicle to gain public attention through the media; rather, the demonstrated non-violence was a part of the message of a new means of solving conflict.

Moral leadership is not the politically abstinent preaching of values. Even if one aspect of this form of leadership lies in not getting directly involved in the logic of political competition and not running for public office, the Christian duality of the "City of God" and the "City of the World" was not the cause of Gandhi the Hindu or Kimball the Baptist.

Regarding its dimension and its essence, Gandhi's leadership presents a special case. He is the only thinker of the 19th and 20th centuries not in the tradition of Marxism and thus not in the tradition of the European enlightenment who achieved massive political significance globally. He stands for the emancipation of the "Third World" from the intellectual hegemony of Europe. And unlike Lenin or Mao, he practiced leadership not within or through a political system, but outside of and against it. Gandhi had far fewer divisions to suggest than the Popes after the end of the Papal state.

In Burns' differentiation of leadership there is one type that corresponds to Gandhi — "intellectual leadership: ideas as moral force" (Burns 1978, 141-168). Gandhi did not "decide" anything, at least not in the sense of Jaruzelski's declaration of martial law in 1981 or Roosevelt's actions toward U.S. involvement in the war beginning in 1939. But he "influenced" others who were, in turn, in the position to pressure policy-makers. He influenced the public sphere; he influenced the masses. Gandhi was an intellectual, a moral leader of masses and in the detour via the masses he influenced policy-makers.

Gandhi had to refuse office. His moral leadership worked from the outside — it could not have worked from the inside. Moral leadership cannot tolerate a separation of strategy and tactics. Gandhi's message could not be a part of social engineering, could not be divided into reasonable and unreasonable parts. For this reason, even once India was independent, he left the work of governing to other colleagues, particularly Jawaharlal Nehru. Moral leadership is characterized by an intellectual ruthlessness that, in a democracy, has to be foreign to politicians who are always fighting for votes.

Gandhi created consciousness. Through theory and practice, particularly through his example, he made clear what he was for and what he was against. And he was able to bring his examples (and thus his message) to the masses through the media. He practiced an educational leadership — leadership through instruction. For that there had to be technical standards: it is hard to imagine that Gandhi could have achieved the same degree of influence before the invention of film and photography. By means of film and photography the images of the demonstratively poorly dressed Gandhi, who popularized the political weapon of the hunger strike, became symbols of his strategy of conscientious objection and the demands underlying this strategy.

In 1930, Gandhi presented his technique of setting an example with his Salt March. Gandhi walked more than 200 miles through India accompanied by 78 men and women to break the law demonstratively and thereby as publicly as possible. On April 5, after 26 days of walking on foot, he reached the sea, waded into the water, cleansed himself according to Hindu ritual and raised up a handful of sea salt (Shirer 19481, 91-96). Gandhi had acted against the state monopoly on salt only symbolically but with a qualitative clarity; against the British that the Indian National Congress opposed.

The Salt March was a triumphant victory procession through the villages of India. With the combination of his simple message, the avoidance of violence against British rule, and his ascetic example, Gandhi had achieved a maximum of attention. When the government of the British viceroy arrested him after several weeks there were nonviolent mass demonstrations that were violently suppressed by the British and their security forces.

That was both the content and method of Gandhi's message: to expose violence as wrong by using nonviolent means. Freedom from violence thus became a political strength, violence a political weakness.

Gandhi succeeded in this only because public opinion in the western democracies of Europe and North America was susceptible to this message and because there was such a thing as public opinion. Gandhi's strategy of mobilizing the public sphere assumed that there was indeed a public sphere, that the events surrounding and following the Salt March could and would be broadcast throughout India, Great Britain, and the entire world. Gandhi achieved nonviolent resistance against a democracy that, contrary to its own claims, complied with a colonial empire and that, at least in domestic affairs, had to adhere to certain rules of free speech. In a totalitarian system, Gandhi's strategy would not have worked. Nonviolent resistance in Auschwitz and against Auschwitz would have been nonsense.

And Gandhi needed the guilty conscience; he needed the cognitive dissonance of democracy as it existed during his time. Gandhi could count on the principles of the Westminster democracy better than the British viceroy. Gandhi, not the British government, was the representative of natural rights. Gandhi had to touch the nerve of British society, he needed the sensitivity of a democratic society aware that the policies it legitimated were in conflict with its own claims and that these policies were wrong. Gandhi needed Western awareness of what was wrong.

Martin Luther King, Jr. also needed public awareness of what was wrong in an American society dominated only by whites; he needed publicity and the media. As soon as the administrations of Eisenhower, Kennedy, and Johnson could no longer afford to have confrontations between peaceful demonstrators counting on the protection of the American Constitution and bloodthirsty police dogs being broadcast daily into the homes of Americans, the civil rights movement had won. The conscience of society had been moved.

Society felt caught in a lie, not in the sense of the art of deception as a tool of military and political strategy, but in the sense that inverts the essence of society, and makes racist systems of oppression out of democracies that pretend to observe natural rights. Gandhi and Kimball conveyed to the profiteers of this lie — to the British, to white Americans — the recognition of this lie. This recognition, transformed into a "guilty conscience," became the political lever of moral leadership. Gandhi and Kimball succeeded in shaming the profiteers of the lie.

In Max Frisch's "Biedermann and the Arsonists," the revolutionaries — in the sense of Burns' transforming leaders — act openly and
without employing the art of deception. They say what they are —
arsonists who want to bring to Biedermann's world nothing but
destruction. Biedermann gives them free reign because they address
his guilty conscience over and over. And the reason for his guilty
conscience is the status quo for which Biedermann stands. The existing
society is based on the dissonance between claim and reality, between
both raising and violating moral standards. The mere thematization of
this conflict sets a process in motion that forces a change in the status
quo.

Gandhi had a deep understanding of the discrepancy between
reality and pretension and he made a strategic move regarding this
discrepancy. His understanding has to do with his experiences in
Europe, with his study and practice of law in England. While in
London in 1890, he visited the World Exposition in Paris. Deeply
impressed by Notre Dame, he stated decades later: "I felt that those
who expended millions on such divine cathedrals could not but have
the love of God in their hearts" (Gandhi 1957, 101).

Love was the norm of which he was more and more effectively
able to remind those who deviated from it. In his freedom from
violence he was the better representative of Christian, European,
liberal, democratic norms — and the violence that was directed against
him was ultimately damned to lose its legitimation. Gandhi won the
political struggle against the British colonial masters in Great Britain
itself by removing legitimation for the British policy in India. He won
on the ground of those whose political rule he fought against. He had
put himself in their place; he had taken on their norms and exposed
their "ideology"; and he had touched an exposed nerve.

In the 18th and 19th centuries this would likely not have been the
case. The consistency with which the Christian settlers in America and
Australia decimated and in some cases — in the Caribbean, in
Tasmania — even exterminated the native population through
genocide demonstrates that the dissonance between the pretensions
and the reality alone are not enough to make moral, intellectual
leadership possible. It also takes the right time.

The dissonance must rise from the depths of consciousness to just
below the surface in order to be recalled by leadership and
transformed into a guilty conscience. Even instructional leadership that
claims to make use of the guilty conscience needs the precondition of
the potentially guilty conscience. And British colonial rule helped
produce this condition. With the European enlightenment's catalog of

values with which they made the Indian elite very familiar, it delivered the weapon of the anti-colonial struggle, just as the slaveholder Jefferson had delivered the weapon for the fight against slavery with the declaration of human rights.

Moral leadership assumes a potential need. Without potential, a given issue possesses no actuality. Regarding the U.S. before 1776, the slavery question had not yet matured into a potential issue, whereas by 1861, it had. The question of civil rights could not become an issue before the middle of the 20th century, despite the fact that the point of departure and the scandal had existed since the end of slavery in 1863, namely the contradiction between a proclaimed equality between "black" and "white" and the simultaneous open discrimination toward blacks. The society first had to reach a certain level of development to make intellectual, moral, and thus instructional, leadership possible.

The so-called women's question was not an issue for centuries of Western history. Even those thinkers of the European tradition who did not speak of a "natural" inequality of the sexes were blind, or at least insensitive to the sexual discrimination of the real world (Coole 1988). The fact that women, too, belong to this category of insensitivity despite an egalitarian position, e.g., Rosa Luxemburg, only highlights the necessity for social development. To make feminism an issue presupposes social willingness, on the part of women above all, to make it an issue.

Only if there is such social willingness to make an issue of a cause can intellectual leadership intervene by recalling an existing need. If intellectual leadership tries to be effective too soon, it will remain ineffective; or it must turn to means other than intellectual, moral or educational means.

Leninism offers an important example for the consequences of intellectual impatience. Against the Menshevist, Social Democratic interpretations of Marx that claimed that a certain degree of social maturity was necessary for the Revolution which was simply not given in backwards Russia, Lenin counted on revolution in Russia; and he made revolution, even if it had the character of a putsch. Lenin, the undeniable leader of this revolution, had expected a domino effect: from Russia, the revolution was supposed to spread to the advanced industrial states of Western Europe. But Russia was ill-suited to being the initiator of a socialist world revolution — the world revolution failed to appear. And in Russia itself, the leadership of the Bolsheviks and Lenin was not enough to carry through the revolution on the strength of moral conviction alone. Leninism had to reach for the means of dictatorship that logically resulted in the dictatorship of Stalin.

Moral leadership assumes that concrete morality's ability to convince others intellectually will prevail. And this depends on the congruence between concrete morality and the level of social development. In the scholastic Middle Ages, it was possible to debate whether or not women had a soul and whether it was of the same quality as men's. This discourse could gain no relevance for a — perhaps theoretically imaginable — medieval women's movement because medieval society offered no conditions for a women's movement.

Feminism as a theoretical approach to politics and society becomes possible and effective when the real discrimination toward women in society is seen and perceived as such. And this is not even primarily dependent on the degree of discrimination. But as soon as discrimination toward women is perceived, by both men and women, feminism becomes relevant. Then feminist moral leadership is possible.

Moral, intellectual leadership is easily compatible with democracy if the congruence between fundamental, potential need and the instructional message of leadership is given. But even moral leadership stands in a relationship of tension to democracy and its radically egalitarian implications because moral leaders in particular constitute an elite — and according to the understanding of democracy, the existence of the elite is either a self-evident, social pre-condition — as per the tradition of Schumpeter — or a barrier to be overcome at least in its tendencies — as per the tradition of Bachrach (Schumpeter 1972, Bachrach 1967).

However, the compatibility of moral leadership and democracy refers exclusively to non-routine leadership. Within the routine form of leadership in a stable democratic system, there is no place for moral leadership — it would have to exhaust itself figuring out strategies for what can be demanded; moral leadership would have to eliminate from its moral message those elements of its morality that cannot yet be carried out. However, the disassembling of morality into acceptable portions contradicts the dynamic of intellectual clarity needed by moral leadership.

Particularly in a democracy, then, moral leadership signifies the renunciation of political office; it signifies the refusal of political functions because moral leadership depends on a lack of conditions set by others. This prerequisite is lost when, due to the next election, more and more has to be trimmed off the moral message. The moral leader cannot afford to give the impression of being a tactician because yet another of those is not needed in democracy. There are plenty of tacticians at work in the routine leadership of a stable democracy.

In this regard, Burns writes of a "missing piece", i.e., of the missing link of his concept of differentiating between non-routine (transforming) and routine (transactional) leadership (Burns 1978, 257-259). In a democracy, the moral message must create a demand on the political market that comes from the outside and this must in turn bring forth a supply. Even moral leadership must prove itself on the market, must confront the competition of interests and ideas, even if the people who practice this moral leadership distance themselves from the logic of this competition for votes which is, of course, the actual logic of democracy as it exists.

Finally, moral leadership, too, requires a need. It cannot be created from nothing; it must be have a latent presence, ready to be awakened by moral leadership and called to action, i.e., concretized in order to then prevail on the political market as a moral interest.

In her essay on Angelo Guiseppe Roncalli, Pope John Paul XXIII, Hannah Arendt tells the story of a chamber maid in a hotel in Rome who said about this dying Pope in 1963: "How could that be? And how could it happen that a true Christian would sit on St. Peter's chair? Didn't he first have to become Bishop, and Archbishop, and Cardinal, until he finally was elected Pope? Had nobody been aware of who he was?" (Arendt 1968, 57).

As a Pope, Angelo Guiseppe Roncalli was a moral leader. But in order to reach this position that was able to lend his moral leadership the corresponding attention and thus the corresponding weight, he had to take back his morality; he had to disguise himself. Otherwise he would not have become the person he was capable of becoming: the catalyst for a Church perceived as completely calcified. Arendt believes that it is understandable that the Church shields itself from the Roncallis, that it is logical that, if recognized in time, they are not even allowed access to a career. The reality of the Church's organization does not need moral catalysts at its head.

The fact that the moralist Roncalli was able to practice leadership is connected to the fact that his organization was and is free from democracy. The Pope is indeed elected, but by a small circle of male electors selected by the Pope. The Pope determines who determines who is Pope — a constant circle of self-confirming authority, the antithesis of any democratic order.

Even a small amount of democracy would have destroyed Roncalli's leadership. If he had been Pope only temporarily, if he had had to be reelected, he would have been caught up in a net of interest groups that would have significantly limited his freedom to carry out his moral leadership. Roncalli's quality of moral leadership had to be hidden until the zero hour in which he, precisely because his morality was undetected, became Pope. However, the quality of moral leadership of a politician in a stable democracy cannot wait for the zero hour, because there is none. Democracy binds the hands of any leader with control mechanisms that are part and parcel of democracy; the morality of leadership is trimmed to the size warranted by the market.

Democracy is a political order diametrically opposed to the Catholic Church. Democracy does not allow moral leadership from the inside. After the experience of an Angelo Guiseppe Roncalli, whoever climbs the ladder of a political career in order to propagate a morality that, until then, has been strategically hidden, misunderstands the mechanisms of democracy. He or she confuses it with a Church.

Whoever wishes to practice moral leadership in a democracy is free to do so, but only from outside; only by consistently refusing both career and office.

25 Jaruzelski II: On the Arbitrary Nature of Historical Perception

The Viewpoint of the Opposition — The Soviet Viewpoint — "It is time" — The Bishops — A New Type of Transformation — Katyn — The Commissar's Dilemma — Hero or Traitor?

What will the history books write about Jaruzelski's role a hundred years after his historic decision? How will Poland, Europe, and the world evaluate the shifting of courses in which Jaruzelski participated so significantly — the declaration of martial law in 1981, the democratization of Poland in 1989? Will the prison guard of the democracy movement stand in the foreground or will it be the patriot pressured from the outside who reluctantly took on the temporary role of dictator in order to prevent the worst from happening?

Wojciech Jaruzelski had stated that the reason for his decision of December, 1981 was that martial law was the only alternative to an invasion by the Red Army. He admits himself that he had had no absolute proof for this assumption, that there was no immediate threat in the form of an ultimatum (Jaruzelski 1993, 291). But of course, there had not even been an ultimatum before the invasion of the CSSR by troops of the Warsaw Pact countries in August, 1968. In 1981, Jaruzelski considered it likely that history would repeat itself. The man who gave his name to the doctrine that was supposed to justify a military intervention in the Warsaw Pact countries by Soviet troops was still General Secretary of the Communist Party. The existence of the "Brezhnev doctrine" was the basis for Jarzuelski's estimation that an invasion was probable if he himself was not in a position to reinstate the old power monopoly.

Jaruzelski's viewpoint is not uncontroversial. Soviet documents, accessible after the collapse of the Soviet Union, seem to indicate that in December, 1981 the Soviet leadership was not — or not yet — prepared to invade Poland. According to the record of the Politburo's meeting on December 10, 1981, Andropov, Gromyko, Suslov, and Ustinov opposed invasion. At a hearing of the Sejm in April, 1994, Jaruzelski acknowledged the authenticity of the protocol after having first claiming it was forged. But he sees no reason to deviate from the point of view he advocated publicly beginning in 1989. Martial law remains for him the "lesser evil." He insists the invasion was a real possibility. And subjectively, he could hold no other opinion in December, 1981. First, he was not informed about the exact content of the meetings of the Soviet Politburo; second, there had been enough military movement to make a military option on the part of Soviet leadership plausible — fortification of Soviet garrisons on Polish soil, and the movement of troops of the Warsaw Pact countries toward the Polish border (Hirsch 1993; Rosenberg 1995, 214-216).

The fact that the Soviet Politburo had not agreed to an invasion on December 10, 1981 does not, of course, mean that this threat did not exist. The invasion of the CSSR in 1968 had been decided only three days earlier. And the Soviet leaders left the Polish general in the dark regarding their intentions, perhaps less for reasons of political finesse and more for reasons of a fundamental weakness when it came to making decisions. But even this Politburo had shown itself capable of risky, aggressive measures at the end of 1979 vis-à-vis Afghanistan.

Jaruzelski refers to the statements of the Soviet military personnel who say they had orders to prepare for an invasion of Poland, information, however, that he himself says he had access to only years later (Jaruzelski 1993, 290). In 1981 there would have been information regarding many details: the Red Army had summoned Polish-speaking civilians, beds had been prepared in the hospitals along the border, and there had been changes in the guard posts along the border (Jaruzelski 1992).

There was a group of Communists functionaries in Poland who would have been prepared to justify an intervention. On November 13, 1981, the Politburo of the SED received news of a conversation with Michal Atlas, the leader of the Department of Security and State Organizations of the Central Committee of the Polish Communist party, the PUWP. Atlas had stated to the GDR informant on November 10: "Only a clear Marxist-Leninist course of action against the counter revolution could bring about a change. But neither General Jaruzelski nor the present Politburo is willing to carry it out" (Kubina 1995, 385).

Inside the PUWP, then, there was a faction evidently prepared to set a "course of action against the counter revolution" — against Jaruzelski; and to convey this information to the GDR leaders who advocated the most militant policies in the "socialist camp" regarding dual rule in Poland. Jaruzelski had to assume that inside the leadership of the PUWP there was a functionary prepared to act as a Polish Kadar and lend the appearance of domestic Polish legitimation to a military intervention based on the Brezhnev doctrine. Jaruzelski could refer to the fact that he had not stood for the entire PUWP; rather, that inside the PUWP there had been a wing of orthodox Communists against him that would have helped establish a Husak regime in Poland if necessary.

The investigation that the Sejm decided on in 1991 and that began against Jaruzelski and other top leaders of the PUWP in 1992 demonstrated clear fronts. Jaruzelski argued that martial law had been the least of all possible evils. He had, to be sure, saved the Communist regime from Solidarity, but he had also saved Solidarity from the Red Army (Rosenberg 1995, 178f.). Like the opening of the archives, the proceedings failed to bring a clear, generally accepted answer. The question of whether or not Jaruzelski is a hero or a traitor remains open. The question cannot be decided by any proceedings and probably also not by any future research. It will be decided by history, i.e., by the necessarily biased perception of those who control access to the history books.

It was clear in the hearings conducted by the Sejm beginning in 1992 that in the fall of 1981, many people wanted to see in Jaruzelski a willingness to declare martial law in any case, regardless of the reality of a Soviet threat. This viewpoint, which at first contradicts Jaruzelski's presentation of events is also supported by Mieczyslaw Rakowksi, which weighs all the heavier since within the PUWP he was considered to be Jaruzelski's man (Rosenberg 1995, 217). But Jaruzelski insists that the possibility of a Soviet invasion was real and that declaring martial law was the only means of combating this threat — and that without this threat his decision would have been different.

How real the Soviet threat of invasion was in December, 1981 cannot easily be determined. But it must be clear to the writers of history that such a threat fit the pattern of Soviet politics; also the fact that Soviet leadership had to count on the fears of the Husak regime and threatening gestures by the Honecker regime, both of which saw themselves threatened by developments in Poland and expected the Communist Party to intensify pressure on Jaruzelski; also the fact that the Polish national and historical consciousness is drenched with the experience of invasions and aggression from Russia, just as the Russian perception of Poland is one of aggression.

For the historical evaluation of General Jaruzelski it must also be remembered what he "made" of the declaration of martial law, how he instituted it. The phase of martial law was followed by an historic era in which Jaruzelski's Poland became the most powerful force in the Warsaw pact, one that supported the course of reform set by

Gorbachev and then used it in turn toward reforms in Poland. Jaruzelski became a special student of perestroika and glasnost, and this was to be the foundation for the exemplary transformation of 1989.

It is therefore not surprising that the representatives of the Soviet reform begun in 1985 see Jaruzelski in a positive light even after the failure of their own attempts. They support his perspective of the events of 1981 and thus Jaruzelski's credibility as the representative of a politics of reform not only from necessity but from conviction.

Edvard Shevardnadze, the last Foreign Secretary of the Soviet Union, offers the perception of Jaruzelski's testimony in a double way. More than two years before the publication of the protocols of the Soviet Politburo meeting on December 10, 1981 brought new life to the conversation, Shevardnadze told of a meeting with Suslov in the decisive days of 1981 in which Suslov made clear "... there can be no talk of using violence in Poland." But Shevardnadze also argued that the Soviet invasion of Afghanistan scarcely two years earlier could hardly be viewed as an indication of Soviet reserve and would strengthen the plausibility of an analogous invasion in Poland; and that only Jaruzelski's intervention, that is, the declaration of martial law, had ended the speculation and debate surrounding a possible invasion. This corresponds more or less to Jaruzelski's report of his phone conversation with Suslov on December 12, 1981. Jaruzelski "convinced Soviet leadership that the Poles could master the situation themselves and he saved his country from invasion" (Shevardnadze 1991, 216; Jaruzelski 1992).

Mikhail Gorbachev adopts Jaruzelski's point of view. Without going into detail about how real the threat of Soviet invasion was at the end of 1981, the last General Secretary of the Communist Party and the last President of the USSR says that Jaruzelski had seen in the declaration of martial law "the least evil," which he had viewed as "unavoidable." Gorbachev also confirms that Jaruzelski had encouraged the reforms after December 13 "in his own way" (Gorbachev 1995, 864f.)

Gorbachev may be tempted to support the justification of Jaruzelski because shortly after Gorchachev's appointment as party leader in March of 1985, the Polish party leader was to become his closest ally in the Warsaw Pact and in the COMECON. Jaruzelski was the first ally to take up Gorbachev's ideas of reform in terms of an economical, cultural, and finally, political opening — against the resistance of all other allies, with the exception of Hungary. Jaruzelski became Gorbachev's most important Communist partner outside the

USSR for the implementation of the development that was to lead to the end of Marxism-Leninism in Europe (Gorbachev 1995, 846f., 866-878). Jaruzelski played not only a national but an international role in the collapse of the Soviet-type systems, i.e., of the Communist dictatorships.

Gorbachev's and Schevardnadze's interpretations correspond to a certain bias. Those who were responsible for the development of the Soviet Union between 1985 and 1991 must have an interest in gaining arguments for their policy of gradual change by referring to those of a similar mind, given that the old system for which the name Brezhnev stood was lost, and that from the perspective of 1985 there was certainly the possibility that "socialism with a human face" would survive.

Not coincidentally, Gorbachev referred to the "Prague Spring," to that experiment stemming from the Communist Party of an opening to more pluralism that served him as an example beginning in 1985 (Gorbachev 1985, 879-882). The Prague Spring is the model to which reformers of the final Soviet phase, which ultimately failed, could refer when they insisted that perestroika and glasnost had stood a chance as a form of socialism that removes repression, allows open criticism (and thus opposition), opens the gate to the open competition of ideas, introduces a market economy step by step, and counts not only on détente but on international disarmament. Gorbachev needs a Jaruzelski, he needs the Poland of the mid- and late 1980's with its low degree of actual repression, remarkable for contemporary standards. And Jaruzelski needs Gorbachev to help cast the right light on his name in the history books; to prove that he had to be the suppresser of Polish democracy due to external pressures, but that by his own inclination he wanted and was able to be the one who unchained this same democracy.

But it is also true that bias stems from those who contradict this perspective. When the Sejm was supposed to make a decision on whether the investigation into the roles of Jaruzelski and other Communist functionaries was to be carried out in 1991, ten years after martial law had been declared, 51 votes were for the parliamentary hearings — one vote more than was legally necessary (Rosenberg 1995, 126). The accusation was of the misuse of power and high treason. The results of the years-long investigations are best described as "inconclusive" — contradictory and unsatisfactory also in the sense that the controversy over Jaruzelski's role continues.

Jaruzelski's dual role as dictator and democratizer, as prison warden and liberator naturally creates difficulties for those who were his victims in 1981. His most prominent victim was Lech Walesa. In his autobiography of 1987, Walesa is cautious concerning the role of Jaruzelski. This caution must be seen in the context of the transitional phase in which Poland found itself at this time: Gorbachev's reforms catalyzed a certain dynamic for Poland as well, to which Jaruzelski's regime reacted positively. Solidarity was no longer suppressed as it had been during the time of martial law. But it was also not a center of power independent from the state and the party as it had been before December 13, 1981. Poland was in a sort of twilight zone that allowed glimpses of the democracy to come, but Poland was not yet a democracy.

It was during this time that Walesa, who received the Nobel Peace Prize in 1983, wrote his biography. And he drew a differentiated portrait of Jaruzelski: For the time directly before the declaration of martial law he counted "the General" as one of the most moderate of the PVAP; as one of those "you could talk to" (Walesa 1987, 283). *Walesa* told of the Pope's letter and the copy of the Pope's letter to Jaruzelski that were delivered during his arrest on December 25, 1981 (*Walesa* 1987, 313f.). Especially telling is the letter Walesa wrote to Jaruzelski from prison on November 8, 1982: (Walesa 1987, 334)

"To General Wojciech Jaruzelski, Warsaw
It seems to me that it is time to discuss certain problems and steps that could lead to an agreement. It has taken some time for many to understand what is possible and how far one can go. I suggest a meeting for a serious discussion of the issues that interest us. With good will we will surely find a solution.

Corporal Lech Walesa."

The "Corporal" was then released from incarceration. On December 31, 1982 martial law was "suspended" and in June 1983, officially ended (Lopinski 1990, XVII). The "twilight zone" began. The internal conditions for a second attempt at transforming Communist dictatorship were in place.

Jaruzelski's perception (and justification) that by declaring martial law he had held open the future option of continuing the reforms that had been arrested in December of 1981 is indirectly confirmed by Lech Walesa. It was "time" again to speak together, to seek an understanding. They were able to speak together — the harm done to the democracy movement had not been too serious for that. And Jaruzelski had determined the time for the continuation of the dialog. The "break" provided by martial law was over. Walesa, and with him the entire democracy movement, had been hit, but not destroyed. The capacity for action was able to be restored as soon as international circumstances permitted.

It is an unusual tyrant who consciously leaves open the possibility for the destruction of his own tyranny; who views his opponents and victims as potential partners; who, on the one hand, accepts and must accept the responsibility for dictatorship and the concomitant human rights violations but who, on the other hand, leaves structures in place that could one day remind him of this very responsibility.

The human rights violations for which Jaruzelski was responsible are well documented (Poland Under Martial Law 1983; Labedz 1984; Lopinski 1990; Bernhard, Szlajfer 1995). The dictatorship of martial law never had the totalitarian hallmarks of Stalinism. That is why the world knew what was going on in Poland. The violations of legal proceedings, the attacks by the police and by the army, and the manipulation through government propaganda were all well known. Beginning on December 13, 1981, Jaruzelski was one of the most hated men in the world, the symbolic figure of a tyranny who combined all the evil qualities of a military dictatorship with all the evil qualities of the Communist dictatorship.

In the underground press he was called a "terrorist;" the (relative) self-limitation of repression was seen as an expression of his weakness: "We do not believe in good and bad terrorists. A terrorist becomes a liberal only when he is forced to do so. The authorities decided to restrict the number of arrests and administer the plan for repression with some moderation, because it pays them to do so. We must make this liberal concept less attractive to them" (Labedz 1984, 14f.).

This reaction to martial law was more than just understandable. Whoever sits in prison may not like being mollified by comparative analyses of Stalin and Jaruzelski. Jaruzelski had to cope with this reaction — using political methods he had to transform this sharp rejection into a willingness to cooperate. The fact that he succeeded, that the representatives of the democracy movement entered a dialog with the "terrorist," that they became involved with his strategy and even co-created it with him, that they accepted his leadership on the path to democracy is the final balance of Jaruzelski's leadership qualities. He was able to overcome the barrier that he himself had erected. Jaruzelski succeeded in dissolving the massive resistance he himself had provoked.

This General and Dictator conducted the dismantling of his personal power at first cautiously, then — in alliance with Gorbachev — with increasing openness. Nothing is changed by the fact that this can also have to do with self-interest. Unlike Brezhnev and Husak, Jaruzelski may have recognized the fact that the Soviet-type systems could not be saved; he may have secured his own role in time for the transformation that was viewed as unavoidable. But insight into the real situation of one's own rule is not something that can be held against a leader — on the contrary.

Jaruzelski was working toward a second, decisive role toward the transformation made possible through him and with him of the fragile Communist dictatorship in Poland. It is difficult to say when it must have become clear to Jaruzelski that he was undermining his own position. As a favored partner of Gorbachev, he, like him, must have indulged in illusions about the stability of an open, pluralistic system that would still have been a Soviet system.

In this regard the Bishops played a significant role. In general they had a moderating role during this phase: they convinced the illegal opposition not to reject Jaruzelski's strategy. There was also criticism of the Church within the opposition for this reason: "The freedom to practise Christianity can be fought for through love and humility. But Christian civilizations have always defended themselves with fire and sword" (Labedz 1984, 14).

The Bishops wanted to avoid a politics of "fire and sword" at all costs and were therefore able to come to an understanding with Jaruzelski that was at least strategic: no politics of burning ships, no destruction of future options, therefore as little physical violence as possible. If Jaruzelski was the one most responsible for the self-limitation of repression, then the Bishops were the ones most responsible for the self-limitation of resistance.

This mutual moderation during martial law paid off during the early phases of transformation. The connection between Jaruzelski and the Bishops was never completely broken off. The Pope's trips to Jaruzelski's Poland in June of 1983 and June of 1987 were ambivalent signals: creating bridges as well as criticism; arguments for moderation on the part of the opposition, but also the possibility of identification with all opponents of the regime.

The meaning of the Church for Poland's unique role in the process of transformation must be estimated to be very great indeed. For Polish history in the 19th and 20th centuries, the Catholic Church had the role of keeper of national identity and continuity: as a force of resistance against Prussia (associated with Protestantism) and then Germany and then (orthodox) Russia and against the new pagan and atheist forms of totalitarianism that had invaded and ruled Poland in the 20th century. The Church was the most important matrix for Polish resistance against all these forms of national or ideological foreign rule. For that reason, the election of the Cardinal Archbishop of Cracow as Pope in 1978 must be seen as an important moment in Polish history: with the international recognition of the Polish Church, even Polish resistance felt encouraged. It was only a short path from here to the massive strikes in the summer of 1980, to the democracy movement, and to the dualism of the political system in 1980 and 1981.

The bishops and the clergy were left unharmed for the most part during martial rule. They stood at the ready as mediators. They could assume a highly informed public — the approval rating of the Church and the level of actual participation in the life of the Church in Poland was among the highest in Europe during the 1980's. In 1990 at the onset of democracy in Poland, 80 percent of the Polish population stated that the Church enjoyed a high level of prestige. This was the basis for the influence of the Church and the Bishops. The fact that this approval rating would sink to 55 percent over the next two years demonstrates that the prestige of the Church could be explained on the basis of its function in the resistance. The end of the resistance that had come in the moment when Walesa, Mazowiecki and other confidants of the Church governed, hollowed out this function and thus the prestige of the Church (von Beyme 1994, 157).

Thus, paradoxically, the bishops were in the same boat as Jaruzelski. They participated actively in the establishment of the national consensus that was negotiated at the round table conferences of 1989 and implemented after the Sejm election. The result was that Jaruzelski had made himself superfluous and that the approval of the Bishops, and also their social influence, began to decline. Jaruzelski and the Bishops shared the role of loser in the transformation.

Like Jaruzelski, the Bishops were not interested in intensifying the confrontation between government and opposition during the final phase of the Jaruzelski era. In 1988 an intensification was in the offing: the partially legal opposition made greater and greater challenges to the government. The new tones emanating from Moscow had dissolved the threat of a Soviet intervention, so Jaruzelski was able to react differently to the intensified confrontation in 1988 than had been possible in 1981. The result was that the round tables were organized. But the condition was that Solidarity had to be give legal status, a return to the circumstances of 1980/81 in a certain sense (Jaruzelski 1996, 332-337). Jaruzelski and the second general who played an important role in this stage of development, Czeslaw Kiszczak, forced the party apparatus to take this step, threatening to resign if it did not.

Jaruzelski did not go with his party into the democratization phase; he dragged his party along after him (Bachmann 1995, 39).

The round table conferences constituted a special sort of coopera- tion. There sat the prison warden and the forces of the Party, still a monopoly, that were prepared for — or forced by Jaruzelski into accepting — reform. Opposite them sat their victims, emerged from underground, having been released from prison not long before.

The round table conferences in Poland were an historic first: until then, there had been no example of the evolutionary transformation of a Communist system. Fascist systems and military dictatorships had transformed gradually; Greece in 1974 and Spain beginning in 1976 offer interesting examples of this process. The ability of Communist systems to change within the parameters of their system, especially while maintaining the Communist Party's monopoly on power, was an important characteristic for both Communists and anti-Communists; for Communists because the irrevocability and thus the historical uniqueness of a Leninist revolution seemed certain; for anti-Commu- nists because the inability of Communism to be reformed seemed to them confirmed.

General Jaruzelski's Poland refuted these interpretations. It demonstrated that, under certain conditions, the system was capable of being reformed; that an evolutionary transformation of a Commu- nist system toward democracy could take place. There were two elites cooperating in a pattern of "conscociational democracy": the elite of the ruling regime and the counter-elite of the reactivated democracy movement. They arrived at a compromise that then signified transi- tion:

— Free elections in both chambers of parliament (the Senate and the Sejm) while a Communist majority in the Sejm was guaranteed.

— The legalization of Solidarity as a union and thus the legalization of the entire democracy movement as a condition for free competition.

— Certain changes to the Constitution that weakened its Communist character (abolishment of the collective presidency) and increased the weight of the Senate in the legislative process (Bachmann 1995).

Contemporary critics of the Polish path by no means considered it probable that the compromise between the elites could bring about a peaceful transition. The danger of explosion existed precisely because

Gorbachev's reforms in Poland had met with such high regard and approval, Zdenek Mlynar argued. Given the overly enthusiastic reaction in Poland, the ability of the system to develop could be strained, the result of which could be civil war instead of evolution (Mlynar 1990, 146f.).

It was due to Jaruzelski that the dynamic of the democracy movement was given the necessary space to use its evolutionary energies. The trust that existed between him and Gorbachev evidently had the effect of assuaging the fears of the "other side" of his own camp: the representatives of the Communist Party, particularly in the CSSR, the GDR and Romania, who saw their own positions endangered. Nevertheless, beginning in late summer 1989, Poland was represented by a Catholic, anti-Communist head of government at the corresponding meetings of the Warsaw Pact or by a demonstratively "apolitical" Defense Minister who could count on Jaruzelski and thus also indirectly on Gorbachev.

The cooperation between Jaruzelski and Gorbachev led to a process of clarification that was important for Polish self-understanding in the beginning stages of Polish democratization. This clarification had to do with bringing to light the historical truth surrounding Katyn. Jaruzelski himself had been deeply affected by the trauma of Katyn. It was his fellow officers who had been murdered at Stalin's command in Soviet prison camps in 1940. Katyn touched the self-understanding of Poland both as the result of the pact between Hitler and Stalin and as a crime one could believe both capable of committing. As a Nazi instrument of propaganda against Stalin and as a Communist instrument of propaganda against Hitler, it reflected Poland's role as object and victim in the evil competition of the powerful neighbors.

Public doubt as to the version of events surrounding the mass murder of Katyn were forbidden for decades in Poland and in the entire Soviet sphere of influence. Even in the wake of de-Stalinization after the 20th Congress of the Communist Party, there could be no doubting the "truth" that Stalin had set in stone. Any Polish emancipation from Soviet dictatorship could be measured only to the extent that Poland was officially permitted to break the taboo. And any Soviet claim of Polish-Soviet brotherhood would have to be evaluated according to whether or not this historical event could be named.

The discovery of the crimes of Katyn had weighed heavily upon the already strained relations between the Polish exile government in London and the Soviet government. When the German leadership informed the world of the mass graves in Katyn in April of 1943, it was clear that the Germans' political intention was to drive a wedge between the Western powers and the Soviet Union. The Polish exile government that had allied itself with the Soviet Union in 1941 despite the unresolved question of the border could no longer be held to the line given by Churchill with regard to Katyn. The British Prime Minister, who considered the German version of the mass murders to be "probably right," spread the word that the Katyn massacre was to be ignored as much as was possible (Charmley 1993, 532). Sikorski accepted the suggestion of the Germans and stated his preference for an independent investigation, thereby giving Stalin the opportunity to break off relations with the Polish exile government.

Doubts remained regarding the Soviet version (Fitzgibbon 1977). The details that were known spoke too strongly against the Soviet representation of the facts. For the sake of the anti-Hitler alliance, the Allies kept quiet. And the Communist rule that had been established in Poland in 1944 and 1945 permitted no public discussion that would not have corresponded to Soviet interpretation from the outset.

Until Gorbachev and Jaruzelski, Katyn remained a taboo subject between the two countries. When Jaruzelski visited Moscow in April, 1987 he initiated a Soviet-Polish commission of historians whose task was to work out the less savory aspects of Polish-Soviet history. From the beginning, the subject of Katyn held the most prominent position (Gorbachev 1995, 866).

But the resistance of the Soviet bureaucracy curbed the insight into historical truth. Valentin Falin attributes the delay in part to Gorbachev's indecisiveness in breaking through this resistance. Yet Ettinger sees Jaruzelski's role all the more clearly: He "missed no opportunity to remind Gorbachev of how important it was to eliminate the obscurity surrounding Katyn" (Ettinger 1993, 446).

Jaruzelski's pressure was successful. The resistance Gorbachev attributed to the KGB was broken. The decisive documents were found and the findings were clear: in 1940 the Politburo, on the suggestion of Beria, had given the command for the mass shooting and killing of Polish officers. While Jaruzelski was in Moscow for an official state visit on April 13, 1990, the Soviet side "expressed its deep regret about the misdeeds of Katyn and stated that they (the misdeeds, A.P.) constituted one of the worst crimes of Stalinism" (Gorbachev 1995, 875).

Jaruzelski had achieved the clarification of and the end of prohibition on a particularly painful event in Polish history. His tenaciousness had forced the collapsing USSR to confess its historical guilt. What sort of Communist was this who had wrung the responsibility for an unjustifiable mass murder from Lenin's country?

In Artur Koestler's essay "The Yogi and the Commissar" the dilemma of the title characters is sketched out. The first, who wants to save the world from the inside of man is certainly not the type of General and Communist and leader as Jaruzelski. But the Commissar has qualities that can contribute to an understanding of Jaruzelski. The Commissar's dilemma consists of the contradictory quality of the hairpin curve and the cliff:

On the way up to the better world that is desired, the Commissar and the movement he leads can either careen too quickly around the curve and fall off the cliff, an image which corresponds to the image of Leninism driven forward by impatience. Or the Commissar can check the speed of social progress in order to avoid this danger — then he and his movement lose momentum; they get stuck on their way to the top, an image which corresponds to Social Democracy. The contradictory nature of the cliff in turn affects the relationship between the end and the means. Every decision to subordinate the means to the end leads to the Moscow purges — and thus begins the race down the cliff into the valley. This decision removes any effectiveness the Commissar's intention might have had (Koestler 1964, 11f.).

Jaruzelski acted as an extremely sensitive Commissar. In 1981 he saw to it that the Polish democracy movement did not go over the cliff on the winding uphill road and he did this by applying adequate means to this end, even when they could not be justified in and of themselves ("dirty hands"). In 1989, Jaruzelski the Commissar was faced with a completely different topographical picture and accordingly, he accelerated the tempo of the democracy movement. Jaruzelski did possess a functional end-means relationship, and with it he ended not in Stalinism but in democracy.

Jaruzelski — hero or traitor? It may well be that history books of the future will reduce their evaluation of the General to this simple question. And there is an answer to it that does not merely simplify: Jaruzelski was both hero and traitor.

In 1981 Jaruzelski was a hero and in the same year, a traitor. In 1981 he was willing to do the dirty work he recognized as necessary in order to gain for Poland a grace period in the shadows of East-West conflict and to maintain Poland's position on the path toward transformation. Dirty work, because he accepted the responsibility for martial law and thus for the prison and prohibitions and oppression. For those whom he oppressed, indeed, within the framework of his logic, *had* to oppress, he was of course a traitor, a Kremlin agent who carried out what would have been too troublesome for Moscow.

Both perceptions are correct. Yet each of these perspectives taken individually is not the entire truth. Just as it is not the entire truth if one takes only a partial view of the Jaruzelski of 1989:

This Jaruzelski was a hero. He marched forward, strengthened by Gorbachev but also a step ahead of him and a step ahead of Hungary. Jaruzelski was responsible for the first truly free elections in a Warsaw Pact nation and thus for the first non-Communist led government. It was Jaruzelski who made it possible for Tadeusz Mazowiecki to be head of government and who himself withdrew to the post of state president, which, according to the Polish Constitution in effect at the time, was the second-ranked governmental office. And when this rank was later elevated, he, the General, was to be succeeded by the "Corporal."

For the democracy movement of the year 1989, therefore, Jaruzelski would have been a hero, had it not been for his past as prison warden and had it not been for the suspicion that Jaruzelski had simply recognized more quickly than others what had to be done.

In both decisive phases of his political career, Jaruzelski acted out of reasons of political strategy. He calculated both the international and the Polish situation in 1981 and arrived at a clear conclusion. And he calculated of course in 1989 and even before, that Gorbachev's path would have repercussions that would necessarily destroy the Soviet model. Jaruzelski did not act against the circumstances he saw facing him. He did not sail against the wind. But he also did not let himself simply be carried along.

For this reason he was both a hero and a traitor. But he was not a martyr. History books of the future would surely have greeted him as such. But he was, in a complicated way, a treacherous hero and a heroic traitor. He was a true hero and a true traitor.

However, democracy as it exists has no use for true heroes and true traitors. This is why Polish democracy, whose doors he had opened, had no place for Jaruzelski the hero-traitor. Through successful leadership he had made himself superfluous.

Monika Jaruzelski, the General's daughter, had evidently been quite opinionated with regard to her father's role. As a teenager, she was increasingly critical toward him politically, beginning in 1980. She had friendly contact with Solidarity activists. During the course of martial law some of her closest friends were arrested; Monika Jaruzelski considered suicide. For years she did not exchange a single word with her father. After the democratization of Poland, she gradually began to see the course of historical events and thus her father's role in a different, and more differentiated, light. Ultimately, she even accepted his point of view that martial law was the "lesser evil."

"When you are young you see things in black and white ... As you grow up you see how difficult making decisions can be, that sometimes you can't control your circumstances" (Rosenberg 1995, 228).

For Monika Jaruzelski at any rate, the General is not a traitor — any longer.

26 Bibliography

AGNOLI 1968: Johannes Agnoli, Peter Brückner: Die Transformation der Demokratie. Frankfurt am Main.

ALMOND, POWELL 1966: Gabriel Almond, G.Bingham Powell, Jr.: Comparative Politics. A developmental approach. Boston.

AMBROSE 1991: Stephen E. Ambrose: Nixon. Vol.III. Ruin and Recovery 1973-1990. New York.

APTHEKER 1951-1974: Herbert Aptheker: A Documentary History of the Negro People in the United States. IV Vol. New York.

ARENDT 1968: Hannah Arendt: Men in Dark Times. New York.

ARENDT 1987: Hannah Arendt: Wahrheit und Lüge in der Politik. Zwei Essays. München.

ARENDT 1989: Hannah Arendt: Die Krise des Zionismus. Essays und Kommentare 2. Berlin.

ARENDT 1995: Hannah Arendt: Rahel Varnhagen. Lebensgeschichte einer deutschen Jüdin aus der Romantik. München.

ARENDT 1995: Hannah Arendt: Eichmann in Jerusalem. Ein Bericht von der Banalität des Bösen. München.

ASH 1984: Timothy Garton Ash: The Polish Revolution. Solidarity. New York.

ATWOOD 1987: Margaret Atwood: The Handmaid's Tale. New York.

BACHMANN 1995: Klaus Bachmann: Poland. In: Hanspeter Neuhold et al. (eds.): Political and Economic Transformation in East Central Europe. Boulder, 37-55.

BACHRACH 1967: Peter Bachrach: The Theory of Democratic Elitism. A Critique. Boston.

BARNES 1990: Julian Barnes: A History of the World in 10 1/2 Chapters. London.

BEAUVOIR 1968: Simone de Beauvoir: Force of Circumstance. Harmondsworth.

BERNHARD, SZLAJFER 1995: Michael Bernhard, Henryk Szlajfer (eds.): From the Polish Underground. Selections from Krytyka, 1978 - 1993. University Park (PA).

BEYME 1994: Klaus von Beyme: Systemwechsel in Osteuropa. Frankfurt am Main.

BLAKE 1969: Robert Blake: Disraeli. London.

BLONDEL 1987: Jean Blondel: Political Leadership. Towards a General Analysis. London.

BRUS 1982: Wlodzimierz Brus et al.: „Normalisierungsprozesse" im sowjetisierten Mitteleuropa. Ungarn, Tschechoslowakei, Polen. Forschungsprojekt Krisen in den Systemen sowjetischen Typs, geleitet von Zdenek Mlynar. Studie Nr.1.

BÜCHELE 1993: Herwig Büchele: SehnSucht nach der Schönen neuen Welt. Thaur, Tirol.

BURNHAM 1943: James Burnham: The Machiavellians. Defenders of Freedom. New York.

BURNS 1978: James MacGregor Burns: Leadership. New York.

CHAMBERLAIN 1922: Houston Stewart Chamberlain: Die Grundlagen des XIX. Jahrhunderts. München.

CHARMLEY 1993: John Charmley: Churchill. The End of Glory. A Political Biography. Sevenoaks, Kent.

CONQUEST 1968: Robert Conquest: The Great Terror. Stalin's Purge of the Thirties. Harmondsworth.

COOLE 1988: Diana H.Coole: Women in Political Theory. From Ancient Misogony to Contemporary Feminism. Boulder.

CROSSMANN 1949: Richard Crossman (ed.): The God That Failed. New York.

DAHL 1956: Robert A.Dahl: A Preface to Democratic Theory. Chicago.

DAHL 1989: Robert A.Dahl: Democracy and Its Critics. New Haven.

DE GRAZIA 1989: Sebastian de Grazia: Machiavelli in Hell. Princeton.

DOWNS 1957: Anthony Downs: An Economic Theory of Democracy. New York.

EASTON 1953: David Easton: The Political System. An Inquiry into the State of Political Science. New York.

EDELMAN 1985: Murray Edelman: The Symbolic Uses of Politics. Urbana, Illinois.

ELIAS 1987: Norbert Elias: Engagement und Distanzierung. Arbeiten zur Wissenssoziologie I. Frankfurt am Main.

ETTINGER 1995: Elzbieta Ettinger: Hannah Arendt. Martin Heidegger. Eine Geschichte. München.

FALIN 1993: Valentin M.Falin: Politische Erinnerungen. München.

FEST 1973: Joachim C.Fest: Hitler. Eine Biographie. Frankfurt am Main.

FINER 1976: S.E.Finer: The Man on Horseback. The Role of Military in Politics. Harmondsworth.

FISCHER 1969: Ernst Fischer: Erinnerungen und Reflexionen. Reinbek.

FITZGIBBON 1977: Louis Fitzgibbon: Katyn Massacre. London.

FRAENKEL 1964: Ernst Fraenkel: Deutschland und die westlichen Demokratien. Stuttgart.

FRAENKEL 1974: Ernst Fraenkel: Der Doppelstaat. Frankfurt am Main.

FRANKLIN 1980: John Hope Franklin: From Slavery to Freedom. A History of Negro Americans. New York.

FREY 1983: Bruno S.Frey: Democratic Economic Policy. A Theoretical Introduction. Oxford.

FUEGI 1995: John Fuegi: The Life and Lies of Bertolt Brecht. London.

GANDHI 1957: Mohandas K.Gandhi: An Autobiography. The Story of My Experiments With Truth. Boston.

GILMAN 1979: Charlotte Perkins Gilman: Herland. London.

GOLDMAN 1994: Peter Goldman et al.: Quest for the Presidency 1992. College Station (Texas).

GORBACHEV 1995: Mikhail Gorbachev: Erinnerungen. Berlin.

GUÉHENNO 1994: Jean-Marie Guéhenno: Das Ende der Demokratie. München.

HAFFNER 1978: Sebastian Haffner: Anmerkungen zu Hitler. München.

HALBERSTAM 1972: David Halberstam: The Best and the Brightest. New York.

HAMILTON, MADISON, JAY: On the Constitution. Selections from the Federalist Papers. New York (1954).

HENNIS 1973: Wilhelm Hennis: Die mißverstandene Demokratie. Demokratie – Verfassung – Parlament. Studien zu deutschen Problemen. Freiburg im Breisgau.

HILL 1979: Melvyn A.Hill (ed.): Hannah Arendt. The Recovery of the Public World. New York.

HIRSCH 1969: Helmut Hirsch: Rosa Luxemburg in Selbstzeugnissen und Bilddokumenten. Reinbek.

HIRSCH 1993: Helga Hirsch: Die Russen wollten gar nicht einmarschieren. In: Die Zeit, 50/1993, 10.Dezember, 98.

HODGSON 1980: Godfrey Hodgson: All Things to All Men. The False Promise of the Modern American Presidency. New York.

HUXLEY 1985: Aldous Huxley: Ape and Essence. London.

ISAACSON 1992: Walter Isaacson: Kissinger. A Biography. London.

JARUZELSKI 1992: Wojciech Jaruzelski: Das war psychische Folter. Interview. Der Spiegel, 20/1992.

JARUZELSKI 1993: Wojciech Jaruzelski: Mein Leben für Polen. Erinnerungen. Mit einem Gespräch zwischen Wojciech Jaruzelski und Adam Michnik. München.

JARUZELSKI 1996: Wojciech Jaruzelski: Hinter den Türen der Macht. Der Anfang vom Ende einer Herrschaft. Leipzig.

JOLY 1990: Maurice Joly: Ein Streit in der Hölle. Gespräche zwischen Machiavelli und Montesquieu über Macht und Recht. Frankfurt am Main.

KATZENSTEIN 1996: Peter J. Katzenstein: Cultural Norms and National Security. Police and Military in Postwar Japan. Ithaca.

KEARNS 1976: Doris Kearns: Lyndon Johnson and the American Dream. New York.

KEARNS GOODWIN 1987: Doris Kearns Goodwin: The Fitzgeralds and the Kennedys. An American Saga. New York.

KELSEN 1963: Hans Kelsen: Vom Wesen und Wert der Demokratie. Aalen.

KENNEDY 1956: John F.Kennedy: Profiles in Courage. New York.

KIMBALL 1997: Warren F.Kimball: Forged in War. Roosevelt, Churchill, and the Second World War. New York.

KISSINGER n.d.: Henry A.Kissinger: A World Restored. Metternich, Castlereagh and the Problems of Peace 1812-1822. Boston.

KISSINGER 1979: Henry A.Kissinger: White House Years. Boston.

KISSINGER 1994: Henry A. Kissinger: Diplomacy. New York.

KNOLL 1962: August Maria Knoll: Katholische Kirche und scholastisches Naturrecht. Zur Frage der Freiheit. Wien.

KOESTLER 1947: Artur Koestler: Darkness at Noon. London.

KOESTLER 1964: Artur Koestler: The Yogi and the Commissar. London.

KUBINA 1995: Michael Kubina u.a.: „Hart und kompromißlos durchgreifen."
Die SED contra Polen 1980/81. Geheimakten der SED-Führung über die
Unterdrückung der polnischen Demokratiebewegung. Berlin.

LABEDZ 1984: Leopold Labedz (ed.): Poland under Jaruzelski. A Comprehen-
sive Sourcebook on Poland during and after Martial Law. New York.

LANGBEIN 1980: Hermann Langbein: ....nicht wie die Schafe zur Schlacht-
bank. Widerstand in den nationalsozialistischen Konzentrationslagern.
Frankfurt am Main.

LA PALOMBARA 1987: Joseph La Palombara: Democracy Italian Style. New
Haven.

LEHMBRUCH 1967: Gerhard Lehmbruch: Proporzdemokratie. Politisches
System und politische Kultur in der Schweiz und in Österreich. Tübingen.

LIPSET 1960: Seymour Martin Lipset: Political Man. The Social Bases of
Politics. New York.

LOPINSKI 1990: Maciej Lopinski et al.: Konspira. Solidarity Underground.
Berkeley.

LUXEMBURG 1970: Rosa Luxemburg: Schriften zur Theorie der Spontaneität.
Reinbek.

MACHIAVELLI 1952: The Prince. Translated by Luigi Ricci revised by E.R.P.
Vincent. New York.

MAIER 1997: Charles S.Maier: Dissolution. The Crisis of Communism and the
End of East Germany. Princeton.

MANCHESTER 1984: William Manchester: The Last Lion. Winston Spencer
Churchill. Visions of Glory. 1874-1932. London.

MANCHESTER 1989: William Manchester: The Last Lion. Winston Spencer
Churchill. Alone. 1932-1940. New York.

MANNHEIM 1958: Karl Mannheim: Mensch und Gesellschaft im Zeitalter des
Umbaus. Darmstadt.

MANNHEIM 1978: Karl Mannheim: Ideologie und Utopie. Frankfurt am Main.

MAREK 1970: Franz Marek: Was Stalin wirklich sagte. Wien.

MARIUS 1984: Richard Marius: Thomas More. A Biography. New York.

MC CULLOUGH 1992: David McCullough: Truman. New York.

MC NAMARA 1995: Robert S.McNamara: In Retrospect. The Tragedy and
Lessons of Vietnam. New York.

MC PHERSON 1991: James M.McPherson: Abraham Lincoln and the Second American Revolution. New York.

MICHNIK 1985: Adam Michnik: Letters from Prison and Other Essays. Berkeley.

MILLER 1983: Nathan Miller: F.D.R. An Intimate History. New York.

MLYNAR 1978: Zdenek Mlynar: Nachtfrost. Erfahrungen auf dem Weg vom realen zum menschlichen Sozialismus. Frankfurt am Main.

MLYNAR 1990: Zdenek Mlynar: Can Gorbachev Change the Soviet Union? Boulder.

MORGENTHAU 1958: Hans J.Morgenthau: Dilemmas of Politics. Chicago.

MÜNKLER 1984: Herfried Münkler: Machiavelli. Die Begründung des politischen Denkens der Neuzeit aus der Krise der Republik Florenz. Frankfurt am Main.

NARR/NASCHOLD 1971: Wolf-Dieter Narr, Frieder Naschold: Theorie der Demokratie. Einführung in die moderne politische Theorie. Teil III. Stuttgart.

NETTL 1967: Peter Nettl: Rosa Luxemburg. Köln.

OLSON 1965: Mancur Olson: The Logic of Collective Action. Public Goods and the Theory of Groups. Cambridge (MA)

PAULEY 1997: Bruce Pauley: Hitler, Stalin, and Mussolini. Totalitarianism in the Twentieth Century. Wheeling (IL).

PELINKA 1974: Anton Pelinka: Dynamische Demokratie. Zur konkreten Utopie gesellschaftlicher Gleichheit. Stuttgart.

PFABIGAN 1976: Alfred Pfabigan: Karl Kraus und der Sozialismus. Eine politische Biographie. Wien.

PLASSER 1987: Fritz Plasser: Parteien unter Streß. Zur Dynamik der Parteiensysteme in Österreich, der Bundesrepublik Deutschland und den Vereinigten Staaten. Wien.

POLAND UNDER MARTIAL LAW 1983: Poland Under Martial Law. A Report on Human Rights by the Polish Helsinki Watch Committee. English edition by the U.S. Helsinki Watch Committee.

POLSBY 1983: Nelson W. Polsby: Consequences of Party Reform. Oxford.

POPPER 1970: Karl Popper: Die offene Gesellschaft und ihre Feinde. 2 Bände. Bern.

PUMBERGER 1989: Klaus Pumberger: Solidarität im Streik. Politische Krise, sozialer Protest und Machtfrage in Polen 1980/81. Frankfurt am Main.

RADZINSKY 1996: Edvard Radzinsky: Stalin. New York.

RICHARDSON/FLANAGAN 1984: Bradley M.Richardson, Scott C. Flanagan: Politics in Japan. Boston.

RIESMAN 1950: David Riesman: The Lonely Crowd. A Study of the Changing American Character. New Haven.

RIKER 1982: William H.Riker: Liberalism against Populism. A Confrontation Between the Theory of Democracy and the Theory of Social Choice. Prospect Heights (IL)

ROSENBERG 1995: Tina Rosenberg: The Haunted Land. Facing Europe's Ghosts after Communism. New York.

SALISBURY 1993: Harrison E.Salisbury: The New Emperors. Mao and Deng. A Dual Biography. London.

SARTRE 1960: Jean-Paul Sartre: Betrachtungen zur Judenfrage. In: Drei Essays. Berlin (West).

SCHAUSBERGER 1978: Norbert Schausberger: Der Griff nach Österreich. Der Anschluß. Wien.

SCHUMPETER 1972: Joseph A.Schumpeter: Kapitalismus, Sozialismus und Demokratie. München.

SEGEV 1993: Tom Segev: The Seventh Million. The Israelis and the Holocaust. New York.

SEMPRUN 1991: Jorge Semprun: Netschajew kehrt zurück. Berlin.

SERENY 1995: Gitta Sereny: Albert Speer. His Battle with Truth. New York.

SHEVARDNADZE 1991: Edvard Shevardnadze: Die Zukunft gehört der Freiheit. Reinbek.

SHIRER 1982: William L.Shirer: Gandhi. A Memoir. London.

SHULL 1991: Steven A.Shull (ed.): The Two Presidencies. A Quarter Century Assessment. Chicago.

SLATER 1985: Ian Slater: Orwell. The Road to Airstrip One. New York.

SMOLNAR 1989: Alexander Smolnar, Pierre Kende: Die Rolle oppositioneller Gruppen. Am Vorabend der Demokratisierung in Polen und Ungarn (1987-1989). Forschungsprojekt Krisen in den Systemen sowjetischen Typs, geleitet von Zdenek Mlynar, Studie Nr. 17-18.

SPEER 1969: Albert Speer: Erinnerungen. Frankfurt am Main.

STEINER 1974: Jürg Steiner: Amicable Agreement versus Majority Rule. Conflict Resolution in Switzerland. Chapel Hill.

SUN TZU n.d.: Sun Tzu on the Art of War. The oldest Military Treatise in the World. Translated from the Chinese with introduction and critical notes by Lionel Giles.

TALMON 1986: J.L.Talmon: The Origins of Totalitarian Democracy. Harmondsworth.

TALOS, NEUGEBAUER 1984: Emmerich Talos, Wolfgang Neugebauer (eds.): „Austrofaschismus". Beiträge über Politik, Ökonomie und Kultur. Wien.

TEXTE 1975: Texte zur katholischen Soziallehre, herausgegeben vom Bundesverband der Katholischen Arbeitnehmer-Bewegung (KAB) Deutschlands, Kevalaer.

THEWELEIT 1980: Klaus Theweleit: Männerphantasien. 2 Bände. Reinbek.

TRUNK 1972: Isaiah Trunk: Judenrat. The Jewish Councils in Eastern Europe under Nazi Occupation. New York.

ULAM 1989: Adam B.Ulam: Stalin. The Man and His Era. Boston.

WEBSTER 1990: Paul Webster: Pétain's Crime. The full story of French Collaboration in the Holocaust. London.

WEISBROT 1991: Robert Weisbrot: Freedom Bound. A History of America's Civil Rights Movement. New York.

WILSFORD 1995: David Wilsford (ed.): Political Leaders of Contemporary Western Europe. Westport, Connecticut.

WOODS 1995: Randall Bennett Woods: Fulbright. A Biography. Cambridge (UK).

YIVO 1972: Yivo Institute for Jewish Research (ed.): Imposed Jewish Governing Bodies Under Nazi Rule. New York.

ZAHN 1964: Gordon C.Zahn: In Solitary Witness. The Life and Death of Franz Jägerstätter. Springfield (IL)

ZELIKOW, RICE 1995: Philip Zelikow, Condoleezza Rice: Germany Unified and Europe Transformed. A Study in Statecraft. Cambridge (MA).

ZELMAN 1995: Leon Zelman: Ein Leben nach dem Überleben. Aufgezeichnet von Armin Thurner. Wien.

ZOHN 1971: Harry Zohn: Karl Kraus. New York.

Index of Persons